PRACTICUM & INTERNSHIP MANUAL

Edited by

Mary-Anne M. Joseph

Alabama State University

PUBLISHED BY

Aspen Professional Services
63 Duffers Drive
Linn Creek, MO 65052

2019

Practicum and Internship Manual
[Edited by] Mary Anne Joseph
ISBN 978-7332488-0-8

To Secure Additional Copies • Contact

Aspen Professional Services
63 Duffers Drive
Linn Creek, MO 65052
jandrew@socket.net
573.286.0418
Aspenprofessionalservices.com

TABLE OF CONTENTS

Acknowledgements..vii

The Editor and Contributors viii

Chapter 1   Finding A Field Site 1
             Tamara P. Thomas, Deanna Henderson,
             Veronica Jackson, and Miranda Clark

Chapter 2   Case Management & Presentation...............................19
             Simone B. Hicks and Jessica S. Henry

Chapter 3   Documentation...34
             Kent Crenshaw

Chapter 4   Consultation and Collaboration...............................43
             Rebecca R. Sametz

Chapter 5   Effective Communication.......................................54
             Danita Henry Stapleton

Chapter 6   Workplace Climate...81
             Dothel W. Edwards, Jr.

Chapter 7   Professionalism..92
             Denise Y. Lewis

Chapter 8   Ethics and Ethical Decision-making...........................102
             Mary-Anne M. Joseph, Kaylin Moss and Christa A.
             Martin

Chapter 9   Self-Care...118
             Mary-Anne M. Joseph, Shayna Hobson and
             Christina Horton

Chapter 10   Résumé Development...137
             Phillip D. Lewis, DeAmber L. Johnson, and
             Bernadette Williams-York

Editor and Contributors

Chapter 11   Job Search and Interview Preparation......................151
              Bernadette Williams-York

Chapter 12   License and Certification.................................167
              Carmela Drake

Chapter 13   What's Next: Taking Your Career to the Next Step........181
              Sabrina Harris Taylor

Chapter 14   Professional Resources...................................199
              Christan Horton

Appendices: Helpful Resources..226

ACKNOWLEDGEMENTS

Developing this textbook was more rewarding than I could have ever imagined and none of this would have been possible without the diverse and dynamic group of professionals who contributed to the development of this textbook. thank you all for your hard work and dedication that made this book possible.

I would like to express my sincerest appreciation to Bernadette York, Kaylin Moss and Christan Horton for the extra time you put into additional research, writing and reviewing of additional contents for this text. Thank you for stepping in and providing me with the extra support that made this project a success.

Additionally, I would like to extend my deepest gratitude to everyone on the Aspen publishing team for your guidance and support throughout the production of this book. I would like to extend special thanks to Jason Andrew for his patience, guidance and support in the completion of this book.

Last but certainly not least, I would be remiss if I did not thank my friends and family. To my mother, Florinda, thank you for always being an affirming voice that knows no boundaries. To my sister, Gail, thank you for always being the voice of reason when despair arises. To my father, Claude, thank you for your continued optimism and can-do attitude. Finally, to my dear friends La'Kisha and Rudy, thank you for your unwavering support, confidence, guidance and encouragement from beginning to end. I could not have done this without all of you.

Mary-Anne M. Joseph

THE EDITOR

Mary-Anne M. Joseph, PH.D, CRC, LPC., has over ten years of experience in the field of Rehabilitation. She has served as a practitioner and a professor in education and vocational rehabilitation. Currently, Dr. Joseph is a tenured Associate Professor in the Department of Rehabilitation Studies at Alabama State University.

Dr. Joseph is a Certified Rehabilitation Counselor, as well as a Licensed Professional Counselor. She holds a Ph.D. in Counselor Education and Supervision from Ohio University and a Master of Science in Rehabilitation Counseling from Winston-Salem State University. Dr. Joseph is committed to research in teaching and learning in Rehabilitation and Human Services and is the author of several publications including: The Ethics of Undergraduate Rehabilitation Education, Development and Implementation of a Quality Curriculum/Program, Ethical Considerations for Working With Transition Aged Youth and Students With Disabilities, and Transition Vocational Rehabilitation.

Dr. Joseph was a recipient of the Sylvia Walker Educator Award in 2017. She was awarded the College of Health Science Faculty of the Year Award in 2014 from Alabama State University. Dr. Joseph regularly teaches both undergraduate and graduate courses in Rehabilitation Services and Rehabilitation Counseling. She often presents scholarly works at state, regional and national conferences. Dr. Joseph is a professional member of the National Rehabilitation Association, the National Association on Multicultural Rehabilitation Concerns, the American Counseling Association, the American Rehabilitation Counseling Association, and the Association for Counselor Education and Supervision.

THE CONTRIBUTERS

Miranda Clark, B.S., M.S., CPSC, received a Bachelor of Science in Family and Consumer Sciences/Secondary Education from Alabama A. & M. University, and a Master of Science in School Counseling, from the University of West Alabama. Bachelor of Science in Family and Consumer Sciences/Secondary Education, Alabama A&M University. Ms. Clark serves as a certified professional school counselor and is employed with the Jefferson County Board of Education in Birmingham, Alabama at Erwin Middle School as the counseling department chair. Ms. Clark has been with the Jefferson County Board of Education for 16 years. Ms. Clark has served as a lead mentor and testing coordinator during her tenure. She also has supervised interns and practicum students in school counseling. Ms. Clark is a member of the American Association of School Counselors, Alpha Zeta Honor Fraternity and Kappa Omicron Nu Honor Society.

Kent Crenshaw, M.S., CRC, is the Executive Director of The Independent Rights and Resources (IRR). During his time at the center, the number of consumers has grown from 12 to over 400. IRR serves any person with a disability who desires to live more independently. The mission is, "To provide a set of core services geared toward promoting self-help, equal access, peer role modeling, personal growth and empowerment." Mr. Crenshaw has advocated for people with disabilities through the county, serving on several boards including National Council on Independent Living, State of Alabama Independent Living Council and Alabama Medical Equipment Board and as a spokesman at several conventions and meetings addressing discrimination and barriers that exist in society for people with disabilities. Mr. Crenshaw is a graduate of Auburn University at Montgomery. He earned his Master of Education from Auburn University and is a Certified Rehabilitation Counselor. He is an instructor at Alabama State University where he involves his students with community service as it relates to people with disabilities.

Carmela Drake, Ph.D., LPC, CAADP, ACGC-III, earned a Ph.D. in Human Services, with a concentration in Counseling Studies, from Capella University and a Master of Science in Counseling and Human Development from Troy State University. Dr. Drake is a Certified Adolescent Alcohol and Drug Professional (CAADP), a Licensed Professional Counselor (LPC), and a Level III Certified Gambling Addiction Counselor (ACGC-III) in the state of Alabama. She has over 20-years of clinical experience working with individuals with substance use and co-occurring disorders. She is an assistant professor and the program coordinator for the Bachelor of Science in the Rehabilitation Services program at Alabama State University. Dr. Drake is a member of NAADAC, the Association for Addiction Professionals, Alabama Counseling Association, and Delta Sigma Theta Sorority, Inc.

Dothel W. Edwards, Jr., Rh.D., CRC, CLCP has 20 years of experience as a rehabilitation educator in higher education. Presently, he is a tenured, full professor, in the Department of Rehabilitation Studies in the College of Health Sciences at Alabama State University (ASU). In addition to his full-time faculty responsibilities at ASU, he provides vocational expert witness testimony (as a contractor) for the Social Security Administration Office of Disabilities Adjudication & Review offices of Atlanta, GA & Orlando, FL; the ODAR National Hearing Center offices of Baltimore, MD & Falls Church, VA, and he was a registered Rehabilitation Supplier under the Georgia State Board of Workers' Compensation.

DeAnna Henderson, Ph.D., is a Licensed Professional Counselor (LPC), National Certified Counselor (NCC) and a Certified Rehabilitation Counselor (CRC). She serves as Dean for the College of Graduate, Adult, and Continuing Education at Wilberforce University. Dr. Henderson's research interests include multicultural issues related to counseling and the academy, mentoring, mentorship of women, and ethical leadership. Dr. Henderson is a member of the American Counseling Association, National Rehabilitation Association, and the National Association for Multicultural Rehabilitation Concerns.

Jessica S. Henry, Ph.D., LPC, CRC, is an Assistant Clinical Professor of Rehabilitation and Human Services (RHS) program in the Department of Education Psychology, Counseling and Special Education at The Pennsylvania State University, University Park. She has devoted her research, practice, and teaching to understanding the essence of wellness through the exploration of stress impacts on performance outcomes and quality of life. Her specific expertise includes counseling individuals with presenting concerns of disability identity development, adjustment to chronic illness, and stress management.

Simone B. Hicks, Ph.D., CRC, is an Assistant Dean & Director of Case Management at Scripps College in Claremont, CA. She earned her Ph.D. in Counselor Education and Supervision from Ohio University. She is a Certified Rehabilitation Counselor. She has dedicated her daily practices to case management in higher education where she collaborates, consult with students, parents, faculty, staff, and other campus resources to best address the diverse needs of each student. Her research interest includes identifying vocational needs for students with disabilities, African American families, and parental involvement.

Shayna Hobson, M.A., is a Therapeutic Behavioral Aide for The National Center on Institutions of Alternatives. Shayna graduate from Maryland University of Integrative Health with a Masters of Arts in Health and Wellness Coaching and a Bachelor of Science in Rehabilitation Services with a concentration in Addiction Studies from Alabama State University.

Christan Horton, Ph.D., CRC, LPCA, is an Assistant Professor in the Rehabilitation Studies Program at Winston Salem State University. In addition to earning her M.S. in Rehabilitation Counseling, she earned a Ph.D. in Rehabilitation Counseling and Rehabilitation Counselor Education from North Carolina Agricultural and Technical State University. Dr. Horton is a Certified Rehabilitation Counselor and Licensed Professional Counselor Associate. She has experience as a mental health and disability case manager, advocate for the aging population, as well as a transitions coordinator for the state of North Carolina. Dr. Horton's research agenda is threefold and includes (a) trauma and trauma informed care, (b) impact of undergraduate mentorship, and (c) maternal mental health and disability. Dr. Horton's mission is to serve as an advocate for individuals diagnosed with disabilities and encourage student scholarship and success. Dr. Horton is a titan in supporting individuals to reach their maximum potential through trauma-informed practices, access, and the development of skills to promote self-advocacy and empowerment.

Veronica Jackson, DPT, LPT, is a licensed physical therapist in the State of Alabama who has 17 years of post-licensure experience including 13 years as a full-time faculty member. She holds a baccalaureate degree in Human Resource Management, a master's degree in physical therapy and doctoral degree in physical therapy (DPT). In addition, she is certified in wound care management, is a credentialed clinical instructor and a credentialed advanced clinical instructor. Dr. Jackson is currently a tenured Associate Professor in the DPT program at Alabama State University, where she has successfully planned and coordinated over 1,000 internships, for 13 cohorts of student physical therapist, serving as the Academic Coordinator of Clinical Education (ACCE)/Director of Clinical Education (DCE). She has experience working with patients in inpatient, outpatient, & home health settings. She currently practices in an acute care setting that allows her to mentor students in the areas she teaches clinical integumentary and patient care concepts. Dr. Jackson is a member of the American Physical Therapy Association, the American Council of Academic Physical Therapy: National Consortia of Clinical Education and Diversity Equity and Inclusion Consortia.

DeAmber Johnson, M.S., LPC-Candidate earned a B.A in Psychology from Langston University-Tulsa in 2007 and went on to earn a Master of Science in Rehabilitation Counseling in 2017. She is a mental health professional (LPC-C) who works with at-risk youth to help them adapt or utilize their strengths at home and in the school. She has over 10 years of experience working with children and their families with disabilities to help them achieve personal, career goals and overcoming adversity. DeAmber, is a member of Chi Sigma Iota and Delta Sigma Theta Sorority, Inc,

Denise Y. Lewis, Ph.D., LPC, NCC, earned a B.A. in Sociology from Ohio Dominican College, an M.A. in Counseling Ministry from Methodist Theological School in Ohio, and a Ph.D. in Counselor Education and Supervision from Ohio University. She is a Principal at a charter school in Ohio and is an Assistant Professor at Grace College and Seminary. In addition to her academic work, Dr. Lewis is the founder and President of The Sankofa Project, a non-profit organization that serves African American youth between the ages of 12-18 in a variety of capacities. Dr. Lewis is currently working on several publications, including a book entitled *"Tea Time for the Soul,"* that speaks to the need for self-care for those in the helping professions.

Phillip D. Lewis, Ph.D., CRC, is an Associate Professor/Graduate Coordinator of the Department of Rehabilitation Counseling and Disabilities Studies at Langston University (LU)—Tulsa, Oklahoma. In addition, he works as a License Mental Health Professional Counselor for the State of Oklahoma Healthcare Authority. At LU he serves as the Chapter Faculty Advisor for the Lambda Upsilon Chapter of Chi Sigma Iota: Counseling Academic and Professional Honor Society International. He earned his Ph.D. in Rehabilitation Counseling Education/Law Health Policy and Disability from the University of Iowa. He earned a M.S. in Rehabilitation Counseling/Administration from Southern Illinois University at Carbondale, IL. He earned a B.S. degree in Social Work/ Political Science from Rust College in Holly Springs, MS. He is a candidate for Licensure as an Alcohol and Drug Counselor. He works as a Mental Healthcare Professional for the State of Oklahoma, often working with at risk youth, and persons with disabilities. His research interest includes, rehabilitation services for persons with mental and physical disabilities, school to work transition for adolescences with disabilities, correctional rehabilitation counseling, suicide prevention, substance abuse counseling, Bullying, Triple Negative Breast Cancer awareness/prevention, and Agrability. He is a member of the American Counseling Association, and Omega Psi Phi Fraternity, Inc.

Christa A. Martin, MRC, CRC, is a Vocational Rehabilitation Specialist-Certified for the Kentucky Office of Vocational Rehabilitation. She graduated from the University of Kentucky with a Master of Rehabilitation Counseling. Christa also graduated from Kentucky State University with a Bachelor of Arts in Psychology with a Human Service concentration, as well as an Associate of Arts in Liberal Studies. At Kentucky State University, she taught psychology and coordinated their Disability Services. She is a Certified Rehabilitation Counselor, Licensed Professional Counselor Associate qualified, and holds a National Certificate of Achievement in Employment Services. Christa provides personal and professional development training around the country, is a trainer with the Southeast ADA Trainer Network, and an avid advocate for individuals with disabilities, as well as the vocational rehabilitation counseling profession. She is a member of the National Rehabilitation Association, the National Rehabilitation Association of Job Placement & Development, and APSE.

Kaylin Moss, M.E., is a Vocational Rehabilitation Counselor for the Tennessee Department of Human Services. Kaylin graduated from Ohio University with a Master of Education in Clinical Mental Health/Clinical Rehabilitation Counseling and a Bachelor of Science degree in Rehabilitation Services with a concentration in Addiction Studies.

Rebecca R. Sametz, Ph.D., LPC, CRC, ETS, is an Assistant Professor and Director of the Master of Science Clinical Rehabilitation Counseling program at Texas Tech University Health Sciences Center. She received a Ph.D in Rehabilitation Counselor Education from Michigan State University, a M.A. in Rehabilitation Counseling from Western Michigan University, and a M.A. in Vision Rehabilitation Therapy from Western Michigan University. Dr. Sametz is a Licensed Professional Counselor (LPC) in the State of Michigan, Certified Rehabilitation Counselor (CRC), and certified Employment Training Specialist (ETS). Previously, Dr. Sametz worked at a non-profit as a Youth Career Development Specialist in which she partnered with local school districts in order to provide youth with disabilities community work experiences who were preparing for transition from school to work. In this role, she also provided career counseling and exploration services to youth with disabilities, job placement and development services, and disability education to employers who served as a placement site for youth with disabilities in understanding the disability and low-cost accommodations.

Dr. Sametz also worked for the State of Michigan's agency for the Blind and Visually Impaired providing career counseling and exploration services for adults and youth with disabilities, as well as served as a job placement and job developer. Dr. Sametz is the past-president of the National Rehabilitation Association Job Placement and Development Division (NRAJPD) and serves on the National Rehabilitation Association Executive Committee and on the Board as the NRAJPD representative. Her research interests lie within the realm of career counseling for individuals with disabilities, veterans and their families, psychosocial adjustment to disability for youth and their families, and mental health concerns of families of children with disabilities. She is currently working on research projects that are addressing the needs of veterans acclimating into civilian life, as well as examining the psychological well-being of parents of children with disabilities.

Danita Henry Stapleton, EdD, LPC-S, CRC, NCC, is an assistant professor and the Program Chair for the Department of Rehabilitation Studies at Alabama State University. She is the Master in Rehabilitation Counseling (MRC) program coordinator. She holds a doctorate in Education Leadership, Policy and Law from Alabama State University and a master's degree in Rehabilitation Counseling from Florida State University.

Sabrina Taylor, Ph.D., is a tenured professor at Coppin State University in the College of Behavioral and Social Sciences and the Department of Psychology, Counseling, and Behavioral Health. She is also the co-project coordinator of the Comprehensive Transition Project at Coppin State University for transitioning high school youth with intellectual disabilities. Over the past decade, Dr. Taylor has worked in the field of rehabilitation counseling serving children, adults, and veterans with disabilities. She is known for teaching and her entrepreneurial spirit. Prior to entering academia, Dr. Taylor owned and operated an adult care home for individuals with Schizophrenia. She received both her doctoral degree and master's degree in rehabilitation counselor education and rehabilitation counseling from North Carolina Agricultural and Technical State University.

Tammara P. Thomas, Ph.D., CADC, is an Assistant Professor of Rehabilitation Studies at Winston-Salem State University. She completed her MS in Rehabilitation Administration and Programming Services at Southern Illinois University at Carbondale and her PhD in Rehabilitation and Counselor Education at the University of Iowa. Throughout her career she has served as a contributor to the field of addictions as a Certified Alcohol and Drug Substance Abuse Counselor in which she has served in the capacity of a director of treatment programs (all levels of care, including corrections), clinical supervisor, trainer, speaker, instructor, program developer, evaluator, and consultant. Additionally, she has also served as a vocational rehabilitation counselor for the Department of Veterans Affairs assisting veterans with disabilities to overcome barriers that impede their ability to reach their vocational goals, and/or independent living needs. Dr. Thomas' research interests include: addiction studies, ethics, administration and programming, gender-responsive treatment, vocational rehabilitation and practices.

Bernadette Williams-York, Ph.D., is an Associate Professor/Associate Head in the Division of Physical Therapy, Department of Rehabilitation Medicine at the University of Washington in Seattle, Washington. Dr. Williams-York received her Bachelor of Science degree from Tulane University in New Orleans, LA, a Master of Science degree from the University of Alabama, Birmingham and a Doctor of Science degree from Rocky Mountain University in Provo, Utah. Dr. Williams-York is a board-certified geriatric specialist and has been a licensed physical therapist for over 30 years. She is also a published author and her teaching and research interests include health disparities, healthcare workforce diversity, health promotion and aging.

Aspen Professional Services would like to thank Dr. Mary-Anne M. Joseph and each of the authors who contributed to this book. It has been our privilege to prepare this book for publication. Many of the authors have been contributors to other books we have published, and we are thankful for their continued contribution to our efforts to produce high quality textbooks for the field of vocational rehabilitation.

Jason D. Andrew, Ph.D., CRC/R, NCC/R

FINDING A FIELD SITE

TAMMARA P. THOMAS
DEANNA HENDERSON
VERONICA JACKSON
MIRANDA CLARK

CHAPTER DESCRIPTION

This chapter provides the reader with knowledge regarding the importance of selecting internship sites that meet academic, professional, and personal needs. Strategies to determine need are examined and presented in detail, including exercises that can be used as resources to determine sites that are a good match. The chapter also provided insight into successfully making connections with the resources within the student's learning communities, with internship site gatekeepers, and with potential internship site supervisors. Strategies aimed at teaching appropriate, efficient, planning and overall professional engagement were presented.

LEARNING OBJECTIVES

> ➢ To teach students the purpose of the internship/fieldwork experience.

> ➢ To teach students about the importance of internship/fieldwork selection.

> ➢ To teach the students how to utilize resources to select and choose appropriate internship placement sites.

> ➢ To provide basic knowledge on how to apply for an internship.

Participation in internship experiences may be required for students at various levels of study and training such as individuals enrolled in baccalaureate and graduate level programs. It is appropriate to acknowledge that each professional discipline uses different terminologies to describe experiential learning experiences. For example, practicum, internship, fieldwork, and field placements have been used interchangeably.

Fieldwork/internship experiences are an essential part of the educational journey for students from various disciplines. Learning experiences that extend outside of the classroom are critical for the personal and professional development of students. These experiential learning opportunities provide pathways to employment by initiating supported transitioning into the workplace, by allowing students to engage in real-world employment experiences. Participation in internship/fieldwork experiences enable student learners to put theory into the practice of what they have learned throughout the years in the classroom setting. Additionally, having the opportunity to practice what was taught in their program's curriculum will also help to solidify career choice, support learning outcomes, acquire new practical skill sets, and gain an experiential understanding of the mission, principles, and values of their chosen professions.

Fieldwork placement experiences provide several benefits. One of the most prevalent advantages of fieldwork is to provide an opportunity to apply classroom-acquired knowledge, attitudes and skills while providing direct services to clients/consumers in the field. While participating in these types of experiential learning opportunities, students will work within various rehabilitation and human service settings. Working within fieldwork placement, students will receive supervision from a licensed or certified rehabilitation professional. They will have access to a network of field experts that can help acclimate students to the profession. Moreover, these learning opportunities allow students to gain exposure to the professional field and gain an understanding of how to put theory into practice.

Additionally, fieldwork placement experiences allow students to explore their chosen career field and ensure that the career field is a right fit. Oftentimes, this entails learning the nuances that are undiscovered in the classroom or textbook. This work experience can serve as a catalyst for future employment after graduation, so it is imperative that the work is taken seriously. Fieldwork experience is often coupled with classroom learning, which helps you process your concerns and clinical experiences (off-campus) that facilitate the development of basic skills.

SELECTING A PLACEMENT SITE

An initial daunting challenge of participating in the internship experience is finding a site that both the faculty internship instructor and the student agree upon as the best fit. It is imperative that there is a collaborative relationship that exists between both parties. Establishing this relationship with the instructor responsible for overseeing the internship experience is critical because they perform duties aimed at maximizing the students learning experience, preserve the integrity of the profession's mission and values, ensure the wellbeing and dignity of consumers, while also upholding the social contract established between the profession, stakeholders, and society.

Each institution and program has established protocols in which internships experiences are conducted and overseen.[2] It is important that students understand the preparation that has been done in an effort to establish longstanding relationships with community partners who have agreed to be an internship site.[2] Keeping this in mind, faculty internship instructors are aware of the needs and expectations of these agencies. Also, as a result of the established working relationship developed between the instructor and the students, the faculty internship advisor may be able to offer valuable feedback that considers the specific needs of the student.

The faculty internship instructor can serve as an invaluable support system who will not only monitor the student's progress but also actively engage with site supervisors and agency staff. Thus, they are well versed on students' strengths and learning needs, while also keeping in mind the needs of various sites. It is vital that the collaborative relationships established between the academic programs and the community partners are preserved and supported.

Securing an appropriate match within an agency that will support quality internship training experiences can be competitive. Internship imbalance, which refers to the lack of available internships positions relative to the number of students seeking internships, can make the process more formidable.[1,3,6] In order to graduate from programs that require students to engage in an internship, it is critically important to maintain existing relationships, while also remaining committed to developing new ones. To ensure that the students maximize the internship learning experience and negotiate the various nuances of selecting and initiating placement, it is essential that the students begin working with the faculty internship instructor, other relevant parties (e.g., advisor), at the onset and throughout the internship experience.

IDENTIFYING RESOURCES

Academic institutions have different procedures in which they approach the internship placement process. The discipline, accreditation requirements, and program preferences can impact the way the placement selection process occurs. In some programs, students are solely responsible for locating and securing their potential internship sites. Other programs may insist that all aspects of establishing the internship placement be strictly controlled by the program, including the decision for site placement.[2,4] Despite the variability in placement approaches determined by respective programs, it is beneficial for the students to recognize that generally the primary resource for internship recommendations and suggestions is the assigned faculty internship instructor.

It is essential that students check with their faculty member to determine if there are policies in place that prohibit students from contacting a clinical site. For example, the field of physical therapy has a national position statement that prohibits students from contacting clinical sites. However, not every discipline has this position statement in place.

In addition to the assigned faculty member, other resources to consider may include other faculty and staff within your institution. Many of the instructors that work within the university setting also have professional connections within the surrounding communities. They may know of sites that hold pre-existing working relationships and agreements with the university or within other departments, or they may have knowledge of agencies that do not have a collaborative partnership with your institution but would like to establish one.

In addition to faculty and staff being a valuable resource for identifying resources, there may also be resources located on campus that are a part of the learning community but are often overlooked. Programs located within the academic institution may also have established a collaborative partnership with agencies within the community. Further, the programs that are available to students can offer helpful services which focus on career development.

THE IMPORTANCE OF "FIT"

Although having an exceptional grade point average is something every scholar should be proud of, it does not guarantee that employers will see the students as an obvious choice for employment. According to the Bureau of Labor Statistics,[3] job openings have reached a new high as of 2017. The statistics show that in September 2017 the level of new hires increased from 63.2 million in 2016 to 65.3 million in 2017.[6] In contrast, the annual total number of separations from jobs increased from 60.9 million in 2016 to 63.0 million in 2017.

Although the labor market has shown marked signs of improvement in recent years, new graduates with little to no work experience may still find it challenging when attempting to compete with more experienced candidates. Also, consideration must be given to the risk of separation from employment (e.g., resignations and terminations) even after a position has been attained. Armed with this knowledge, it is vital that students understand the pitfalls that can occur as they transition into the workforce. Additionally, when selecting a fieldwork/internship, students should not only select a position that is congruent with their knowledge, skills and abilities, but the student should also remain diligent in ensuring that the internship position is in keeping with their interest and career goals.

The Theory of Work Adjustment (TWA) was developed by Dawis and Lofquist.[5] The TWA theory considers the psychological nature of the interaction between persons and their environments. Dawis and Lofquist defined work adjustment as a "continuous and dynamic process by which a worker seeks to achieve and maintain correspondence with a work environment."[6] This correspondence between the two is a process of reciprocity in which there is an interplay between the worker's satisfaction and the employer's satisfactoriness.[7]

An employee's satisfaction is dependent on reinforcers that exist within the environment. The TWA suggests that there is a reciprocal nature that exists between people and the environments in which they work. Although the employee lends their knowledge, skills, and abilities to the working environment with the intent on contributing to the mission of the organization, the employee, in turn receives internal and external rewards. TWA supports the idea that matching people to the most suitable work experiences can contribute to a sense of satisfaction. Therefore, it stands to reason that meticulous attention should be given to selecting a placement that considers the individual needs of students concerning career development and internship site placement.

When selecting an internship, students should aim to select a placement that allows them to gain more practical knowledge of how to perform in workplace settings that support their career choice. Additionally, the learning opportunity should also provide a formalized presentation of relevant work experience gained upon the completion of the internship. This means that selecting an internship placement must be intentional and methodical in the sense that it should be relevant, challenging, and congruent with their career interests and goals.

Further, selecting an internship placement site should not be based on money and simple convenience. When students begin their internship preparation one common question is, "Do you know where I can get a paid internship?" The truth of the matter is that paid internships are not as readily available as unpaid ones. Moreover, although paid internships are extremely desirable, it may not always be the appropriate choice when considering long-term career goals. Besides, there are incidences of unpaid internship positions becoming paid full-time positions. So, the thought of giving so much time without compensation is daunting, the short-term benefit of a poorly selected paid internship pales in comparison to the financial and professional gains associated with securing a meaningful internship that leads to a successful career.

There may also be other unique considerations that student interns must consider when determining the appropriate internship selection. Students should be diligent in gathering information about various placement settings of interest. Keep in mind that that faculty internship supervisors will be invested in working collaboratively during this process. A critical reason, as mentioned earlier, is the important need to preserve longstanding established relationships with community partners.[10] Another important reason is, it is essential for the school to have trust in the community partner as well as the student who will represent the institution during the internship experience.[11]

Therefore, gathering as much information as possible about potential sites, can help students effectively evaluate the "fit." According to Chatman,[4] the assessment and establishment of "fit" suggests that once this match between the person and the organization occurs, then behavioral outcomes, values, and norms can be predicted.[4,11] The assumption is—the better the "fit," the more favorable performance outcomes. When students are informed, they will be able to make better decisions regarding internship selection.

In order to select the internship placement that best meets their individual needs:

➤ Students must have thoroughly researched sites of interest,

➤ Students must clearly identify what factors are important to them.

Each student has uniquely different life circumstances which must be acknowledged and taken into consideration in order to determine how those circumstances may impact participation in the internship experience. An example of this may be that there are students who desire to work at a specific site which has all the elements that make the site desirable. However, the location of the site may not be within a reasonable distance, and students do not have access to transportation. In this case, students may have to reconsider and evaluate alternate placement sites that could also provide a similar learning experience.

EXERCISE #1

CARD SORTING

This card sorting exercise is designed to help you identify important factors that are critical in determining if the internship site of interest is a good "fit" for you and matches your professional and personal needs. Items needed include sticky notes (2 colors), marker, paper, or colored stickers, and your phone to take a photo of the results. Here are the steps to engaging in a card sorting process that will help you prioritize what factors are most important. The steps are as follows:

Step 1. Lay down 4-5 sticky notes on a spacious table horizontally (e.g., yellow colored). Each sticky note will represent a scaled category. For example, Label #1 may read: *Extremely Important*, #2 may read *Very Important,* Label #3 may read *Important,* Label #4 may read *Somewhat Important*, and Label #5 may read *Not Important.* Use the marker to label each sticky note.

Step 2. Use the second set of sticky notes (e.g., pink colored) to write down all the factors associated with the selected sites being considered. Include details such as the agency type, clientele (adolescents vs. adults), settings, distance from where you reside, the mission of the agency, supervisor qualities, and other relevant pros and cons. Make sure to include personal factors that may impact your participation in the internship. Relevant factors may include family responsibilities, transportation, personal and professional values, flexibility, helping others, decision-making, freedom, and other perks. Remember, this is your wish list, so to speak, and you may very well end up with 50 or more cards (sticky notes). Therefore, be as exhaustive as possible.

Step 3. Begin to sort the cards under each category based on how important the factor is to you.

Step 4. Once you have completed the process of sorting your sticky notes according to how important the factor is, you will need to take a picture of your results or use paper to write down each category and the factors that were categorized underneath them. This way you will have a list of what you found to be the most important to the least important factors that may impact your internship placement and ultimate choice in sites.

After you have completed the card sorting exercise and have analyzed the results of the exercise, you will now have a better gauge on what aspects of your internship site selection are most important. You will also have a snapshot of what factors are most important to you and what work experiences are best suited to expand and develop your knowledge, skills, and abilities. This pragmatic approach to sorting out your preferences will provide an excellent foundation when collaborating with your faculty intern supervisor or academic advisor. This information will also help you to narrow down the most suitable sites and can increase the likelihood of fit.

STRATEGIES FOR SECURING A SITE

STRATEGIES FOR SECURING A SITE INCLUDE BUT ARE NOT LIMITED TO THE FOLLOWING:

Review your institution's established database of field sites. Identify three to five potential field sites that match your career interests. Construct a professional email or letter request for information about the agency's fieldwork/internship application process addressed to the field site or internship liaison at the site. Request a tour of the field sites so you can see firsthand what happens in the facility.

Be sure to research the agency and ensure that you are fully knowledgeable of the services provided by this agency. Prepare for an interview with the agency as many fieldwork/internship sites prefer to interview students before admitting them as an intern. The purpose of the interview is to ensure that the student is well prepared and a best fit for the agency. Additionally, expand your opportunities for fieldwork/internship experiences by attending professional conferences, and identify mentors within your field of study and in other areas.

Educating and equipping students with professional generic abilities and concepts is essential in the process of securing a field site. Since you as the students may initiate the first contact with the site, it is essential that you demonstrate professional behavior. Rejection or confirmation of your request for admittance into a field site can be a direct result of the lack of professionalism. Therefore, it is best practice to always consult your faculty member prior to engaging with professionals at a field site to ensure that you are fully equipped for the encounter.

Additionally, consult with your university advisor or instructor to gain an understanding of the requirements of their fieldwork. This would include identification of how many service hours are needed to complete the internship/fieldwork experience and a clarification of how these hours are to be spent. More specifically, what activities do you need to be engaged in during your fieldwork experience. Additionally, be sure to acquire information regarding the objectives or learning targets you are responsible for during the internship/fieldwork and be prepared to share this information with your field site contact.

THE PROCESS

INITIATING CONTACT

You have decided which internship site(s) are most desirable. You have completed the hard work of thoroughly researching the prospective organizations, you have narrowed down "fit", and you have met and discussed your choices with your faculty internship supervisor and any other relevant parties that may be involved in the decision-making process. Now that you have completed the groundwork, it is time to take the formal steps necessary to apply for your desired internship placement. It is imperative to take note of deadlines established by the prospective organization in which you are interested in for an internship, as well as the process involved in applying for the internship. Additionally, it is a good idea to identify who the internship manager is at the internship site so that you can communicate directly with that person. Upon this initial contact, it is critical that you present yourself in the most professional manner possible.

Your initial contact plays an important role in setting the tone for your interview. Initially, you may be making a "cold" call. In other words, you are contacting a prospective site without an appointment or previous introduction! Well, this can be awkward if you have not prepared to make these calls professionally. The best-case scenario is if you have been referred by another individual who has an established relationship with the organization. However, this may not always be possible. Therefore, here are a few tips to ensure that you are representing yourself in the most professional light when reaching out to prospective internship sites:

STEP 1: PREPARE, PREPARE, PREPARE. TAKE THE TIME TO SCRIPT OUT AN OPENING STATEMENT.

Time is of the essence, so you do not want to waste anyone's time, including yours. Creating a script gives you the opportunity to organize your thoughts **before** calling. Your script should include an introduction, a reference point (something about your program, and the internship), and a transition to your question or dialogue. **Note:** Speak using a natural voice. Do not read the script like a robot. For example:

"Good morning, Ms. Daniels. This is Jonathan Stampley, and I am a student at (university name) and (program name). I am contacting your agency because I am interested in applying to participate in your internship program. May I have the name of the person to whom I should speak regarding the possibility of interning at your facility?"

STEP 2: PREPARE A SCRIPT FOR THE REST OF YOUR CALL.

You should be prepared to ask follow-up questions during the initial call such as:

"Could you please provide me with a direct contact phone number or email? What is the best time to reach him or her? May I leave my contact information?"

The person you may need to speak with could be available to take the call at that time or you may already be speaking to the contact person. Therefore, be prepared to answer detailed questions about your internship. Questions that you may be asked could require you to give more detail and may include the following:

➢ Information about your academic program.

➢ How many hours will you need?

➢ What learning opportunities are you interested in?

➢ What credentials will be required to oversee your internship?

➢ Who is your academic advisor or internship supervisor?

➢ Do you have an email or contact number in which your faculty internship supervisor or advisor can be reached?

➢ Do you have the internship manual so that I may learn more?

➢ When will you begin and when will it end?

Make sure that your voice tone is warm, polite, clearly articulated, confident, and your responses are clear and concise. During this part of the conversation, you should avoid sounding as if you are uninformed regarding the details and the requirements of your internship. If you do not know the answer to an inquiry, make sure to acknowledge this and inform the agency personnel that you will find out the answer and contact them with the correct information. The mode of professional communication should be either by phone (not texting, unless requested) or through email.

STEP 3: ASK FOR AN APPOINTMENT

You should ask for an appointment at a specific time but remain flexible if the time does not work for the contact. Your aim is to gain a commitment to meet during the initial call, as opposed to remaining vague and leaving to chance that you would have to start this process all over again.

Remember time is of the essence, and you may have other prospective agencies you are considering. **Ask** for the best method of applying and what necessary supporting documents are needed. Refrain from asking questions that are readily available on the organization's website. Do not hesitate to ask for clarification on information that is unclear.

STEP 4: FOLLOW UP BY EMAIL.

Upon the completion of the call, it is proper etiquette to follow up with an email expressing your gratitude. The content should not only express your appreciation, but it should also review and inform (humbly). In the email, you may want to summarize the discussion, provide any information that you indicated that you would provide, as well as any relevant contact information, and website links. You may also include, at this time, any relevant and appropriate documents if indicated by the organization's representative.

Please note that it is not professional to send out application documents without first clarifying with the organization's internship supervisor or representative that the method of transmission is acceptable. The application may be required to be submitted through an online applicant portal. If you make the mistake of sending your information without clarification, you will run the risk of your documents being overlooked, "misplaced," or rejected. Moreover, by forwarding unsolicited information, you run the risk that the internship position(s) are already secured by other applicants or unavailable for a variety of reasons.

Remember, each organization will have their own internship application process. Some processes may be more formalized and may require that the procedures for applying for an internship begins six months or more in advance. An example of this may be state and federal agencies that have a more vigorous vetting process and may have more bureaucratic processes than local not-for-profit agencies. Additionally, these placements tend to be more competitive. So, make sure that you are aware of the established timeframes and deadlines so that you may allow yourself enough time to submit a completed application.

VISITING A SITE

Students who decide to visit a facility should always check to see what times are best to visit. When possible, it is always best practice to make an appointment to tour the facility. The facilities' clinicians are normally busy providing care to clients, so an unexpected visit may not be welcomed. This could leave a bad impression. Students should dress appropriately in business attire and show courtesy while at the field site whether they are visiting or working in an official capacity. Consult both your faculty member and your field site liaison to determine if there is a required dress code to which you should adhere.

APPLICATION PACKETS AND LETTERS

When applying for the internship, most organizations require an application to be completed. This application packet may require the submission of a letter of interest or cover letter, as well as letters of support or reference. You may also be required to submit a resume along with the other supportive documents. These are more formalized procedures, and you want to be efficient. These documents serve as your "calling card" or "formal introduction" as to who you are and what assets you possess that will contribute to the overall mission of the organization. Make sure that the application is readable and free of errors. It may be beneficial to download the application (if available) and create a draft to be used as a template before completing the original document. If the application form is fillable, then type in your responses and do not handwrite them on the form.

It is good practice to utilize the resources that are available to you within your institution and your program. Before submitting your final documents, it is beneficial to solicit the assistance of the faculty internship supervisor, academic advisor, campus resources such as the career center, and writing coaches. These individuals can assist you by reviewing your documents and providing feedback to you regarding the quality of the completed packet. This will provide you with the opportunity to make any necessary corrections before submitting them. Documents that contain grammatical errors, misspellings, and appear ill-prepared and rushed will only serve to weaken your application. If you do not understand something on the application, then contact your resources (such as your university faculty) or the organization to obtain clarification.

Some internship sites require students to submit letters of recommendation or support. As students negotiate their academic and professional journey, they have become increasingly aware of the need to utilize resources in their program and community to vouch for their qualities and abilities. Therefore, it is critical that you choose individuals who can not only make favorable statements about who you are, but they can also provide information that is relevant and beneficial to the goal that you are aiming to accomplish. Please see the chapter on Resume Writing for more information about letters of recommendation.

While pursuing your fieldwork/internship site you may find that some sites may invite you to interview for the position. Once you have received confirmation that you will be interviewing for the position, do not leave any detail of this process to chance. You will continue to be just as diligent in your efforts as you were in your preparation to secure this meeting. As you prepare for your face-to-face interview, begin with a review of the organization's website and any other literature that is available for you to study. Information that you may pay attention to is the history, mission, goals, and values of the organization. Have a clear understanding of the consumers the organization serves. Be well-versed on the programs and services offered within the organization. More information about the interview process can be found in the chapter on Interview Preparation.

CONTRACT AGREEMENTS

Fieldwork experiences require a contract agreement between the field site and the academic institution. Students need to be aware that effective written agreements between the institution and the clinical education sites should be current and describe the rights and responsibilities of both parties. At a minimum, agreements address four key areas.

First, the contract will address the purpose of the agreement. Second, it will address the objectives of the institution and the clinical education site. Third the contract will address the rights and responsibilities of the institution and the clinical education site. This includes those related to responsibility for patient/client care and responsibilities for supervision and evaluation of students. Fourth, the contract will include the procedures to be followed in reviewing, revising, and terminating the agreement.

Prior to the fieldwork experience, students should inquire whether there is a current agreement in place in order to be in compliance with the agencies policies and procedures. The faculty or the fieldwork coordinator should have this information. For liability purposes, a contract between the university and the field site must be established before the student can engage in any activities at the field site. The following are special issues that may arise.

HOUSING NEEDS

When internship/fieldwork students are required to move away from their place of residence to complete their internship/fieldwork experience, they are often left with the burden of securing housing. It is essential that students know that many states typically provide a listing of available housing for some allied health students who are in their internship/fieldwork. Students should remain mindful that taking time to research housing assistance can save money and allow them an opportunity to secure a fieldwork/internship site away from their place of residence.

GRIEVANCES

The authors would like to briefly address student grievances. Any student who has a problem or concern with the internship/fieldwork site should discuss the concern with the course instructor as soon as possible. Fieldwork/Internship instructors have the resources to manage challenges students may encounter during their experience. However, if the concern remains unresolved, the student should follow up with their instructor. In extreme cases where consultation with the course instructor does not prove to be beneficial, the student should consult the Program Coordinator for guidance on the university's policy for managing such challenges. These policies and procedures, as well as the chain of command, may vary from school to school.

CONCLUSION

Finding a fieldwork/internship site can be a complicated process, however it is one that requires dedication and research. Engagement in an effective fieldwork/internship site can provide many benefits to students. These benefits can include; improved skill level, the establishment of professional relationships, the expansion of resources and references and potentially a source of longterm, full-time employment. Students should engage in this process with great caution and consideration as it has the potential to shape their career.

Moving forward, once students have successfully secured their internship site placement, they will begin the process of being indoctrinated into the organizational practices and professional responsibilities. Students will work with their assigned faculty internship supervisor, internship site supervisor, and other staff to discuss roles, expectations, and responsibilities of all individuals involved in this process. It is important that the lines of communication remain open between all parties involved. Using effective communication skills will be critical as students embark of the journey of putting theory into practice.

> PLEASE SEE THE EXTENSIVE APPENDICES FOR THIS CHAPTER WHICH ARE LOCATED AFTER CHAPTER 14.

DISCUSSION QUESTIONS

1. What is the purpose of a fieldwork/internship experience?

2. Discuss how the concept of "fit" impacts the selection of internship sites and placement.

3. Discuss the importance of displaying professional behavior when seeking a fieldwork site and maintaining that level of professionalism during the internship.

4. Describe and discuss at least three strategies that you should use when seeking an internship/fieldwork site.

5. Describe and discuss the primary components of a clinical contract discussed in this chapter.

CASE STUDIES

CASE STUDY 1, GRADUATE LEVEL

Tammy is a second-year physical therapy student who is scheduled for an inpatient rehabilitation affiliation 6 months from now, that will be 10 weeks in length. The Clinical Coordinator has provided the student with a list of appropriate inpatient rehabilitation facilities to select from, and clinical site information via website. The student is confirmed for a five-star inpatient rehab teaching hospital, where she will need to secure housing. The student is required to submit a letter of interest with goals, a resume, and undergo a phone interview, in order to secure official confirmation of the internship learning experience within three weeks.

QUESTION:
1. How should this student prepare for this phone interview to secure this internship learning experience over the next three weeks?

CASE STUDY 2, UNDERGRADUATE LEVEL

Rachel is a Rehabilitation Services major, in her senior year, who needed to secure observation clinical time to meet graduation requirements in a Fieldwork course, with no Fieldwork Coordinator. A listing of clinics was not available to the student. Therefore, the student had to research sites in the desired area, gather contact information, and have a clinical contract set up between the university and the clinical site.

QUESTION:
1. How should this student proceed to secure the required observation hours with a clinical facility?

CASE STUDY 3, GRADUATE LEVEL

A graduate student is scheduled to start a clinical rotation in three months in an inpatient rehab setting. The student has been identified as having bipolar depression, ADHD, and a personality disorder and faculty members have devised a plan of action for the student to address. The student has been referred to Student Disability services, a professional psychologist, and Medical Doctor for evaluation, treatment, and recommendations. The student is following through on

what he/she needs to do in order to receive appropriate
accommodations for this learning experience.

QUESTIONS:
1. How should this student proceed to prepare for this clinical learning experience?
2. What information should the student seek from the professionals above?
3. Who should the student meet with and why?
4. What communication should be shared with the internship site Instructor?
5. What specific learning strategies and considerations should be put into place on behalf of this student?
6. What reasonable accommodations should be advocated for on behalf of the student?

CASE STUDY 4, GRADUATE LEVEL

A graduate student contacts the local board of education three
days before they need to start the school counseling internship to
complete the required internship hours before the student's deadline.
The local board of education accepts the request and places the
student with a secondary school counselor. The school counselor is
notified two days before the internship is to start.

The student stated upon arrival at the internship that there was a
mix up in placement since the student had notified the board three
months before, but the person responsible for placement of the
internship resigned. The student does not bring any documentation as
to standards to learn or experience during this fieldwork experience.
The student does not bring a time log documentation form for the
supervising counselor to sign for the hours worked on day one.

QUESTIONS:
1. What should the student provide to the supervising counselor on the next day of the internship?
2. Identify two areas of weakness by the student in setting up in the internship.
3. After identifying the areas of weakness, consider how the student could have been proactive.
4. What is the significance of the time log documentation?

5. Why is follow up important in this case study, from the student's point of view?

CASE STUDY 5, GRADUATE LEVEL

A graduate student directly contacts the possible supervising counselor and asks if there are other ways besides being present for direct contact hours to acquire the total amount of hours needed, such as an individual assignment to do on the student's own time or online webinars. The student also states that the program of study was started before the internship hours increased from 300 to 600 and asks if doing the lower amount of fieldwork hours will work. The student follows up with the possible supervising counselor after speaking to the advisor and receiving written instructions that states the increased amount of internship hours will have to be completed for graduation.

QUESTIONS:
1. From this case study, did the student discuss any options with the college or university's site coordinator, advisor, or professor first, before contacting the possible supervising counselor?

2. Is it ethically appropriate to ask to do fewer work hours if your college or university advisor has put in writing that you must complete the program of study under the new guidelines for internship hours?

3. How could an ethics violation occur for both the student and possible supervising counselor, if this was carried out with the lower amount of field site hours?

4. What is the possible outcome for both the student and possibly the supervising counselor if the scenario in question number three played out?

CASE STUDY 6, UNDERGRADUATE LEVEL

An undergraduate student sets an appointment to speak with his/her advisor about possible sites for student teaching the semester prior to the planned fieldwork. The advisor sets up the student teaching with a school and gives the student the school name, the supervising teacher's name, and the start date. The student enrolls in the Directed Teaching course. The student teacher provides the supervising teacher with all required documentation that will be needed for the duration of the internship. The Directed Teaching class meets periodically throughout the student teaching timeframe for the student to meet on

17

campus to complete paperwork and to work on the culminating product. During these meetings, additional information is given for the next steps to take during the fieldwork experience to prepare for graduation.

QUESTIONS:
1. What is different in case study number six from the other case studies?
2. How was the student proactive in the search for a field site?
3. Explain how communication is a key component to securing a site?
4. Explain why consideration of timing is important to secure a site?

REFERENCES

[1]Anderson, N. (2009). Rebalancing the internship balance. Monitor on Psychology. Retrieved from https://www.apa.org/monitor/2009/06/ceo.aspx

[2]Baird, B.N. (2011). *The internship, practicum, and field placement handbook (6th ed.).* Allen & Bacon: Prentice Hall. Upper Saddle River, NJ.

[3]Bureau of Labor Statistics (2018). Job openings reach a new high in 2017, hires and quits also increase. Retrieved from https://www.bls.gov/opub/mlr/2018/article/job-openings-reach

[4]Chatman, J. A. (1989). Improving interactional organizational research: A model of person-organization fit. *Academy of Management Review, 14*(3), 333-349.

[5]Dawis, R. V., & Lofquist, L. H. (1984). *A psychological theory of work adjustment.* Minneapolis, MN: University of Minnesota Press.

[6]Doran, J.M., & Cimbora, D.M., (2016). Solving the internship imbalance: Opportunities and obstacles. *Training and Education in Professional Psychology, 10*(2), 61-70. Retrieved from http://psycnet.apa.org.proxy.lib.uiowa.edu/fulltext/2016-07823

[7]Eggerth, D.E. (2008). From theory of work adjustments to person-environment https://journals-sagepub-com.proxy.lib.uiowa.edu

[8]Glassdoor. (2018). 50 most common interview questions. Retrieved from https://www.glassdoor.com/blog/common-interview-questions/

[9]Hodges, S. (2015). *The counseling practicum and internship manual: A resource for graduate counseling student (2nd ed).* New York, NY: Springer Publishing Company.

[10]Pitts, J.H. (1992). Organizing a practicum and internship programs in counselor education. Retrieved from: https://eds-a-ebscohost-com.proxy.lib.uiowa.edu/ehost

CASE MANAGEMENT & PRESENTATION

SIMONE B. HICKS

JESSICA S. HENRY

CHAPTER DESCRIPTION

The purpose of this chapter is to provide readers with a refresher in case management. This chapter will define case management and present readers with the primary phases and processes of case management as well as a discussion of the varying roles of the case manager. Discussion about case assessment will also be provided to aid readers in preparing to review and assess client cases as may be necessary as a rehabilitation professional. The chapter will also provide practical activities and mini case studies that will allow readers the opportunities to engage in case assessment and review. Strategies for effective case management will be provided in addition to resources such as an introduction to professional organizations that aid with and promote effective case management. Knowledge of case management is essential during the internship and fieldwork process. In addition, this chapter tackles the notion that the case management process relies on self- awareness, self-care and cultural competence.

LEARNING OBJECTIVES

➢   Students will explore the key components of case management.

➢   Students will explore effective case assessment considerations including, cultural competence and goal development.

➢   Students will learn how to develop a comprehensive case presentation.

INTRODUCTION

As you familiarize yourself with knowledge pertaining to becoming a helping professional and the many functions roles provides, one essential task of care surrounds proficiency in case management. This pattern of documentation and specialty of service delivery outcomes aid in ensuring the wellness standards for consumers of health-related services through measures of advocacy and autonomy.[13] Case management is a specialty practice which enhances treatment procedures for consumers across a range of service industries and is rooted in health care delivery models.

The theory of case management can be traced back to the1920s, when psychiatry and social work were first noticed for a documentation-centered treatment system. Case management is known as an evidence-based practice use to provide a framework of systems supports. This type of monitoring procedures assists in observing and responding to the individual needs of the consumer. Likewise, case management; when done correctly, outlines the expectation of case managers to ensure collaborative care efforts between themselves and consumers. This two-way coordination structure (i.e. plans for care both written and approved by the service provider and consumer) helps to provide treatment methods that are considered timely, efficient, equitable, and client-centered[3]. In this chapter, we will explore the different phases and activities of case management; which include: collecting, and interpreting information that indicates the needs of the consumer across the case management process.

DEFINING CASE MANAGEMENT

There is no one formal definition of case management, per say. Defining case management becomes more explicit as managers understand that the overarching aim is to audit progress of service effectiveness. Using case management, service providers are able to determine what a plan of treatment must look like and whether or not the plan illustrated effectiveness in reaching a goal. Case managers view the purposefulness of this multidisciplinary technique according to the focus of the profession within which services are being provided. For the purpose of this chapter and providing a definition of case management, we look to the Commission on Case Management Society of America (CMSA), which employs case management as "a collaborative process of assessment, planning, facilitation, care coordination, evaluation, and advocacy for services to meet individual and/or family comprehensive health needs through communication and available resources to promote, cost-effective outcomes". Case management serves as a foundational tool throughout the fields of human services and rehabilitation. As a result, professional organizations such as the American Case Management Association (ACMA) provide a collaborative practice model for a variety of professions in health care and education. Examples of professions that may be influenced by the ACMA model include: social work, nursing, rehabilitation counseling, mental health, occupational therapy and education, to name a few.[1]

As mentioned above, case management, as a specialty practice, is utilized across a variety of service-delivery based professions. As you prepare to enter the world of work you are encouraged to refer to the specific standards of practice for the particular profession you select. These standards typically outline in a written document the performance expectations with regard to case management. For example, if we were to turn to the Rehabilitation Counseling profession, the Commission on Rehabilitation Counseling (CRC) highlights case management in the 2018 CRC Scope of Practice as:

A systematic process merging counseling and managerial concepts and skills through the application of techniques derived from intuitive and researched methods, thereby advancing efficient and effective decision-making for functional control of self, client, setting, and other relevant factors for anchoring a proactive practice. In case management, the counselor's role is focused on interviewing, counseling, planning rehabilitation programs, coordinating services, interacting with significant others, placing clients and following up with them, monitoring progress, and solving problems.

CRCC, 2018

For a new human service provider, you will be able to easily access the role expectancies of case management for the specific profession that you work by exploring documents that highlight standards of practice and/or ethical codes. These documents outline the criteria for which practitioners are expected to follow while involvement in the case management process. These professional standards play a unique role in ensuring the effectiveness of services and in promoting respect for human dignity and diversity.[2] Recognizing the importance of case management with assist you as you may be deciding to pursue an array of professional careers; furthermore, your training in the specialty practice of case management has the potential to translate across professions which is considered an asset with the occupational agenda of any organization.

Occupational Therapy is another helping profession that utilizes case management and care coordination strategies to direct the services provided for consumers. According to this profession, case management helps to reduce costs as well as bridge health and social services for coordination efforts.[8] Overall, as a profession, following the development of the Commission for Case Manager Certification (CCMC), Occupational therapists have adopted the Certified Case Manager (CCM) credential to conduct case management according to a unified scope of practice.

Through the lens of a rehabilitation professional, case management is a strategy that assists practitioners to arrange services, monitor program outcomes, arrange and accommodate placement, monitor ethical decisions, control for multicultural concerns that may arise, and respond to the needs of vocational rehabilitation consumers.[14] Similarly, case management in mental health is influenced by the supply and demand service model, and is a "way of tailoring help to meet individual needs through placing the responsibility for assessment and service coordination with one individual worker or team."[10] There are five core tasks of case management which include: 1) assessment, 2) planning, 3) implementation, 4) monitoring, and 5) reviewing.

THE PHASES OF CASE MANAGEMENT

The effectiveness of case management relies on the expertise of the human service professional. In order for the case management process to be successful, case managers must have regard for the significance in developing an individualized plan that considers the specific needs and desires of the consumer from start to finish. The lack of personalization in the case management process increases a risk that the plan will be less or completely ineffective. Let's consider a situation where a client is mandated by court to enter a drug treatment program in response to addiction related behaviors that has led to his children being placed in foster care. Case management or the lack thereof could make or break the consumers success. The case management process must consider not only the overarching needs of the client, for instance, addressing addiction and getting his children out of foster care; but also, consider his mental and emotional status towards managing addiction and raising his children.

The phases of case management include referral, intake & screening, assessment, care plan & service coordination, and follow-up & reassessment.[6, 9, 15] In addition to varying professions upholding slightly different aims of case management, the agencies for which you may work might also adopt different processes to gather information, yet theses phases will all-in-all remain consistent. We begin our discussion by considering how the first phase, referral phase has evolved over time.

REFERRAL

In traditional case management, a client was referred for services by a secondary source. However, as healthcare services evolve and become more autonomous in nature, consumers may now self-refer for treatment. Indicating the source of referral and making appropriate referrals serve as an intricate part of the case management process. The aim of referral in case management is to ensure that the consumer receives the most appropriate connection to a service that will help with their rehabilitation. These referrals must be documented in the consumer's case file as they help paint a picture of the individual toward rehabilitation readiness.

INTAKE, ENGAGEMENT, AND SCREENING

In case management you may see the terms, intake, engagement and screening used interchangeably; however, there are some distant differences that should be considered during these phases. Intake, engagement, and screening all refer to the practice of obtaining information and all are considered foundational to the development of a helping alliance critical for planning to begin.[3,16] The intake phase involves gathering basic information about the client, such as, name, age, date of birth, family history, employment history, and in some cases, other important information like medical history, substance use/dependency, or criminal background. The intake interview phase of case management allows the manager to infer information about the consumer and build a therapeutic alliance by becoming familiar with one another.

Intakes are scheduled to gather pertinent information; such as demographics, mental health assessment, medical history, family support, and job history. Further, intake information helps determine a baseline for the client current standing before treatment or services have been initiated to create change. The intake process can be conducted in a variety of ways: a standard set of questions, the client shares a narrative, or the referral source will share information. According to the Commission for Case Manager Certification (CCMC),[3] the intake assessment phase serves to identify key concerns/ issues to address with the client. In all, the case manager hopes to gain comprehensive knowledge to assess the client's immediate needs. In addition to the assessment phase, assessing a client's risk is important as well.[16] For example, as mentioned previously, identifying the client's baseline will gauge where the client is and determine the trajectory for case management services.

Screening on the other hand is considered an additional layer. The case manager collects information about the appropriateness of services and determines eligibility.[3,16] If a client does not meet certain criteria of a program or service, the case manager can then make referrals for other services that are more closely related to the needs identified during initial contact. Case managers should not continue to the assessment phase if discrepancies in eligibility are observed.

MULTICULTURAL COMPETENCIES DURING INTAKE

Across all phases of case management, but particularly the intake phase, the case manager or human service practitioner must begin to consider the role of multicultural competence. While case management in the past has not necessarily considered the impact of multicultural properties, today as we continue to serve more diverse populations seeking services, the case managers own awareness of potential bias must be considered. This type of exploration throughout the case management process is vital to refrain from imposing preconceived ideas about the client based on the bias for which they may hold. Furthermore, awareness will help decrease any negative effects of microaggressions and biases within the helper-client relationship. Beginning this practice of self-awareness in your role as case manager during this phase will be an additional benefit to the rapport and relationship as it progresses.

ASSESSMENT

The primary objective of the assessment phase is to gain additional information about the consumer and assist in determining a baseline before treatment begins in order to observe changes over time. The assessment phase of case management serves as the initial indicator to determine if case management is effective. Assessment is rendered in an objective manner and utilized as another means of gathering data about the client.[4] For example, the assessment may use properties of some standardized or non-standardized form but should also consider input of the consumer, staff/case managers, and other key community stakeholders.

Care Plan and Service Coordination

The next two phases run parallel with one another. The care plan is comparable to a blueprint that outlines the goals, objectives, and intended actions of the service provider and the client as they work together to carry out the client's service plan.[3] In this chapter, thus far, we have discussed how case management is a specialty practice that is used across many human service and rehabilitation professions. This allows us to understand the need for gaining knowledge of the multidisciplinary case management process. In order to impose such a universal view of care plan development, the healthcare profession has adopted the use of SMART goals and objectives for universality of treatment and development of the rehabilitation care plan.

SMART Goals

Ideologies of the SMART system of goal development trace back to George T. Doran of Spokane, Washington in 1981.[5] The acronym SMART consists of five key criteria of goal and objective development. These include:

- ➢ Specific,
- ➢ Measurable,
- ➢ Attainable,
- ➢ Realistic, and
- ➢ Time-Specific.

The criteria "Specific" surveys the major concerns that are presented about the client and seeks to foster improvement across that designated area.[3] When developing the "measurable" criteria of a SMART goal, the case manager is deliberately quantifying progress in order to measure change. A major criteria of goal development requires the case manager to consider the following questions:

1) can the desired goal be achieved?

2) is there a path to assure that the goal can be accomplished?[5]

Additionally, the client's goal must be realistic, which means the goal should focus on ensuring that the plans for services are achievable when compared to resources that are available.[5] For example, developing a plan for a consumer with an intellectual disability which involves an ultimate goal of becoming an astronaut, may not be realistic. In this situation the human service or rehabilitation professional may have considered the limitations of their client's disability. It is also noteworthy to consider the ethical ramifications of such a plan. Failure of the plan may cause undue harm to the client.

Finally, when writing goals with the client the service provided should remember to make them "time specific." Time-specific represents the criteria which indicates an anticipated time frame for which evidence of results will be achieved.[5] The client's involvement during this phase is critical as they guide their process. Allowing the client to drive their goals serves as an empowerment tool and demonstrates their belief in the process. Further, this phase is an opportunity for the case manager to service, help maintain compliance, and support the client's goal.

Goal development serves as the opportunity to note improvement as the client receives services. Timelines may be adjusted as needed; however, documentation should occur to explain the changes accordingly. Throughout the case manager/client relationship, the case manager assists in coordinating services, helps to maintain compliance, and supports the client to reach outlined goals.

Service coordination follows the outline of the care plan and highlights what services will be initiated, how they will be organized in order to ensure timely, efficient, equitable and client-centered regard for rehabilitation, and is expected to postulate in what way services will benefit the overall goal of the service delivery progression. The main goal is to commence action toward rehabilitation by way of structured activities and/or referral. One of the major components of a case manager is to recognize what services exist within the community. Case management and other care plan coordinators are encouraged to familiarize themselves with community assets. Building rapport and having knowledge about what services are available would be beneficial to the consumers to reach the goal of optimal and holistic wellness.

FOLLOW-UP & REASSESSMENT

The final phase of case management are follow-up and/or reassessment. The focus of this phase is to review progress of service interventions through monitoring closely what has been achieved and how services have encouraged evolution since initiation. The treatment regimen and the client advancement toward obtaining goals are included as the targeted focus of the follow-up phase. Reassessment occurs if the consumer has not had progress towards outlined goals. In the instance that client function has not improved, managers should begin to look closely at effectiveness of the intervention through an evaluation of services and the development of a new care plan.

CASE REVIEW & ASSESSMENT

A significant proportion of the case management process is reviewing and assessing each case. These procedures occur after the case manager has obtained substantial information to structure care coordination.[3] Understanding and further clarifying the difference between reviewing a case and assessing a case is crucial. Reviewing a case consists of gathering basic information given at the time the client referral is received and the intake process initiated. Case management is not a linear model as it relates to the assessment phase; but is an ongoing assessment process for the case manager. The assessment phase is a comprehensive needs-based approach; which identifies critical areas to explore in the case management process.[19] During this phase, the case manager may identify missing information or concerns that need to be addressed as goals are developed. As a case manager, the more attentive and critical you are during the assessment phase to the needs of the consumer, the easier it will be to create a more efficient plan of care and rehabilitation.

Creating and providing services unique to the consumers' needs is paramount to the success of case management services. Over time, developments in the field of case management support the idea of objectively assessing each case individually. For example, some agencies adhere to rubrics that assess the needs of each client. According to the Alabama Department of Mental Health, the Service Utilization Needs Assessment-Revised (SUN-R) is used to define consumer concerns across five key areas, including: 1) social needs, vocational needs, transportation needs, behavioral need, and basic needs. This assessment requires the case manager to examines these pertinent areas of need by providing a score of "1" if attention is required, score of "0" if no further attention is required. Regardless of the score of "1" or "0", the assessment provides space for the case manager to give description and thorough explanation of the evaluation. While this model seeks to increase effectiveness, one challenge for the case manager is to avoid temptation to adopt a one-size-fits-all mentality. Instead remember the importance of assessing each case individually and thoroughly.

Case managers have a responsibility to assess consumer needs holistically (i.e. physical, mental, emotional, social, financial, spiritual, and intellectual). The Strengths Model was developed to support adults through the rehabilitation process and now accommodates adolescents as well. This model focuses on the strengths of the client while simultaneously serving as an objective toolbox for the case manager throughout phases of the process.[12]

STRATEGIES FOR EFFECTIVE CASE MANAGEMENT

There are several strategies to achieve effective case management services. This section will highlight a few. Based on agency cultures, the execution of strategies may vary. Generally, when one thinks of case management actions certain words are common; such as: linking, facilitating, corresponding, accessing, and connecting. These strategies can lead to the delivery of effective case management services. Additionally, case managers should consider the importance of rapport building between the case manager and client, awareness of resources, and time management. Below will provide examples of case management actions.

Linking is the process of pairing clients with services that address the identified need to accomplish their goals.[18] For example, if the need is training in laundry, hygiene, appearance, and dressing for a consumer with Autism Spectrum Disorder (ASD), the case manager may find it appropriate to link them to an occupational therapist who specialized in ASD. Similarly, connecting occurs when the case manager establishes association to services providers who can in achieving their goals and improving their quality of life. In a facilitative role the case manager guides the process of service provision. This and many other roles played by case managers require them to communicate with other service providers in the community and access a wide range of agencies and services that have the potential to benefit their clientele.

An additionally pertinent component is to establish trust in the case manager/ client relationship.[7] Perhaps the consumer has interacted with professionals, family, or friends who created a feeling of mistrust when the individual reached out for help. It is essential to create a safe and open space for a client to be expressive and share their experience. Building trust takes time. The initial interaction is a critical point for clients as they can possibly be entering a new experience or repeating another experience.

A central component of a case manager's role is being aware of the resources locally, regionally, and statewide. Serving as a liaison requires these professionals to build community relationships. It is also a recommended practice to visit the agencies to understand the services provided within these agencies. In doing so, the case manager can enhance service delivery and gain the ability to describe agency services to clients.

Awareness of resources increases the delivery of efficient and effective services. To illustrate, a case manager meets with the client and assesses their needs. Based on the assessment, the client may exhibit issues that require immediate referral to more appropriate resources. Having a relationship built with community partners and understanding their services will enable the case manager to link the client with appropriate resources.

Discussed above is the emphasis on building relationships with clients and community partners. Equally important is the ability to prioritize and practice time management. In the case management process, it is essential for case managers to prioritize and manage time while with a client so that the most efficient service can be rendered.

CASE PRESENTATION

While in their internship/fieldwork experiences, students are often actively engaged in case management services. During their in-class experience, students are also often asked to present their knowledge of the case management process by way of a case presentation. The purpose of this particular learning tool seeks to allow students the opportunity to present their knowledge about the process, discuss the work they have engaged in with a particular client, lead the class through the case management process, and gain feedback from both their colleagues and instructor in regard to how they are managing the case and what tactics they could employ to enhance the successful goal achievement for their client.

When conducting an in-class case presentation there are eight content areas that should be discussed. These areas include but are limited to: (Depending on the instructor's preference some of these sections may not be included in your case presentation):

> ➤ Background information about the site,

> ➤ Client background information with presenting issues,

> ➤ Symptoms and behaviors of the client,

> ➤ Focus of the session,

> ➤ Issues that were addressed,

> ➤ Counseling theory used or would use,

> ➤ Treatment plan/objectives, and

> ➤ Questions.

In the following section we will briefly describe each of these areas.

BACKGROUND INFORMATION

This section should have information about the company or agency where the student is completing his or her fieldwork/internship experience. This section of the case presentation should include the basic demographics of the company and its hierarchy. It should also include a list and description of the services the agency provides and the population they serve.

CLIENT BACKGROUND

This section of the case presentation should include a detailed summary of the clients' background information and presenting issues. Such information would include the clients' basic demographic information, relevant familial, educational, and vocational statuses as well as any challenges, barriers, and or limitations the client may be experiencing. Additionally, this section should include a listing and description of any symptoms, behaviors, and diagnostic information relevant to the client. In cases where information is delivered to outside sources, use pseudonyms (fake names) to protect anonymity of the consumer.

TREATMENT/SERVICE PLAN

If you have a clearly developed or partially developed plan for working with your client, it should be included in your case presentation. A treatment or service plan outlines the clients' challenges and limitations, the goals of the client that will aid in eliminating their challenges and limitations as well as the services that will be provided in order to help the client achieve his or her goals. This plan helps to keep both the service provider and the client on track throughout the service provision process.

FOCUS OF SESSION

Every time you meet with the client you should have a sense of direction, whether that is building rapport or focusing on a particular area such as self-esteem. This is to say that every session that you have with a client is to have a clear purpose. In this section of your case presentation you are to let your audience know the purpose of your most recent meeting with the client. What goals were to be accomplished as a result of the session.

ISSUES THAT WERE ADDRESSED

In this section you will discuss what challenges or limitations you addressed with the client during your most recent session. In your discussion it may be helpful to reflect on previous challenges and limitations that were addressed with or overcome by the client. Examples of things that may have been addressed with your client include coping skills, problem behaviors, relationship issues, or service needs.

THEORY OF PRACTICE USED

As professionals we develop a framework/philosophy from which we operate when serving clients in the fields of Human Services and Rehabilitation. This guides you in how you work with your clients. Very often, when working with members of the public, we are trained to do so with a framework/philosophy in mind. We draw upon theories, techniques, and varied approaches we are taught during our academic training. In this section of the case presentation, students are asked to share the framework/philosophy from which they gleaned to serve the needs of their client. You should describe any theories and theory specific techniques you may have employed or plan to implement when helping your client. Be sure to include a clear rationale that describes why you believed this approach to be most suitable for your client.

QUESTIONS

As Human Services and Rehabilitation professionals one of the most important things to remember is that two heads are indeed often better than one. Students should take the Questions section of their case presentation to ask for suggestions, resources, and/or ideas from their colleagues and instructor. This is an opportunity for you to gain valuable information or ideas that you may not have considered which you could utilize to better serve your client(s).

Please be mindful that during or at the end of your case presentation you may be asked to address questions regarding your client, the treatment plan, or any other information that you present. Always take such opportunities to enhance your knowledge and skill. If someone asks a question it is often because the presenter has piqued their interest and curiosity. Take all feedback and questions as opportunities to expand your knowledge and skill, rather than criticism or signs of failure.

In addition to addressing the eight areas outlined above students should consider a few other factors when engaging in such an assignment. It is always best practice to begin preparing your presentation as far in advance as possible. If you are using power point or another presentation medium, ensure that you keep your slides neat, organized, simple, and creative. Practice your presentation ahead of time to ensure that you are familiar with all the information you have placed in your presentation. Additionally, include some creative components into your presentation, keep your audience engaged, and find a few ways to involve them in the presentation.

CONCLUSION

Case management is an essential role of human service and rehabilitation professionals. The phases and components of case management are essential to gathering, assessing, and implementing information about the client to ensure effective service provision. Human service and rehabilitation professionals would do well to ensure that they are well versed in the case management process when working with clients who have physical, educational, socioeconomic, vocational, medical, and psychosocial needs.

MINI CASE STUDIES

CASE STUDY: MARK

Mark is a 20-year-old college student from a small rural town in the Midwestern part of the United States. He is a first-generation student and navigating his college experience with limited family support. He has a work-study job to help support his daily needs. Mark entered the counseling center requesting to speak to someone regarding additional resources to help with his mental health. He was later connected with an intake counselor to identify his needs. He indicated that he was feeling anxious and getting behind in his schoolwork because of lack of focus. Mark stated that he has the school insurance but there is limited availability in the counseling center, and he has limited time due to his class and work schedule. Further, he mentions that his family does not believe in sharing his problems outside the household, so he is hesitant about therapy and does not want to upset his mom. Consider the five stages of case management as you process the next steps.

QUESTIONS RELATED TO THE CASE STUDY?
  ➤ Develop a case presentation of Mark's case.

  ➤ What additional information is needed?

  ➤ What are additional resources needed to consider for this case based on the details provided?

CASE STUDY: JOSEPHINE

Josephine is a 36-year-old female residing in Northern California. She is a mother of two. Her daughter is a high school senior and she has a 10-year-old son. She is a single mother with the support of her mother. Josephine has type II diabetes. She is currently working a part-time job at a local store. Josephine was recently referred to her community agency for additional support and linkage to community resources. Consider the five stages of case management as you process the next steps.

QUESTIONS RELATED TO THE CASE STUDY?
  ➤ What additional information is needed?

  ➤ What are some possible limitations for Josephine based on her listed diagnosis?
  ➤

REFERENCES/RESOURCES

[1] American Case Management Association (2019). Retrieved from: https://www.acmaweb.org/

[2] American Counseling Association. (2014). ACA Code of professional ethics. Alexandria, VA.: Author.

[3] Commission for Case Management (2018). Case management philosophy and guiding principles. Case Management Body of Knowledge. Retrieved from https://www.cmbodyofknowledge.com/content/case-management-philosophy-and-guiding-principles

[4] Denzin, Norman K. (1973). *The research act: A theoretical introduction to sociological methods.* New Jersey: Transaction Publishers.

[5] Doran, G. T. (1981). There's a S.M.A.R.T. way to write management's goals and objectives. *Management Review, 70,* 35-36.

[6] Fabbri, E., De Maria, M., & Bertolaccini, L. (2017). Case management: an up-to-date review of literature and a proposal of a county utilization. *Annals of Transitional Medicine, 5*(20), 396.

[7] Ganske, K., Gnilka, P. B., Ashby, J., & Rice, K. G. (2015). The relationship between counseling trainee perfectionism and the working alliance with supervisor and client. *Journal of Counseling and Development, 93,* 14–24.

[8]Golden, R. (2015). The importance of collaboration. *Case Management Society of America Today, 4*, 21–22.

[9]Jensen, S. (2013). Case management and care coordination: Best-practice workplace solution. *Occupational Medicine and Health Affairs, 1*(4).

[10]Mendenhall, A. N. & Grube, W. (2016). Developing a New Approach to Case Management in Youth Mental Health: Strengths Model for Youth Case Management. Child and Adolescent Social Work Journal, 34(4), 369-379. DOI:10.1007/s10560-016-0467-z

[11]Onyett, S. (1998). *Case management in mental health.* London, UK: Nelson Thornes Ltd.

[12]Prochaska, J. O., DiClemente, C.C., & Norcross, J.C. (1992). In search of how people change: Applications to the addictive behaviors. *American Psychologist, 47*, 1102-1114.

[13]Rapp, C. & Goscha, R. (2006). *The strengths model.* N.Y: Oxford University Press.

[14]Robinson, M., Fisher, T. F. & Broussard, K. (2016). Role of occupational therapy in case management and care coordination for clients with complex conditions. *The American Journal of Occupational Therapy, 70*(2), 1–6.

[15]Roessler, R., & Rubin, S.E. (2006). *Case management and rehabilitation Counseling: Procedures and techniques.* Austin, TX: PRO-ED.

[16]Shelesky, K., Weatherford, R., & Janelle, S. (2016). Responding to the Increased Needs of College Students: A Case Study of Case Management. *Journal of College Student Psychotherapy, 30*(4), 284–299.

[17]Shlonsky, A., & Wagner, D. (2005). The next step: Integrating actuarial risk assessment and clinical judgment into an evidence-based practice framework in CPS case management. *Children and Youth Services Review, 27*(4), 409-427.

[18]Service Utilization Needs Assessment Revised. (n.d.). Retrieved from http://www.mh.alabama.gov/downloads/IDCP/SUN-R_Form_Problem_Areas_Unmet_Needs.pd

[19]Woodside, M. & McClam, T. (2013) Generalist case management: A method of human service delivery (4th Ed). Belmont, CA: Brooks/Cole Cengage Learning.

[20]Wright, J., Williams, R., & Wilkinson, J. R. (1998). Development and importance of health needs assessment. BMJ (Clinical research ed.), 316(7140), 1310-1313. DOI: 10.1136/bmj.316.7140.1310

DOCUMENTATION

KENT CRENSHAW

ABSTRACT

The purpose of this chapter is to provide readers with information about the importance, purpose, and practice of documentation. This chapter will define documentation and provide readers with information regarding the varying types of documentation. Information about the implementation of varying types of documentation will be provided in addition to practical application activities for practicing accurate and appropriate documentation. This chapter will also provide strategies for employing effective and efficient documentation in the field in order to ensure clarity and accuracy. Additionally, readers will be provided with helpful resources to enhance their documentation skills, development, and growth. This information is essential during the internship/fieldwork process because it will assist students in their ability to develop and maintain accurate and clinical documentation and will raise the students' awareness of the importance of timely and clear documentation.

LEARNING OBJECTIVES

- ➢ Students will understand the importance of documentation.
- ➢ Students will understand what information needs to be documented, and the guidelines for documentation.
- ➢ Students will learn the key principles of documentation.
- ➢ Students will practice the development of SOAP notes.

DEFINING DOCUMENTATION

The Collins English dictionary[2] defines documentation as "documents supplied as proof of evidence of something." Records have been defined as "a document or other thing that preserves information."[2] Documentation is the interactions between and among health professions, clients, their families, and health care organizations. Record keeping has been stated as "part of the professional duty of care owed by nurses to the patient."[3] Documentation serves as a permanent record of client information and care. Documentation is considered as a communication tool to exchange the information stored in records between practitioners and other service providers.

Documentation can enhance and ease communication and referrals between practitioners and other stakeholders involved in the client's life such as parents, teachers, medical providers, and other professionals. A proficient record keeping system helps track and organize these contacts.[19] Good documentation ensures continuity and consistency of services, regardless of which colleague or staff member provides services. This is especially important if there are staff changes or when a staff member is on leave or away from the office for other reasons. The bottom line is that careful and diligent documentation enhances the quality of services provided to clients and, ultimately, can protect practitioners. Records can provide a history and current status if a client seeks services from another health professional.[14]

TYPES OF DOCUMENTATION

There is a wide range of documentation, such as:

➢ Health record,

➢ Regulation and legislation,

➢ Reimbursement Documentation,

➢ Research Data SOAP notes,

➢ Progress note,

➢ Legal documentation, etc.

It is essential to note that this section does not contain an exhaustive list of the various types of documentation.

Health records or documentation provide evidence about the care and treatment patients receive. They include progress notes, assessments and care plans, as well as letters written to and about patients, and written communication between colleagues about patients.[1] This type of record is not only evidence of care, it also is a clinical tool, enabling continuity of care and appropriate decision making about future care and treatment. It offers an up-to-date account of the duties of health and social care organizations to handle confidential information.[1]

Regulation and legislation Audits of reports and clinical documentation provide a method to evaluate and improve the quality of patient care, maintain current standards of care, or provide evaluative evidence when standards require modification in order to achieve the goals, legislative mandates, or address quality initiatives.

Reimbursement Documentation is utilized to determine the severity of illness, the intensity of services, and the quality of care provided upon which payment or reimbursement of health care services is based.

Research Data from documentation provides information about patient characteristics and care outcomes. Evaluation and analysis of documentation data are essential for attaining the goals of evidence-based practice and quality health care.

The *SOAP* note (an acronym for subjective, objective, assessment, and plan) is a method of documentation that was a widely adopted and structurally theorized by Larry Weed almost 50 years ago. According to Many & Many,[6] SOAP notes are an essential piece of information about the health status of the patient as well as a communication document between health professionals. Subjective data are based on personal feelings, emotion, and experience. Objective data are data that are not influenced by emotions, opinions, or personal feelings. Assessment is the diagnosis or condition of the client. Plan refers to how you are going to address the patient's needs and follow-up.[6] Progress notes are made in a chart to record interactions with your patients/clients. The primary purpose of a progress note, however, is to allow another practitioner to readily assume the management of a patient if you are not available.[15]

Legal documentation. What is Legal documentation? Dimond [3] stated that a legal document is any document requested by the court and he goes on to identify some of the documents and records that may be requested. In the preoperative setting, the courts may request any of the documents we complete, so it is essential that all records are completed correctly.

PURPOSE OF DOCUMENTATION

The basic purpose of documentation is the creation of information or records of an interaction between the practitioner and client. Human service and rehabilitation programs stress the importance of best practice guidelines and ethical obligations in working with clients.[18] This includes documentation of all interactions with clients such as intake interviews, individual planning, career counseling, responsive services, and consultation with teachers, parents, administrators, and outside agencies.[18]

According to Beach and Oates,[1] documentation provides evidence of the level of care, treatment, or service given to a consumer/client. There are reasons why quality documentation is important in today's service context: Communication, continuity of care, professional accountability, legal, quality assurance, funding, and resource management and reach.[18] Communication among practitioner provides efficient and effective exchange of pertinent client information to the interprofessional care team. Continuity of care requires accurate information about the client to develop and provide an accurate plan of care for the client.[13]

In regard to professional accountability, documentation is one-way practitioner's knowledge, judgment, and skill are demonstrated.[17] Legal documentation or client's records are admissible as evidence in a court of law or professional conduct proceeding to establish time, date, and quality of service.[17] Audit and Quality assurance is used to evaluate the quality of service to the client and the appropriateness of care from documentation. Funding and resource management is documented to support the allocation of resources, workload management, and reimbursement to the agency.[13] Research provides valuable information to evaluate client's outcomes and to determine the efficiency and effectiveness of care.[13]

WHEN TO DOCUMENT

We have all heard the cliché, if you did not document it, you did not do it, or it did not happen.[1] Therefore, what you write does matter. According to the Nursing and Midwifery Council Code,[11] it is the duty of practitioners to keep clear and accurate documentations relevant to their practice; and considers documentation to be a crucial aspect of duty. Document any progress when each contact is made. Making and keeping records is an essential part of care and you must keep records for everyone you treat or who asks for your advice or services.[4] Remember, documentation needs to be created as close to the service delivery as possible so that records are timely, detailed and accurate.[5]

Here is why practitioners and staff should want to carefully document. According to Heathfield,[5] documentation provides evidence of service or treatment and offers a history of the practitioner and the client interactions. The interaction can be either or both positive and/or negative. Heathfield[5] stated that practitioners needs to document client performance, both positive contributions and performance failures, and document exactly what was said and what the client did and said in response during the meeting or conversation. Document any agreements made during the conversation, goals set, improvements required and expected, and the timeline for improvement.[5] Documentation should also contain commitments that the practitioner makes to assist the client. Documentation is a chronological and a precise description of the services provided and the actions of the client. Also, documentation can provide proof that the services were offered and/or provided to the client, so the client can have the opportunity to accept or decline the services. Documentation provides support to justify the reason services are offered and the continuation of service.[5]

Documentation should include progress notes, assessments and care plans, as well as written communication between colleagues about the clients.[1] Good clinical notes document the medical history of the patient. By documenting all relevant clinical information, you are recording this information for future reference.[8] Documentation is not only evidence of service but can be used as tools to make appropriate decisions about the continuation of care and future treatment.[1]

HOW DOCUMENTATION IS USED

Documentation is used to keep track of your work with a client and to assist should a client return after a long absence from receiving your services. Making and keeping records is an essential part of care and you must keep records for everyone you treat or who asks for your advice or services.[4] Also, documentation is used to assist with continuity of care should you refer a client to other practitioners or colleagues and to use as a resource should you experience an ethical or legal challenge regarding your work with a client.

There are several uses for and potential readers of documentations. Whatever those uses and whoever those readers, the primary aim is to communicate accurately any observations, actions, and discussions relevant to the patient or service user. Practitioners keep well-documented records to help protect themselves from professional liability in the event they become the subject of legal or ethical proceedings.[7]

According to Rhyne-Winkler and Wooten,[16] most counselors provide quality services that enhance the lives of their clients; however, counselors have failed to evaluate, document, and communicate the evidence of their effectiveness. With a move towards collaborative and shared approaches to care, both with colleagues from other disciplines and patients, you need to adopt a style of writing that suits this way of working. This means that prospective readers who may not have the specific professional knowledge of the person writing the health record should understand recorded documentation.

The use of archaic terms, acronyms, abbreviations, or professional jargon may confuse and unnecessarily complicate communication, particularly for lay readers.[12] According to Heathfield,[5] you need your documentation to appear professional, neat, and organized. Remember to write documentation as if you are talking about the history to a third party. You never know who may read your documentation one day; so, make sure that it reflects your professionalism.

STRATEGIES FOR EFFECTIVE DOCUMENTATION

Effective documentation should be written in an objective, legal, fair, factual and timely manner. You need your documentation to appear professional, neat, and organized. According to the Nursing and Midwifery Council, you must keep clear and accurate notes of the discussions you have, the assessments you make, the treatment and medicines you give, and how effective these have been. You must complete documentations as soon as possible after an event has occurred. According to Heathfield,[5] documentation should be written during or immediately following the meeting or conversation with the client. At no time should you miss writing down the conversation on the day when it occurred. Waiting until later affects the quality of the documentation because it is based on memory. Utilizing strategies that help minimize time spent in documenting interactions will, in turn, maximize time spent providing direct service to students.[18]

Wilson[19] writes that careful and consistent documentation assists with organizing and accessing information, evaluating time spent in delivering direct services to clients, and reflecting on successful interventions. Orwell[12] suggested it is a good idea to write documentation as if the client might request to read them. Additionally, human service and rehabilitation professionals may be asked to rely on them as evidence in a court of law. Your documentation should correspond with what the session includes. You must not tamper with original records in any way. You must ensure any entries you make in someone's paper or electronic records are clearly and legibly signed, dated, and timed.[18] Also, documentation should include information required by payers in addition to relevant clinical information. You must ensure all records are kept securely.

Finally, document any contact and meetings, agreements, commitments, timelines, improvements needed, and other details that might slip from memory. Make certain that you set a date and time for completions, goal completion, and meeting dates so that mix-up will not occur.[5] Effective documentation can serve as a tool to assist agencies with year to year planning, to organize continuity of interventions, and increase reporting and accountability for services provided, as well as to validate the necessity of providing direct service.[18]

CONCLUSION

When working with clientele from varying populations human services and rehabilitation professionals should ensure that they are effectively managing client records using effective documentation. Fields of human services and rehabilitation use documentation to track client progress toward goal acquisition, service provision, session progression and much more. It is essential the human service and rehabilitation professionals gain a clear understanding of the multifaceted purpose of documentation and the varying types of documentation.

Additionally, knowledge of the use and purpose of documentation will aid human service and rehabilitation professionals in developing effective strategies for documentation of client records. Many agencies have a pre-existing preference for documentation of client records; therefore, fieldwork/internship students would do well to learn the basics of case management and apply their knowledge to the specified method of documentation preferred by their fieldwork/internship agency. A review of examples of case notes, plans, and documentation can aid students in learning how to more effectively compile case documentation.

Remember, if you did not document it, it did not happen. As human services and rehabilitation professionals we often work with agencies who may receive subpoenas for records. Therefore, we have an ethical obligation to ensure that we are keeping client records that are accurate, appropriate, effective, timely, and professional.

HELPFUL RESOURCES

[1]Mitchell, B., (2007). Documentation in counseling records: an overview of ethical, legal, and clinical issues. *American Counseling Association.*
[2]Mosby, A., (2006). Mosby's Surefire Documentation: How, What, and when Nurses Need to Document. Elsevier Mosby.
[3]Ruebsaat, G. (2006). Records Management Guidelines. B.C. Association of Specialized Victim Assistance and Counselling Programs and B.C./Yukon
[4]Society of Transition Houses.
www.endingviolence.org/files/uploads/RMGApril2006.pdf.

DISCUSSION QUESTIONS

1. What is documentation and why is it important?

2. List and explain the different types of documentation?

3. What is the main purpose of documentation?

4. What is documentation used for?

5. List and discuss four strategies for effective documentation.

REFERENCES

[1]Beach, J., & Oates, J. (2014). Maintaining best practice in record-keeping and documentation. *Nursing Standard, 28*(36), 45-50.
[2]Collins English Dictionary (2003). Glasgow, *HarperCollins Publishers*
[3]Dimond, B., (2008). *Legal Aspects of nursing (5th Ed).* Harlow, Pearson Education Limited.
[4]Health Professions Council (2008). *Standards of conduct, performance and ethics.* London, HPC
[5]Heathfield, S. (2018). *The importance of documentation in human resources.* The Balance Dotdash Publishing. NewYork.
[6]LeFebvre R., Lynch, O., & Williams, D. (2013). S-O-A-P / Progress notes. university of western states college of chiropractic.
[7]Many, T. W., & Many, B. T., (2014). SOAP notes: A Tool to promote reflective dialogue about student learning: Best Practices. TEPSA News.
8Mathioudakis, A., Rousalova, I., Gagnat, A. A., Saad, N., & Hardavella, G., (2016). How to keep good clinical records. *Breathe (Sheffield, England), 12*(4), 369-373. doi:10.1183/20734735.018016

[9]Mitchell, R. W., (2007). *Documentation in counseling records: An overview of ethical, legal, and clinical issues.* American Counseling Association. Alexandria, VA.

[10]Nursing and Midwifery Council. (2009). *Record keeping Guidance for Nurses and Midwives.* London, NMC.

[11]Nursing and Midwifery Council. (2015) *The code professional standards of practice and behaviour for nurses and midwives.* NMC, London.

[12]Orwell, G., (1962). *Inside the whale and other essays. Penguin Books,* London.

[13]Pirie, S., (2011). Documentation and record keeping. *Journal of Perioperative Practice, 21*(1), 22-27.

[14]Potter, P.A., Perry, A. G, Stockert, P.A. & Hall, A.M. (2017). *Fundamentals of Nursing.* Elsevier. St. Louis, Missouri.

[15]Psychotherapy & Counselling Federation of Australia. (2014). *Draft Guidelines on Client Records.* PACFA.

[16]Rhyne-Winkler, M. C., & Wooten, H. R. (1996). The school counselor portfolio: Professional development and accountability. *School Counselor, 44*(2), 146-150.

[17]The College of Practical Nurses of Nova Scotia (2017). *Documentation Guidelines for registered nurses.* Halifax, NS Author.

[18]Wehrman, J. D., Williams, R.; Field, J., & Schroeder, S. D., (2010). Accountability through documentation: What are best practices for school counselors. *Journal of School Counseling,* 8(38), 23.

[19]Wilson, J., (1997). A record-keeping system for school counselors. *Professional School Counseling, 1*(2), 61-62.

CONSULTATION AND COLLABORATION

REBECCA R. SAMETZ

CHAPTER DESCRIPTION

The purpose of this chapter is to provide students with the understanding of consultation and collaboration within the rehabilitation and human services field. The chapter will discuss the concepts and varying types of consultation and collaboration and provide strategies for employing consultation and collaboration within the students' perspective field. The concepts discussed in this chapter aim to prepare students for field work experiences where they may be asked to perform consultation and collaboration services. The case study at the end of the chapter, as well as the discussion questions, encourage students to utilize different consultation and collaboration methods within rehabilitation and human service settings. This information is essential during the internship/fieldwork process because it will assist students in knowing how to facilitate consultation and collaboration services with other professionals.

KEYWORDS:

- ➢ consultation
- ➢ collaboration
- ➢ strategies

LEARNING OBJECTIVES

- ➢ Define the concepts of consultation and collaboration in the rehabilitation and human services community.
- ➢ Discuss the varying types of consultation and collaboration.
- ➢ Discuss strategies for employing consultation and collaboration in the rehabilitation and human services field.

INTRODUCTION

Rehabilitation and human service professionals are often trained to provide direct services to their clients and integrate the knowledge from various academic courses into their practice. However, rehabilitation and human service professionals have various roles and wear several different 'hats' throughout the rehabilitation process. Regardless of where one may work, at some point in their careers they will be asked to collaborate with and provide consultation services for other professionals. Consultation and collaboration are closely related processes that give rehabilitation and human service professionals opportunities to engage in cooperative relationships with other professionals. These processes involve individuals working together to address a problem, share resources, stimulate change or improvement, and use specialized information to achieve a common goal.[1] Unfortunately, consultation and collaboration with other human service professionals seems disproportionate in the literature when comparing to other roles and functions of rehabilitation and human service professionals.[18]

CONSULTATION

Literature talks about consultation as it pertains to other professionals outside of health services but is discussed more often in the literature within school settings. Consultation is a form of indirect education and mental health service delivery involving a professional with specialized knowledge and skills (i.e. a consultant) working with another professional (i.e. a consultee) to support clients' needs.[8] Dougherty[7] suggested that consultant roles may include that of advocate, expert, trainer/educator, collaborator, and other less common roles. However, consultants are considered 'experts' in most situations.

However, to embrace the role of a consultant, it is important to understand that there is no such thing as failure. The goal of the consultant is to provide the best services that meets the client's needs and open the door for future opportunities for consultation with human service professionals. For example, if a rehabilitation counselor meets with an employer to discuss the opportunities for hiring their client with a disability, and the employer is not interested in hiring that client, it does not mean that the consultant has failed. The consultant should remember that even if they are just sharing secondary resources with employer or community constituents, it does not mean that they have failed. This can be viewed as an opportunity to educate the community about resources available, and advocate for the use of these services. This is still considered consultation, and this type of relationship creates a mutually beneficial environment.

TYPES OF CONSULTATION

There are many models of consultation that exist. Models of consultation include mental health, process (organizational), and behavioral. Mental health consultation focuses on primary prevention, with the consultant (considered to be an expert) diagnosing a problem and providing a solution while having no responsibility for carrying out the recommended changes.[9] Within the role as an expert, the consultant would then come in and diagnose the problem and recommend a course of action in order to resolve the problem. Then, the consultant would provide a report that discusses and outlines his or her recommendation for the rehabilitation or human service professional who made the referral to the consultant to implement the recommended service. What is important to make clear is consultants are not part of the implementation of the recommended service to resolve the problems at hand; they are not part of the team that is implementing the recommendations made by the consultants. There are different types of consultations that can take place, meaning that they may not involve diagnosing. There can be times when a consultant is asked to come in and evaluate processes, programs, or general services being provided in additional to behavioral interventions and diagnoses.

Another common model of consultation is process consultation. Process consultation focuses on the ways problems are solved as well as the system in which problems occur.[15] The focus of process consultation is on the *how* of interpersonal and group interactions rather than on the *what* of the content.[19] The consultant and consultee examine communication patterns, group member roles, group problem solving and decision making, group norms and growth, leadership and authority, and intergroup cooperation and competition. The consultant then provides help with methods of communication and problem solving and with procedures for planning, decision making, and implementing the recommendations.[15] This form of consultation requires the consultant to build humanized interpersonal relationships with those that they are working with in order to get a better understanding of the structure, processes, and overall culture of the environment that is being evaluated.

Psychological or behavioral consultation is the application of systems theory and principles of learning to the problem-solving process. Further, it focuses on the needs of the individuals, groups, programs, and organizations.[3] The sequence of behavioral consultation is the following:

➢ problem identification/evaluation,

➢ problem analysis,

➢ behavior objectives,

➢ plan design and implementation, and

➢ evaluation of the behavior change.[10,17]

Psychological and behavioral consultation is based on principles and procedures found within psychology and related disciplines which a professional psychologist applies to their areas of expertise in response to the presenting needs and stated objectives of consultees.[3] This is more commonly seen within hospital settings and inpatient type settings where the consultant from a different department within a specific specialty may be asked to come and conduct a consult. For example, a psychiatrist may be asked by hospital emergency staff to perform a consult on a patient that has recently entered the hospital. This is more of a focused evaluation where the consultant, in this case the psychiatrist, may be focusing on one reported behavior or observed behaviors, and not considering the environmental factors that can potentially impact the plan design and implementation of a particular form of treatment. This is also known as consultant and emergency management.

STRATEGIES FOR CONSULTATION

As a potential consultant for other rehabilitation and human service professionals, it is important to recognize that one is not better or more of an expert, but the consultant merely has a different role at this time in the process.[9] A consultant may feel inclined to tell the consultee how to collect data, or how to perform a particular service because he or she is the designated expert. However, the consultant can be less directive and focus more on the side of being nondirective and collaborative with the consultee to utilize the resources they have and implement recommendations within the scope of their resources.

Further, the consultant may not necessarily receive a referral from another professional. The consultant may need to take the necessary steps in building relationships with those in the community in order to educate them about what services are offered,[17] and what areas of expertise one may have. While an influx of opportunities for consultation would be preferred, that is not a realistic expectation to have. It is the consultant's responsibility to create a partnership with other professionals and community members, and a partnership is formed when their investment in your unique combination of abilities and resources equals the investment in their unique combination of opportunities.

Lastly, the consultant may have a specific specialty that they are most knowledgeable in, but it does not always lead to knowing how to remedy the situation in a setting. For example, if a rehabilitation counselor were to be asked to consult on a case regarding an adolescent that has Autism within a local school, the rehabilitation counselor (the consultant) may know methods of treatment that could work, but may not have knowledge of the school system to make a recommendation that will be effective. Therefore, the consultant should create a climate and environment in which learning and change can take place.[4] What is meant by this is simply that it would be beneficial for the consultant to work with teachers, administration, and staff as a 'team' to brainstorm the best plan once the consultant delivers his/her expertise on the situation.

This method of consultation began because the consultant may not have the knowledge or expertise about a particular disability or situation, but can create a situation where the knowledge emerges from a group of professionals from various specialties.[4] This example leads us to collaboration and demonstrates how collaboration and consultation can fit into one another, especially in diverse human service settings. Nevertheless, consultation is a powerful helping process that continues to adapt and change in our changing environment, with the goal being to help whole systems function in a more collaborative and interdependent fashion in order to provide the best services to our clients.

COLLABORATION

Collaboration among rehabilitation and human service professionals happens more often than many may think, but there is still plenty of room to grow in terms of "breaking down" our silos and coming together as "one team." Collaboration, in the general sense, is a partnership of two or more equals who share in the decision-making responsibilities and work toward a common goal.[12] With effective teamwork and communication along rehabilitation and human service professionals, it can assist in maintaining client safety,[22] effective execution of services, and reduction of repetitive services.

The steps for this process are coming together, defining a shared vision, developing a strategic plan, taking action on the plan, and evaluating progress.[16] For example, within the school, counselors can collaborate with administrators to collect and share school performance data, to develop programs for overcoming barriers, to design strategies for school problems, and to emphasize a healthy school climate.[7] Another example is, rehabilitation and human service professionals can collaborate with community agencies to help with the coordination of services such as outreach, that the agency may not have the resources to provide.

STRATEGIES FOR COLLABORATION

Collaboration can take place in specialized groups called teams that have a specific work purpose. Teams share one or more common goals. Effective teams are committed to their constructive cooperation; have goals and identified roles; and are composed of members who are aware of the focus of the team, the responsibilities of the members, and the strategies of goal attainment. It has also been reported that teams are productive when team members trust, rely on, and respect each other, have problem-solving, conflict-resolution, and relationship-building skills, feel accountable, and encourage and help every other's efforts.

Making services more accessible and effective is a potential benefit of collaboration. It assists clients with complex problems that may require a great many services to have a team of professionals working together to reach the same goal. By working together, professionals do not potentially duplicate services and can potentially reduce costs associated with their agency. What is being said is that collaboration can reduce individual expenses in planning, research, training, and other development activities throughout the rehabilitation process.[12] When the overhead costs are shared among all agencies involved in the rehabilitation process, duplication of cost and effort is avoided.

A strategy that has come to the forefront of the research and within the literature is interprofessional collaboration among rehabilitation and human service professionals.[1] Interprofessional collaboration is when professionals with different backgrounds and from different specialties come together and work as a team to assist a client through the rehabilitation process. Having an opportunity to meet as a team with a group of professionals from various professions and specialties provides opportunities for interprofessional interaction and enables decision-making, as well as identification of the relevant problems in a case.[22] Rehabilitation and human services opportunities need more opportunities to explore such practices and to better articulate what works in different clinical settings.[6] Interprofessional collaboration and consultation promotes new ideas, goals, and practices that may benefit the greater good of an organization, profession, or group of people.[2,5,11,21]

CONCLUSION

The intent of this chapter is to encourage rehabilitation and human service professionals that provide consultant work to move toward taking a more active part in planning and decision-making for their clients.[13] Collaboration became an important and central tenet in consultation. As we previously learned, consultants would generally get called in to provide their "expert" opinion. At some point, there may be recognition that there was a critical problem with the consultant being the expert; this strategy or model often did not lead to change.[20] Why you ask? Well, think about it. Let's say you were the professional that was reading a report from a consultant that you asked to come in and observe and potentially diagnose a child. While reading the report from the consultant, you may decide that the recommended services are too costly, or that it requires too much staff time be taken away from other clients. Therefore, you disregard the consultant's recommendations and may only implement a small part of the recommendation. This may result in a lack of results because the child is not receiving all parts of the recommended services. Therefore, there have been recommendations within the literature to have the consultant be involved in the implementation of recommended services. This naturally creates opportunities for collaboration between the consultee and other staff working with that client to eliminate barriers to reaching client goals.

In conclusion, consultation and collaboration exist among the rehabilitation and humans service profession. While professional expectations regarding consultation and collaboration roles may differ among the different human service specialties, it still exists and is utilized throughout the rehabilitation process. There is a huge push for consultation and collaboration to occur that includes different professional backgrounds not only so that staff are exposed to different models, but also understand the responsibilities of their colleagues within the rehabilitation process.

CASE STUDY

Mrs. Jones is a Disability Services counselor at a local university with several years of experience in her position, and an additional five years' experience working as a special education teacher. She has a student who has trouble staying focused on a single task, bothers others, and often fails to complete assignments. Mrs. Jones only has what the school psychologist provided about the student's work while he was in high school, but the report is more than four years old. Mrs. Jones asks a local vocational rehabilitation agency to assist in re-evaluating the student.

A psychologist, who is a new graduate and in her mid-20's, has considerable experience with functional behavior analysis and classroom interventions for the management of attention deficit hyperactivity disorder. The psychologist chats briefly with the teacher and then completes an observation of the student within several of his classrooms, in a monitored environment. During the observation, she finds the class to be well managed, with engaging academic instruction from the college professor. However, she also notes that the teacher attends to students that most often ask questions throughout the lecture, and she disregards others in the classroom. The psychologist meets with Mrs. Jones to discuss the observation and next steps in their work together. The psychologist shares with Mrs. Jones that the college professor only interacts with the students who ask questions, and that the student being observed struggles sitting still.

CASE STUDY DISCUSSION QUESTIONS
Please answer the following questions regarding the case study:

1. If the psychologist proceeds through a series of questions designed to elicit a behavioral definition of the student's difficulty and keeps the discussion focused on the classroom environment when the

professor attempts to discuss her frustration with the lack of support for this student, is the psychologist operating in a collaborative manner?

2. If the psychologist offers to devise a behavior contract and bring it to the professor and Mrs. Jones, and the professor agrees to work directly with the student, is this still consultation, or is it collaborative?

3. If the professor modifies the student's assignments to decrease the amount of writing and the psychologist works directly with the student to teach him to use a self-monitoring and self-reward system for work completion, is this still consultation, or is it collaborative?

4. If, during the psychologists' and professor's work together, the professor decides she no longer has time to work with the psychologist, is the professor's decision to termination consultation a violation of the tenets of collaboration because it was made unilaterally?

DISCUSSION QUESTIONS

1. What is the role of consultants in rehabilitation and human service professions?

2. What are the goals of a consultant?

3. What are important consultant skills and abilities for working with a teacher in a school-age setting?

4. What are essential elements of a collaborative consultation relationship?

5. As a consultant, how can you be collaborative?

6. If you were asked to be part of an interprofessional team, what do you believe is important to understand about others involved in the group? What strategies would you use in working with a diverse group of professionals who have roles you may not be aware of?

7. In what types of settings does consultation and collaboration occur for rehabilitation and human service professionals?

REFERENCES

[1]Aguirre-Duarte, N. A. (2015). Increasing collaboration between health professionals. Clues and challenges. *Columbia Medica, 46*(2), 66-70.

[2]Arredondo, P. (1996). *Successful diversity management initiatives.* Thousand Oaks, CA: Sage.

[3]Arredondo, P., Shealy, C., Neale, M., & Winfrey, L. L. (2004). Consultation and interprofessional collaboration: Modeling for the future. *Journal of Clinical Psychology, 60*(7), 787-800.

[4]Backer, T., Blanton, J., Barclay, A., Golembiewski, R., Kurpius, D., Levinson, H., Leonard, S. (1992). What is consultation? That's an interesting question! *Consulting Psychology Journal, 44*(2), 18-23.

[5]Cox, T. (1993). *Cultural diversity in organizations: Theory, practice, and research.* San Francisco, CA: Berret-Koehler.

[6]Di Giulio, P., Arnfield, A., & English, M. W. (2013). Collaboration between doctors and nurses in children's cancer care: Insights from a European project. *European Journal Oncol Nursing, 17*(6), 745-749.

[7]Dougherty, A. M. (2000b). *Psychological consultation and collaboration in school and community settings (3rd ed.).* Belmont, CA: Brooks/Cole.

[8]Erchul, W. P., & Sheridan, S. P. (2014). Overview: The state of scientific research in school consultation. In W. P. Erchul, & S. P. Sheridan, *Handbook of research in school consultation (2nd Ed.)* (pp. 3-17). New York, New York: Routledge.

[9]Kurpius, D. (1978). Consultation theory and process: An integrated model. *Personnel and Guidance Journal, 56,* 335-338.

[10]Labott, S. M. (2019). Consultation Models and content. In S. M. Labott, *Health psychology consultation in the inpatient medical setting* (pp. 23-31). American Psychological Association.

[11]Loden, M., & Rossener, J. B. (1991). *Workforce America.* Homewood, IL: Business One Irwin.

[12]Mattessich, P. W., & Monsey, B. R. (1992). *Collaboration: What makes it work. A review of research literature on factors influencing successful collaboration.* Saint Paul, MN: Wilder Research Center.

[13]Michaels, C. A., & Lopez, E. (2005). Collaboration and consultation in transition planning: Introduction to the mini-theme. 16(4), 255-261.

[14]Newman, D. S., Guiney, M. C., & Barrett, C. A. (2017). Language in consultation: The effect of affect and verb tense. *Psychology in Schools, 54*(6), 624-639.

[15]Nolan, A., & Moreland, N. (2014). The process of psychological consultation. *Educational Psychology in Practice, 30*(1), 63-77.

[16]Prelock, P. (1995). Rethinking collaboration: A speech-language pathology perspective. *Journal of Educational and Psychological Consultation, 6*(1), 95-99.

[17]Sanchez, D., & King-Toler, E. (2007). Addressing disparities consultation and outreach strategies for university settings. *Consulting Psychology Journal: Practice and Research, 59*(4), 286-295.

[18]Sangganjananich, V. F., & Lenz, A. S. (2012). The experiential consultation training model. *Counselor Education and Supervision, 51*(4), 296-307.

[19]Schmuck, R. A. (1995). Process consultation and organization development. *Journal of Educational and Psychological Consultation, 6*(3), 199-205.

[20]Schulte, A. C., & Osborne, S. S. (2003). When assumptive worlds collide: A review of definitions of collaboration in consultation. *Journal of Educational and Psychological Consultation, 14*(2), 109-138.

[21]Thomas, R. R. (1991). *Beyond race and gender.* New York, New York: AMACOM.

[22]Xia, L., Wu, H., & Cheng, Y. (2016, November). Interprofessional collaboration strategies: A hematology unit case study. *Journal of Nursing Education and Practice, 7*(4), 51-54.

EFFECTIVE COMMUNICATION

D. HENRY STAPLETON

CHAPTER DESCRIPTION

The value of communication in the workplace is well articulated in the scholarly literature.[2,21,31,48] Due to the magnitude of the topic, this chapter centers on aspects of communication relevant to rehabilitation and human services fieldwork students. The overarching goal of this chapter is to highlight the important role effective communication plays in the professional world of work.

The chapter will discuss the connection between the business world and the realm of education. Students will be provided with information about various communication styles, communication fundamentals in the workplace, typical communication barriers, and the practical use of communication skills. Strategies for effective communication will be infused throughout each section of the chapter. The final section depicts communication challenges student workers might face during their field experiences. Each depiction (case scenario) is followed by discussion question(s).

OBJECTIVES:
After reading this chapter, students will demonstrate:

➢ increased knowledge, understanding, and appreciation of collaborative behaviors in the workplace,

➢ increased appreciation for the development of soft skills,

➢ increased knowledge, understanding, and appreciation of communication fundamentals and communication styles,

➢ increased knowledge and understanding of communication barriers, and

➢ increased mastery of effective communication skills.

INTRODUCTION

John Donne said it best, "no man is an island entire of itself; every man is a piece of the continent." As members of this great continent, human beings must communicate in order to accomplish goals both simple and complex. In order to do so effectively one must comprehend the meaning of not only communication, but effective communication as well as emotional intelligence. These three terms embody the very essence of communicating.

Communication is defined as a "two-way process of reaching mutual understanding, in which participants not only exchange (encode-decode) information, news, ideas, and feelings but also create and share meaning. In general, communication is a means of connecting people or places. In business, it is a key function of management. An organization cannot operate without communication between levels, departments, and employees."[4]

More expansively, effective communication includes "speaking effectively, writing concisely, listening attentively, expressing ideas, facilitating group discussion, providing appropriate feedback, negotiating, perceiving nonverbal messages, persuading, reporting information, describing feelings, interviewing, and editing."[48] A person's ability to engage in effective communication has been found to be linked to emotional intelligence. Good communication skills are an outcome of emotional intelligence.[16] Emotional intelligence is a navigation for successful interactions in the workplace; it enables student workers to succeed in diverse work environments and to keep their eye on the bigger picture (the agency's mission).

Emotional intelligence "is the ability to monitor one's own and others' feelings and emotions, to discriminate among them and to use this information to guide one's thinking and actions."[28, 29] Emotional intelligence serves as a safety net for student workers, preventing them from being carried away by emotions and subjectivity. Emotionally intelligent students' actions and decisions (communications) are guided by a mindfulness of their feelings and emotions, as well as the feelings and emotions of others.

Students who are emotionally intelligent can regulate their emotions, problem solve, and resolve conflicts. The emotionally intelligent person recognizes emotions and their impact on self and others.[1] This individual pauses before speaking or acting, thus refraining from making a permanent decision based on emotion. The emotionally intelligent person benefits from constructive feedback, demonstrates authenticity and empathy, and acknowledges the good in others. Lastly, the emotionally intelligent person offers constructive criticisms, apologizes when appropriate, forgives and forgets, honors commitments, and willingly aids others. Bariso[1] emphasized the importance of emotionally intelligent persons continuing to sharpen their intelligence in order to thrive in every aspect of their lives.

Communication errors and ineffective communication have resulted in calamities and tragedies in the financial and healthcare industries, and in the wider environment.[22] Hence, it is essential for students to have a comprehensive view of what the term means. In order to fully appreciate the vital role communication plays in their lives, students must "personalize" the term by asking themselves two essential questions:

> ➢ What losses have they experienced as a result of poor (ineffective) communication?

> ➢ What joys have they experienced as a result of good (effective) communication?

Students must objectively evaluate their capacity to effectively communicate with others and maintain constructive relationships. This personal appraisal is not static; it involves continuous refinement of interpersonal skills. If students are to succeed in the workplace, they must commit to a continued course of improvement. This requires students to maintain a sufficient level of self-awareness and an openness to mentoring and constructive feedback.

Communication in the 21st century involves more than two-way processes. Communication frequently involves multiple processes, which often occur simultaneously. There are various facets of effective communication in which students should strive to attain proficiency. These features include speaking effectively, writing concisely, listening attentively, expressing ideas, facilitating group discussions, providing appropriate feedback, negotiating, perceiving nonverbal messages, persuading, reporting information, describing feelings, interviewing, and editing.[48]

THE NEXUS BETWEEN THE BUSINESS WORLD AND EDUCATION

The primary purpose of higher education is to prepare students for the workplace. In developed countries, communication is viewed as one of the most important skill sets in (new) college graduates. These skill sets encompass both oral and written communication and require graduates to communicate virtually, face-to-face, informally, and formally on a national and international basis with a multi-cultural and multi-generational audience.[21] Despite effective communication being one of the most desired skill sets for employers, it is one of the most lacking in recent college graduates.[31]

Employers report a lack of communication skills preparation in undergraduate curricula,[20] arguing current offerings are inadequate.[5,8] Specifically, there are significant variances between industry's expectations and higher education's provision of oral communication skills. These oral communication skills gaps can influence job satisfaction and significantly impede job performance, organizational productivity, and adaptability.[10] There is also evidence that students perceive a substantial disparity between the professed value of oral communication and the time actually dedicated to its development in degree studies[5, 8, 20, 24].

There are four oral communication skills that have been cited as the most critical for entry-level workers: following instructions, listening, conversing, and receiving feedback.[26] These core competencies often dictate the selection of college graduates for entry-level jobs. While pursuing their educational training students should actively seek out opportunities to cultivate these critical entry level competencies. In the development of these and many other skills that students will be working to harness during the fieldwork/internship process, students should not fear but embrace feedback they receive from their instructor(s), site supervisor and peers. Such feedback and other assessments are strategies for developing student proficiency.

In order to develop effective communication skills, students should be exposed to diverse communication settings.[6] Preferably, these settings should explore cross-cultural, gender, generational, and personal styles of communication. Crosling and Ward,[5] revealed limitations pertaining to the sole use of oral presentations in the classroom to develop communication skills in students, noting that most workplace communication is informal in nature. Hence, classroom activities (e.g., small group activities and role plays) should prepare students for effectively communicating with supervisors and similar staff, negotiating and working successfully in groups, approaching issues critically, and assertively presenting one's view. With practice and exposure, students become adept at selecting from their repertoire the skills most appropriate to any given work situation.

Rehabilitation and human services professionals who fail to view communication as a core clinical skill may endanger the efficacy of service delivery. Areas impacted range from establishment of rapport during consultations, to the accuracy and completeness of data, to the accurate identification of symptoms, to precise efficacy of treatment, to adherence to drug regiments and diets, to pain control improvements.[13, 14, 27, 34, 44] Additionally, subpar communication skills can lead to uncertainty about diagnosis and prognosis, confusion about the results of diagnostic tests, doubts about future service or care recommendations, as well as the therapeutic intent of treatment.

It has become obvious overtime that communication skills training renders positive outcomes for health consumers. Health care organizations implementing communication skills training experience fewer complaints to medical boards and accrediting bodies. Effective communication between physicians and patients positively influences emotional health, symptom resolution, physiologic status, and pain control. There is a positive correlation between effective physician-patient communications and enhanced patient health outcomes.[44] This specific finding, in conjunction with other related research findings, support the need for communication skills training in medical school curricula, and these findings can certainly be applied to the fields of human services and rehabilitation.

DEVELOPING COMMUNICATION SKILLS

There are several means by which fieldwork/internship students can develop and refine their communication skills. In this section we will discuss project-based learning, the development of soft skills, and communication styles.

PROJECT-BASED LEARNING
Project-based learning (PBL) is a model that organizes learning around projects. Projects are complex tasks, based on challenging questions or

problems, that involve students in design, problem-solving, decision making, or investigative activities; give students the opportunity to work relatively autonomously over extended periods of time; and culminate in realistic products or presentations.[23, 47] Project-based learning skills are highly sought by today's employers. Project-based learning affords opportunities to work collaboratively with others, handle interpersonal conflicts, and solve complex problems. Moreover, this pedagogical approach provides opportunities for deeper in-context learning and for the development of important skills tied to career readiness.

When engaged in project-based learning, students can refine key social, communication, and self-management skills. More specifically, when engaged in project-based learning students acquire generic attributes such as problem solving, computer literacy, information literacy, collaboration, and teamwork skills. Other essentials of project-based learning include establishing clear relations and roles, openness, self-confidence, organization, clearly defining project successes, and re-evaluating when necessary.[9,35] Project-based learning is experiential learning. Students become adept at overcoming challenges associated with working in teams, managing projects, and meeting organizational deadlines. Project-based learning affords opportunities for students to engage in authentic projects and performance tasks that are tied to real-world careers and experiences.[18]

SOFT SKILLS (PEOPLE SKILLS)

As professionals in the fields of human services and rehabilitation, students will be called to demonstrate their abilities through the application of both hard and soft skills. The term Soft Skills is used to indicate all the competencies that are not directly connected to a specific task; they are necessary in any position as they mainly refer to interpersonal interactions with others in the work setting. Hard Skills, on the other hand, include specific capabilities required to perform a particular job. Often soft skills are referred to as people skills, and hard skills as technical skills.

Interpersonal skills, often referred to as soft skills, include communication, listening, team problem solving, cross-cultural relations, and customer service.[11] Soft skills have emerged as the top skills business and industry look for in job candidates.[32] Research supports that when workers are terminated, it is usually because they lack skills to create and maintain productive relationships. This means that in order to succeed in the world of work students must possess much more than a good grade point average or procedural expertise within their field of study. No company will retain a worker whose interpersonal deficits jeopardize profits or consumer relations. Consumers need to experience empathy and personal concern—they need to feel valued.[19] Fundamental soft (people) skills are not innate. Hence, they must be cultivated in the classroom and fieldwork settings.

Eight soft skills are perceived as particularly important by most business executives: communication, courtesy, responsibility, sociability, positive attitude, professionalism, integrity, and teamwork.[41] The following are recommendations for incorporating and practicing soft skills throughout your academic and fieldwork experiences:

> ➤ Engage in and evaluate your personal practice of basic people skills.

> ➤ Practice effective customer service skills.

> ➤ Engage in problem-solving discussions based on real life situations.

> ➤ Take advantage of opportunities to engage in role-play exercises in mock business settings.

You can adhere to these recommendations by routinely soliciting feedback regarding soft skills proficiency from your supervisor, family members, and peers and making the necessary adjustments. The author cannot overly emphasize the importance of practice, learning from mistakes, and being open to constructive feedback. Keep a journal of soft skills mistakes, particularly as they relate to problem solving or conflict resolution and be open to processing these with your field work instructor and peers within the classroom setting.

COMMUNICATION STYLES WITHIN THE WORKPLACE

Communication styles are specific ways of receiving messages; personal ways of interpreting messages; and specific ways of expressing the response or feedback.[17] Communication styles are indicators of how a person structures the world of social relations, interprets the information, and transforms that information into active behavior in social settings.

According to Karl Sun, co-founder and CEO at Lucidchart and prior business developer at Google's China office, there are four basic styles of communication in the workplace: analytical, intuitive, functional, and personal.[46] Workers with analytical communication styles have a preference for data, facts, specifics, and precise language. Conversely, those with intuitive communication styles demonstrate a preference for the big picture and not being bogged down in too much detail. Those workers with a functional communication styles hold a preference for process and thinking through plans methodically. And last, but certainly not least, workers with personal communication styles demonstrate a preference for relationships. They tend to focus on establishing personal connections, and understanding what others are thinking. Sun underscored how diverse communication styles can benefit organizations because every style has its strengths. Valuing diversity of communication styles can promote synergistic, industrious, and inclusive environments where relationships are based on mutual trust and respect.

WHAT TYPE OF COMMUNICATOR AM I?

> Take some time and consider what type of communicator you are according to Sun's communication descriptions.

> List three benefits associated with being this type of communicator.

> List three challenges that may be associated with being this type of communicator.

> Discuss three methods for overcoming the challenges associated with being this type of communicator.

> To gain an objective perspective, ask others about your communication style. Gather this information from a diverse group of individuals. Consider asking a good friend who will tell you the truth, a professor with whom you have a strong relationship, and a former or current supervisor. This will give you a variety of perspectives on how others view your communication style.

CULTURAL CONSIDERATIONS IN COMMUNICATION

Taking a different approach to communication styles, Waldherr & Muck,[48] derived a circumplex model of communication styles. The model has eight distinct numbered sectors, with each sector having a positive and negative pole.[pg. 18] The communication styles are:

> Assertive-submissive (sectors 1 and 5),

> expressive-reticent (sectors 2 and 6),

> responsive-inconsiderate (sectors 3 and 7), and

> agreeable-aggressive (sectors 4 and 8).[49]

To further illustrate, the researchers provided the following examples of communication styles.[pg. 21]

TABLE 1

EXAMPLE OF COMMUNICATION STYLE COMPLEX

Sector	Style	Example
1	Assertive	Dictates the issue to debate
2	Expressive	Social butterfly, chats easily with strangers
3	Responsive	Always has a comforting word if someone does not feel well
4	Agreeable	If verbally attacked, tries to ease the situation rather than defend self
5	Submissive	Usually agrees if others talk about their views
6	Reticent	While in the company of others, only talks when directly addressed
7	Inconsiderate	Inconsiderate, bluntly communicates a lack of interest in others' problems
8	Aggressive	Overly attacks people who disagree with personal position

As previously mentioned, understanding differences in communication styles promotes greater awareness of self and others.[25] This understanding provides an interpretive context for understanding the communication patterns of colleagues and consumers from diverse backgrounds. Cultural differences in communication styles, along with underlying differences in cultural values and thinking styles, can become a major source of misunderstanding, distrust, and conflict in intercultural communication.

Cultural differences are often associated with group-based identity perceptions, as well as corresponding stereotypes and prejudices toward culturally diverse groups. These differences can be seen in the verbal communication styles of varied cultural groups. An exploration of communication styles of diverse cultural groups revealed low-context and high-context communication cultures. Table 1 depicts major differences between the two concepts.[25]

Low-context cultures are considered individualistic, while high-context cultures are considered collectivistic.[25] The individualistic culture values independence, freedom, and privacy. Members of this culture also value being unique and free to express themselves. Members of collectivistic cultures demonstrate major societal values such as interdependence, relational harmony, and connectedness. They view themselves as part of encompassing social relationships whose behaviors are largely influenced by the thoughts, feelings, and actions of others in the relationships.

TABLE 2

CHARACTERISTICS OF LOW-TEXT VS. HIGH-TEXT COMMUNICATION CULTURES

Low Context Cultures	High Context Cultures
United States and most European cultures	Latin America, Africa, East Asia, Middle East, Native Americans
Analytical thinking	Holistic thinking
Attention given to specific, focal objects independent of the surrounding environment	The larger context is taken into consideration when evaluating an action or event, emphasis on maintaining social harmony as the primary function of speech in interpersonal interactions
Messages are direct (revealing the speaker's true intentions), elaborate, with rich expressions	Messages are indirect (camouflaged), with pauses and understatements, courtesy often takes precedence over truthfulness
Promotes positive aspects of self	Deemphasizes positive aspects of self
Sender-oriented	Receiver-oriented
More attention is paid to actual verbal message than contextual cues	Persons are more sensitive to situational cues

MY CULTURAL COMMUNICATION

1. With which cultural group are you associated, low-text culture or high-text culture?

2. How does your cultural upbringing impact your communication style? What are the benefits? And what are the challenges?

3. What can you do to overcome the communication challenges that are directly related to your culture?

THE APPLICATION OF COMMUNICATION IN THE FIELD

CASE RECORDING AND REPORTING

The importance of oral communication was discussed previously. However, communication also occurs in written formats. Those in the fields of human services and rehabilitation are required to document their casework and consumer contacts. Students must fully appreciate the relevance of documentation as a tool to protect consumers and practitioners in the event of an ethics complaint or lawsuit.[37] Students' ability to effectively communicate in writing is essential to their success in the fields of human services and rehabilitation.

Many students struggle with professional writing. Hence, it is essential that students take advantage of opportunities to improve their written communication skills by practicing case documentation.[30] Students can accomplish this by completing case management activities and assignments required in their courses. Obtaining feedback on these assignments and correcting errors are means of improving skills in this area. Believe it or not, writing papers can assist students in improving written communication skills needed for case recording and documentation. Additionally, students develop both oral and written communication skills when they actively prepare for and participate in class discussions.[7]

Case documentation and recording requires a variety of communication competences: writing case notes and summaries so that others can understand a consumer's progress; reporting verbally on consumer's progress to a rehabilitation team or other collaborators; preparing a summary report or letter to describe the consumer to cooperating individuals or agencies; reporting to referral sources case progress or disposition; abiding by ethical and legal considerations of case communications and recording; compiling and interpreting consumer information to maintain a current case record; and participating in case conferences.[39]

SERVICE INTERVIEWS

Good communication skills are the basis for an effective interview. Students may be required to conduct service interviews during their fieldwork/internship experiences. Evans, et al., in their 3-Stage Model of Interviewing specified the following communication skills as important:

➢ attending,

➢ questioning,

➢ reflecting content and feeling,

➢ confronting,

➢ communicating personal observations and reactions, self-disclosing, and

➢ interpreting.[12]

Similarly, Rovers reported guidelines for good interviews within medical settings that are transferrable to other work settings such as human services and rehabilitation:[42]

➢ Greet the client and introduce yourself.

> Explain the interview process.

> Explain the need to collect personal information, how the information will be used, and that it will be treated confidentially.

> Indicate the approximate length of the interview.

> Use words/manners that convey professionalism.

> Pay attention to body language.

> Ask open-ended questions.

> Begin with broad questions, then get more specific.

> Use active listening skills and demonstrate empathy.

> Ask the client to restate any unclear information and use paraphrasing feedback strategies to ensure understanding.

> Communicate at an appropriate educational level, avoiding professional jargon.

These tips are not only instrumental during the intake process but throughout the helping relationship.

QUALITY RELATIONSHIPS

Quality relationships are at the crux of agency productivity. Bolton and Bolton outlined the following realisms as being central to success at work:

> Work organizations are clusters of collaborative relationships.

> The quality of relationships greatly impacts organizational success.

> The quality of relationships can affect customer retention.

> Quality work relationships increase access to useful information.[3]

Bolton & Bolton[3] conveyed how all employees benefit from the development and maintenance of mutually supportive relationships. In this increasingly interconnected world, seventy percent of work is collaborative. Being successful in the workplace requires cooperation (the ability to give and take). Cooperative relationships increase productivity and profit and decrease absenteeism and job dissatisfaction.[36] Poor relations at work have been found to impede the transfer of knowledge, and to decrease employee motivation, job satisfaction, and organizational effectiveness. When work relationships are strained, employees tend to avoid one another, and interpersonal interactions are kept to a minimum.

Regarding relationship building with consumers, Evans, et al.,[12] introduced three stages: exploration, clarification, and action. During the exploration stage the practitioner is building working relationships and discovering consumer problems. In the clarification stage the practitioner is defining consumer problems, prioritizing the problems for actions and redefining problems into attainable goals. Finally, during the action stage the practitioner is identifying an optimal action plan for each goal, working with consumer to implement and complete the chosen actions, and then moving to termination of the relationship once the goals have been attained.

Each stage requires mastery of basic helping competencies on the part of the practitioner. Perhaps the most fundamental workplace communication skill that contributes to the development of positive consumer and colleague relationships is listening. Bolton & Bolton [3] highlight three listening skill clusters; attending, following, and reflecting that are necessary to ensure that one is engaging in effective listening. Attending refers to posture of involvement, appropriate body motion, eye contact, and a none distracting environment. Following involves the use of door openers, minimal encouragers, infrequent questions, and attentive silence that encourages the other party to openly share. Additionally, reflecting involves paraphrasing, reflecting feelings, reflecting meanings, and summative reflection for clarity and understanding.

It has been stated that subpar listening in the workplace can lead to wasted time, unnecessary mistakes, alienation of coworkers, lost opportunities, diminished profits, and decreased effectiveness.[3] There are documented instances in business and industry where a single listening mistake proved catastrophic. Listening with empathy is also a desirable interpersonal skill. The capacity for empathy is important. Stephen Covey, a renowned educator and executive, postulated that the root cause of all interpersonal conflict is the inability to listen with empathy.

SOCIAL MEDIA/ELECTRONIC COMMUNICATION/FRATERNIZING

Most agencies will disclose their social media policies during the orientation or onboarding phase. It is very important that students adhere to these directives. Most agencies prohibit the use of agency computers or equipment for personal communication. Many agencies monitor the email and internet activity of both employees and field students. Correspondingly, there should be no personal phone calls or texting during the fieldwork shift unless the student is on an official break from work tasks. Students should communicate to family, friends, and significant others that fieldwork is not only an extension of classroom instruction but an avenue for job training and employment. If an emergency arises, family, friends, and significant others should be instructed to contact the student's direct supervisor.

Students are cautioned against befriending (on social media) employees within the fieldwork venue. Such friendships can occur, if desirable, after the fieldwork period formally ends. Students should not lose sight of the fact that the fieldwork opportunity is a business opportunity and not a social opportunity. Students also need to be mindful of their social media activities. Could the content adversely influence future employment? Could the content negatively impact the reputation of the agency? Another area of concern is communicating (interacting) with consumers via social media. It is important that students adhere to agency directives regarding fraternization with consumers, their friends, and family members. When in doubt, students should confer with their site or faculty supervisor. Lastly, students should inform supervisors of any existing (or dual) roles they might have with employees or consumers of the agency.

As students get to know team members and supervisors, they should inquire about preferred methods of communication. Students will find that some colleagues prefer emails, some prefer text messages, and some prefer to be contacted on their office phones. Some colleagues will prefer face-to-face contacts and updates. Regarding emailing, student workers must be mindful of proper email etiquette and avoid using text lingo. Student workers may be required to provide their mobile contact numbers to site supervisor(s) and other team members. Such requests are not unusual in settings that provide 24-7 supports or crisis or emergency services. Students who are not comfortable with being 'on call' should promptly discuss the issue with their faculty supervisor.

Bolton and Bolton[3] posited that overuse of digital devices erodes empathy, blocks the formation of meaningful relationships, obstructs learning, and hampers productivity. In TED Talk, "Connected but Alone," MIT's Sherry Turke stated her concerns over the misuse of digital devices; specifically, people are developing problems relating to others, they expect more from technology and less from each other, they are losing the capacity for being alone, and traditional conversation has been replaced with mediated connection leading to the loss of valuable interpersonal skills.

COMMUNICATION BARRIERS

According to Bolton & Bolton,[3] 12 barriers to communication can be divided into three major categories: judging, sending solutions, and avoiding the other's concerns. Carl Rogers believed the major barrier to interpersonal communication was our innate tendency to judge others. Sending solutions may involve advice giving, threatening, or moralizing. Avoiding the other's concerns encompasses a group of actions noted for getting conversations off track and making the person feel unheard or uncared about. Another barrier to effective communication is the use of aggression and subpar conflict resolution skills. Bolton & Bolton[3] speak of a personal space that each person has a right to defend (assertively). He defines assertiveness as the balance between submissiveness and aggression. Assertiveness involves the skill of expressing one's feelings openly and honestly while still respecting others. Assertiveness can facilitate resolution of conflicts within the workplace, while aggressiveness can impede conflict resolution.

Nelson-Jones[33] described the capacity to resolve conflicts within the workplace as a relevant interpersonal skill. He listed the following responses as important when resolving conflicts: paraphrasing and restating, partial agreement without self-indictment, asking for specifics when the other person presents as angry, taking ownership of language and tone of message, and contracting to talk later. The conflict resolution process[3] involves treating others with respect, listening until you "experience" the other side (reflect content, feelings, and meaning), and briefly stating your own feelings, needs, and view.

Another barrier to effectively communicating in the workplace is failing to understand and appreciate cultural differences. Communication patterns may differ among ethnic and racial groups, genders, socio-economic categories, geographies, and age groups. Sanchez-Burks, et al.,[42] discussed how East-West differences in indirectness are more pronounced in the work setting, leading to miscommunications and misunderstanding and a cross-cultural divide.

Roessler and Rubin[39] stressed the importance of acquiring knowledge of relevant characteristics of minority cultures, realizing that knowledge provides a basis for understanding the unique personal experiences of others. When striving to effectively communicate with others of a different cultural group, it is important to avoid overgeneralizations, stereotypes, and preconceived notions. Proficient communicators cross cultural divides by: studying the research literature on nonverbal communication patterns of diverse cultural groups; making conscious and concerted efforts to observe the ways in which people communicate and act; becoming aware of their own communication styles; and understanding the impact their style of communication has on others. Knowing how we affect others allows us to modify our behaviors should our impact be negative. Hence, skilled and effective communicators are open to feedback on how their behaviors influence others.[45]

It is important to note that cultural proficiency is a lifelong learning process of professional and personal development. There are several strategies that can be implemented to reduce communication barriers within diverse work settings: listening attentively and asking questions when one does not understand; reading, listening, and broadening one's experience base about diverse people; acknowledging prejudices and biases and committing to reduce them; seeking feedback from diverse others about how well one is communicating respect for them and valuing their diversity; recognizing that diversity exists and learning to value and respect fundamental differences; and dismissing myths about diverse others when in a group of associates.

CONCLUSION

As discussed in this chapter communication is an essential function of our practice as human services and rehabilitation professionals. Effective communication is a valued skill that is coveted by employers and essential to the success of budding professionals. Therefore, fieldwork/internship students should actively participate in project-based learning, actively develop soft skills and receptive communication patterns, and actively explore cultural considerations that can enhance communication skills and remove communication barriers. Effective communicators should also strive to maintain high emotional intelligence.

Fieldwork/internship students would do well to recognize how effective communication (both oral and written) directly connects to the work that they do as human services and rehabilitation practitioners. Effective communication is a compulsory component of quality service provision (from intake, to service plan development and implementation, to case management and recording, to teaming and collaboration, to discharge and case termination). Regarding effective communication, the old age adage "practice makes perfect" or at least practice makes better, still rings true. Hence, it is essential to note that while striving to develop and implement effective communications skills, students, like all professionals, will encounter barriers to effective communication. However, such barriers can be overcome, and success can be achieved through the continued practice of effective communication.

CASE STUDIES

CASE STUDY 1
C- COURAGE (pushing beyond one's comfort zone, communicating vulnerabilities)

Supervisor Bill: *Jean, I will let you take the lead on the next home visit. Do you have your home visit guide with you?*

Jean: *Yes, I do. I appreciate the opportunity to take the lead during my second week on the job. I will do my best, but I need to admit that I'm nervous. I don't think I am ready.*

Supervisor Bill: *Let's discuss the aspects of the home visit that are causing you anxiety.*

Jean: *O.K.*

DISCUSSION QUESTIONS:

> What interpersonal communication skills did Jean display?

> How did the demonstration of these skills benefit Jean?

> How did they benefit the consumer?

> How did they benefit Jean's relationship with her supervisor?

CASE STUDY 2
O- OPENNESS (TO GROWTH, CHANGE)

Supervisor Bill: *Jean, you did a good job with the Jones family interview on Tuesday (outlines several strengths). I want you to work on improving your eye contact and pausing at least 10 seconds after asking a question. You want to make certain that you give all family members adequate time to answer your questions.*

Jean: *Thank you. I really appreciate the feedback. I will work on improving in these two areas. Maintaining eye contact has always been difficult for me. Has it always been easy for you?*

Supervisor Bill: *No, it has not always been easy, but I learned how eye contact could strengthen the consumer–provider relationship. Not only does it put the consumer at ease, but it communicates that you are confident in your ability to provide the needed services.*

Jean: *I didn't realize I was rushing through the interview. I was trying to complete the interview within the allotted time.*

Supervisor Bill: *The most important thing is that you obtain useful information. I would prefer that you complete the interview over 2-3 sessions verses rushing the process and obtaining information that is not pertinent to case planning or service delivery. With time, you will learn to better pace the interview.*

DISCUSSION QUESTIONS

> What communication skills are being exhibited by Bill? By Jean?

> Who benefits from this level of interpersonal communication?

CASE STUDY 3
M-MUTUALITY (conditions of sharing, reciprocity)

Team Leader Sara: *Jean, I thought we agreed that all team members would have their assignments to me by midnight. I have yet to receive yours. We are not going to meet our deadline.*

Jean: *I ran into a problem. I am so sorry.*

Team Leader Sara: *Jean, sorry is not good enough. If you were having problems, you should have let me know or reached out to other members of the team. Communicating any delays is important when working with a team and trying to meet a deadline. Making deadlines as promised is important. Your inability to ask for help when needed will reflect poorly on the team and our division.*

DISCUSSION QUESTIONS
- ➤ What interpersonal conflict has occurred in the above scenario?
- ➤ What could Jean have done differently?
- ➤ How would you describe Sara's interpersonal skills?

CASE STUDY 4:
M-MANNERS
(politeness, courtesy, respectful interactions)
(The following are seven examples of Jean displaying
good manners (courtesy) within the work setting)

Jean: *Bill, I want you to know I appreciate your guidance and feedback.*

Jean: *Team, before we get started, I want to apologize to everyone for the lateness of my assignment. You have my word that it will not happen again.*

Jean: *Tom, I apologize for interrupting your phone call earlier.*

Jean: *Mary, I apologize for being late to the meeting. I appreciate you waiting. I know your time is valuable.*

Jean: *Bill, I know it's important for me to sign the attendance log when I arrive in the mornings and depart in the afternoons. I apologize for failing to routinely sign the log.*

Jean: *Mary, you told me the best method of contacting you was by text. I apologize for emailing you. I am so sorry that you did not receive the information you needed in a timely manner. I apologize, it will not happen again.*

Jean: *Bill, I apologize for not calling to let you know that I was ill on Tuesday and unable to report to work. My actions were unprofessional. Is there any way I can make up the work that I missed?*

DISCUSSION QUESTIONS

➢ What benefits will occur due to Jean's demonstration of good manners and courtesy in the above circumstances?

➢ What do good manners communicate about a worker?

CASE STUDY 5
U- UNDERSTANDING
(in order to be understood, you must first understand, suspension of judgement, respect for differences)

Mary: *Jean, your comments about the Korean family appear to be a bit prejudicial. I wonder if your views are affecting your work with the family.*

Jean: *Mary, I am not certain I understand.... Could you provide some examples? I really do not want the family to think I am prejudiced against them.*

Mary: *Have you worked with Korean families before?*

Jean: *No*

Mary: *Ok, so how did you prepare for your work with the family?*

Jean: *I am not sure I am following you...*

Mary: *Jean, when working with an ethnic group for the first time, you must prepare.*

Jean: *I didn't prepare. I didn't do any research; I guess it shows.*

Mary: *Yes, it does. Well, I have some information on Korean culture that I will gladly share with you. The more you understand about the Korean culture, the better you will be able to service the family.*

DISCUSSION QUESTIONS

1) Jean displayed a lack of what important interpersonal communication skill(s)?

2) How could Jean improve her communication?

CASE STUDY 6
N- NEED FULFILLMENT
(Maslow's Hierarchy)

According to Maslow's motivational theory (1943), human beings have five basic needs: physiological, safety, belonging/love, esteem, and self-actualization. Unfulfilled needs can affect communication and, subsequently, work performance. During supervision, students should openly discuss their needs. Unrealized needs can result in work complications as reflected in the following vignette.

Scenario A

Supervisor Bill: *Jean, Ms. Smith telephoned about the date and time of your next visit. I was surprised to hear that you have not been out to see her since the initial visit.*

Jean: *I have been planning to go. To be truthful, the neighborhood makes me a bit uncomfortable. There appears to be a lot of unemployed men in the area who stand on the corners during the daytime. I guess I am afraid to go back alone.*

Supervisor Bill: *Your safety is important to the agency. Let's process your thoughts and feelings and see if we can come up with an appropriate plan of action. It's important that you feel safe when doing your home visits.*

Scenario B

Supervisor Bill: *Jean, you are really doing a great job. I see improvements every week. Are you working well with the team?*

Jean: *Thank you, Bill. I really appreciate the feedback. I thought things were going well with the team...but I don't know. The team went bowling the other night. I didn't get an invitation. I don't know why. But, I was a bit bothered by it.*

DISCUSSION QUESTIONS

1) What two needs are not being met/addressed by Jean?

2) How could Jean's failure to verbalize her needs lead to problems within the work setting? What interpersonal skills did Bill demonstrate?

CASE STUDY 7
I-INTEGRITY (oral and verbal reporting and recording, congruency between oral and written reports)

Team Leader Sara: *Jean, your written report did not indicate any concerns about Ms. Thomas' medical condition. During last week's case staffing, you verbalized several concerns. Is she doing better?*

Jean: *No, she is not doing better. I did not intend to leave out that important bit of information. I will review the report and resubmit it for your approval.*

Team Leader Sara: *Thank you, Jean. It is very important that your written reports reflect your actual case concerns and what is really happening on a case. You always want to show integrity in your report writing by being as accurate as possible. Remember, these reports are often viewed by the funding source or they may end up in court.*

DISCUSSION QUESTIONS

1) Explain how oral and verbal reporting involves integrity.

2) What interpersonal skills did Sara demonstrate?

CASE STUDY 8
C- CLARIFICATION AND COLLABORATION
(never make assumptions when stuck)

Supervisor Bill: *Jean, you must have spent hours on this project. I appreciate the time you spent on the assignment, but you failed to address three major components.*

Jean: *Really? I attempted to follow the report format you provided last time. I struggled a lot with this project. I wasn't sure if I was on the right track.*

Supervisor Bill: *What could you have done differently?*

Jean: *I assumed I was doing it correctly, even though I struggled. Next time I will ask for help.*

Supervisor Bill: *Jean, seeking clarification is important; it saves a lot of time and effort. Unfortunately, you are going to have to put more time and effort into the report. The current format is not acceptable. Jean collaboration is an important aspect of teamwork.*

DISCUSSION QUESTION:

1) What could Jean have done differently?

2) Could such deficits jeopardize Jean's fieldwork experience?

3) What can Jean do to improve in this area?

CASE STUDY 9:
A-ASSERTIVENESS

Supervisor Bill: *Jean, I hear you've had a bad day. Do you want to talk about it?*

Jean: *I don't want to get anyone in trouble.*

Supervisor Bill: *I can appreciate your position, Jean. No one is going to get in trouble. My role is to prepare you for eventual employment in the field, so it's important that we work through any challenges you might face here at the agency.*

Jean: *Well, Lisa and I have been working on the Smith case, but she is not pulling her weight. She has not completed any of the agreed upon tasks. I am doing both my work and hers. I am feeling overwhelmed. When I tried to speak to her about it, I became so angry, I burst into tears.*

Supervisor Bill: *Jean, your intentions were good. You tried to talk it over with Lisa. This issue with Lisa must be addressed. It is not going to go away by itself. Would you like me to intervene?*

Jean: *No, I would like to be able to handle conflicts on the job without bursting into tears. I want to try and maturely work through this situation.*

Supervisor Bill: *Okay, let's role-play what you plan to say to Lisa.*

DISCUSSION QUESTION:

1. What interpersonal skills were lacking in this scenario?

CASE STUDY 10
T-TEAM BUILDING

Jean: *Bill, things are going really well with the team. I feel like I belong. I have an invite to the next bowling night!*

Supervisor Bill: *I am glad to hear that things are going well. Why do you think things are better?*

Jean: *I realized that as a new worker, I had to earn my place on the team. Therefore, I read up on how to become a valued team member. I have been trying hard to exhibit some of the skills that I read about and that we have discussed during supervision.*

Supervisor Bill: *Can you share some of the skills that you have been exhibiting?*

Jean: *Well, I communicate regularly and provide frequent updates. I am polite and courteous. I try to be reliable, open to feedback, honest, solution-focused, and cooperative.*

DISCUSSION QUESTIONS:

1) What are your thoughts about Jean's new efforts?

2) Discuss the specific interpersonal skills identified above. Which skills are you proficient in?

CASE STUDY 11:
E- EMPATHY

Supervisor Bill: *Jean, how are things going with Lisa?*

Jean: *Things are much better. You know I used the 3-part message for assertiveness that we role-played, and it worked! Lisa was very receptive to the discussion. She has a lot on her plate right now. I didn't realize she was recently widowed, with four children, and that she has been trying to find a new place to stay.*

Supervisor Bill: *So, do you regret the confrontation, the use of assertion training?*

Jean: *Yes, I feel badly. I wish I knew about everything she was going through. I didn't' think to ask Lisa if things were okay in her life or if there was anything that she needed...*

Supervisor Bill: *If you knew all about the personal stuff, what you would have done differently? Remember the agency's top priorities are productivity and client outcomes.*

Jean: *Well, I would not have displayed anger; I would have displayed empathy.*

DISCUSSION QUESTIONS:

1) How can a worker exhibit empathy without compromising productivity or client outcomes?

2) Can the display of empathy ever be detrimental to the work environment?

REFERENCES

[1]Bariso, J. (2018). *EQ Applied.* Borough Hall: Germany.

[2]Beebe, Beebe, Redmond, Geerink, & Wiseman (2015). *Interpersonal Communication Relating to Others. 6th Canadian Edition.* Toronto: Pearson.

[3]Bolton, R. & Bolton, D.G. (2018). *Listen up or lose out.* New York: American Management Association.

[4]Business Dictionary. (2018). Communication. Retrieved from: http://www.businessdictionary.com/definition/communication.html

[5]Courtis, J and Zaid, O. (2002). Early employment problems of Australian accounting graduates: an exploratory study. *Accounting Form, 26*(3), 320-339.

[6]Crosling, G., Ward, I. (2002) Oral communication: The needs and uses of business graduate employees. *English for Specific Purposes. An International Journal, 21*, 41-57.

[7]Dallimore, E.J., Hertenstein, J.H. & Platt, M.B. (2010). Using discussion pedagogy to enhance oral and written communication skills *College Teaching, 56*(3), 163-172 https://doi.org/10.3200/CTCH.56.3.163-172

[8]DeLange, P., Jackling, & B. Gut, A. (2006) Accounting graduates' perception of skills emphasis in undergraduate courses: An investigation from two victorian universities. *Accounting & Finance, 46*(3), 365-386.

[9]Dubois, M., Hanlon, J., Koch, J., Nyatuga, B., & Kerr, N. (2015). Leadership Styles of Effective Project Managers: Techniques and Traits to Lead High Performance Teams. *Journal of Economic Development, Management, IT, Finance and Marketing, 7*(1), 30-46

[10]Duke University (2011). Meeting the upgrading challenge: Dynamic workforces for diversified economics. Durham, N.C., USA: Duke Center on Globalization, Governance, and Competiveness.

[11]Durbrin, A. (2004). *Human relations: interpersonal, job-oriented skills, 8th Edition.* Pearson Prentice Hall.

[12]Evans, D. R., Hearn, M. T., Uhlemann, M. R. & Ivey, A, E. (2008). *Effective communication: A Programmed approach to effective communication. 7th Edition.* Brooks & Cole Cengage Learning: Belmont, CA

[13]Fallowfield, L.J. & Jenkins, V.A. (1993). Effective communication skills are the key to good cancer care. *European Journal of Cancer, 35,* 1592-1597.

[14]Fallowfield, L., Jenkins,V., Farewell, V., and Solis-Trapala, I. (2003). Enduring impact of communication skills training: results of a 12-month follow-up. British Journal on Cancer, 89(8): 1445–1449, Published online 2003 Oct 14. doi: 10.1038/sj.bjc.6601309

[15]Fallowfield, L.J., Lipkin, M., Hall, A., (1998). Teaching senior oncologists communication skills: Results from phase one of a comprehensive longitudinal program in the United Kingdom. *Journal of Clinical Oncology, 16,* 1961-1968.

[16]Gardenswartz, L., Cherbosque, J., & Davies-Black, A.R. Reprint Edition (2008). *Emotional intelligence for managing results in a diverse world the hard truth about soft skills.* Davis-Black: Mountain View, California.

[17]Georgeta, P. Cristina, S., Pânişoarăa, I., Duţăa, N. (2015) Comparative Study Regarding Communication Styles of The Students. *Procedia - Social and Behavioral Sciences, 186,* 202 – 208.

[18]Hansen, R.S. (2010). Benefits and problems with student teams: Suggestions for improving team projects. Retrieved from: https://doi.org/10.3200/JOEB.82.1.11-19

[19]Harari, O. (1993). The lab test: A Tale of quality. *Clincal Laboratory Management Review 82*(3), 55-59.

[20]Holtzman, D. M., & Kraft, E. M. (2011). Skills needed in the 21st century workplace: A comparison of feedback from undergraduate business alumni and employers with a national study. *Business Education & Administration, 3*(1), 61-76.

[21]Jackson, D. (2014). Business graduate performance in oral communication skills and strategies for improvement. *The International Journal of Management Education 12,* 22-34.

[22]Jelphs, K. (2006). Communication: Soft skill, hard impact? Clinician in management, 14, 32-37.

[23]Jones, B. F., Rasmussen, C. M., & Moffitt, M. C. (1997). *Real-life problem solving: A collaborative approach to interdisciplinary learning.* Washington, DC: American Psychological Association.

[24]Kavanaugh, M.H. and Drennan, L. (2008). What skills and attributes does an accounting graduate need? Evidence from student perceptions and employer expectations. *Accounting, and Finance, 48*(2), 279-300.

[25]Lui, M. (2016). Verbal communication styles and culture. Oxford Research Encyclopedia of communication, DOI: 10.1093/acrefore/9780190228613.013.162. Retrieved from: https://oxfordindex.oup.com/view/10.1093/acrefore/9780190228613.013.1 62

[26]Maes, J.D., Weldy, T.G., Icenogle, M.L. (1997). Oral communication identified consistently as the most important competency in evaluating entry-level candidates. *The Journal of Business Communication, 34*(11). 167-80.

[27]Maquire, P. (1999). Improving communication with cancer patients. *European Journal of Cancer, 35*, 2058-2065.

[28]Mayer, J. D.; Salovey, P. & Caruso, D. R. (2004a). Emotional Intelligence: Theory, Findings, and Implications. *Psychological Inquiry. 15*(3), 197-215. DOI: 10.1207/s15327965pli1503_02.

[29]Mayer, J. D., Salovey, P. & Caruso, D. R. (2004b). A Further Consideration of the Issues of Emotional Intelligence. *Psychological Inquiry. 15*(3), 249-255. DOI: 10.1207/s15327965pli1503_05.

[30]McDonough, R.P. & Bennett, M. S. (2006). Improving communication skills of pharmacy students through effective precepting. *American Journal of Pharmaceutical Education, 70*(3): 58.

[31]National Association of Colleges and Employers (NACE) (2010). *Job outlook.* Bethlehem, PA.

[32]Nealy, C. (2005). Integrating soft skills through active learning in the management classroom. *Journal of College Teaching and Learning, 2*(4), 1-6

[33]Nelson-Jones, R. (1999). *Introduction to counselling skills.* Thousand Oaks, CA: SAGE.

[34]Ong, L.M., deHaes, J.C, Hoos, A.M., Lammes, F.B. (1995). Doctor-patient communication: A review of the literature. *Sci Med, 40*, 903-918

[35]Project Management Institute. (2013). The high cost of low performance: The essential role of communications. Retrieved from: https://www.pmi.org/-/media/pmi/documents/public/pdf/learning/thought-leadership/pulse/the-essential-role-of-communications.pdf

[36]Rath, T. (2006). *Vital friends.* New York: Gallop Press.

[37]Reamer, F. G. (2005). Documentation in social work evolving ethical and risk management standards. *Social Work, 50*(4), 325-334. DOI: 10.1093/sw/50.4.325.

[38]Robles, M. M. (2012). Executive perceptions of the top ten soft skills needed in today's workplace. *Business Communication Quarterly, 75*(4), 453-465. DOI: 10.1177/1080569912460400

[39]Roessler, R.T. & Rubin, S. E. (2006). *Case management and rehabilitation counseling. 4th Edition.* Pro-Ed. Austin, Texas:

[40]Robles, M.M. (December 2012) Executive Perceptions of the Top 10 Soft Skills Needed in Today's Workplace. *Business Communication Quarterly, 75*(4) 453 –46 DOI: 10.1177/1080569912460400

[41]Rovers, J.P. (2003). *Patient data collection. In: A Practical guide to pharmaceutical care, (2nd ed).* American Pharmaceutical Association, Washington, DC:

[42]Sanchez-Burks, J., Lee, F., Choi, I., Nesbit, R., Zhao, S., & Koo, J. (2003). Implications for bridging cultural divides. *Journal of Personality and Social Psychology, 85*(2), 363–372 0022-3514/03/$12.00 DOI: 10.1037/0022-3514.85.2.363

[43]Stewart, M.A. (1996). Effective physician-patient communication and health outcomes: A review. *Canadian Medical Association Journal, 152*(9), 1423-1433.

[44]Sue, D.W. & Sue, D. (2013). *Counseling the culturally diverse: Theory & practice. 6th Edition.* John Wiley & Sons, Inc. Hoboken, New Jersey.

[45]Sun, K. (2018) Four ways to combat workplace communication breakdown. Retrieved from: https://www.forbes.com/sites/karlsun/2018/04/24/4-ways-to-combat-workplace-communication-breakdowns/#6c7547042d5b

[46]Thomas, J. W., Mergendoller, J. R. & Michaelson, A. (1999). *Project-based learning: A handbook for middle and high school teachers.* Novato, CA: The Buck Institute for Education.

[47]Urciuoli, B. (2008). Skills and services in the new workplace. *American Ethnologist, 35*(2), pp. 211-228.

[48]Waldherr, A. & P. M. Muck (2011). Towards an integrative approach to communication styles: The interpersonal circumplex and the five-factor theory of personality as frames of reference. *Communications, 36*, 1-27.

WORKPLACE CLIMATE

DOTHEL W. EDWARDS, JR.

CHAPTER DESCRIPTION

The focus of this chapter is to provide definitions of organizational culture, workplace climate, the effects of conflict in the workplace, work climate and ethics, workplace burnout, peer support groups, self-care, and benefits of a positive work climate. Further, it is the focus of this chapter to delve into the subjective and often convoluted aspects of these terms and to offer supportive coping mechanisms.

OBJECTIVES

1. To teach students about the varying types of work settings and climates.

2. To teach students about building relationships in the workplace.

3. To teach students about workplace etiquette.

ORIENTATION

In lieu of academic requirements of the fieldwork/internship site, it is paramount that students be made aware of the formal and informal challenges of the climate of the work site prior to placement. The function of the orientation is to introduce students to the formal day to day activities of the organization. Much of this information is presented in a straightforward format, usually in the form of videos, individual and group classroom setting by which the policy and procedures of the organization are being shared with the new hire and fieldwork/internship students.

The function of policy and procedures is to introduce and indoctrinate new hires and fieldwork/internship students how one should conduct one's self by way of established rules of the organization. In most cases, the organization's mission and objectives are provided during this process. During the orientation fieldwork/internship students can begin to observe their site, where they will spend a good portion of their time.

An agency is made up of a variety of persons based on position and function which is usually illustrated in the agency policy and procedures handbook via an organizational chart that lists each employee's position/title, role, and function as it relates to the services that are being rendered. Each person brings a unique outlook on life and brings varying personalities that formulate "a way of doing things" that may not necessarily match an organization's policies and procedures. In a sense, an informal culture is established which presents unique values, attitudes, and beliefs that the fieldwork/internship student will need to fully understand to properly function within the organization.

ORGANIZATIONAL STRUCTURE: CHAIN OF COMMAND

During the orientation period, fieldwork/internship students should be exposed to the formal structure of an organization or more commonly described as the "chain of command." This offers the fieldwork/internship student an explanation of the employees' responsibilities and their association to each other across the organization.[15] These responsibilities are associated with the concepts of centralization and formalization.

Centralization refers to the distribution of authority among personnel in the organization and consists of two subcomponents: participation in decision-making and hierarchy of authority.[12] Participation in decision-making refers to the extent to which employees possess autonomy within their job. A centralized structure is indicated by lower levels of participation in decision-making and higher levels of authority, which creates freedom for employees. Communication in the form of complaints or questions is done by the rank of the employee within the hierarchy.

Formalization refers to the degree to which rules and procedures are formally written and communicated through members of the organization. Hierarchy of authority refers to the degree to which employees possess autonomy within their jobs.[12] Higher levels of formalization offer employees little to no flexibility in their job roles, while abundant flexibility is given in lower levels of formalization employees can contribute to the decision-making process. A centralized structure is indicated by lower levels of participation in decision-making and higher levels within the hierarchy of authority, which create less autonomy for employees.

It is essential that fieldwork/internship students understand these concepts and prepare themselves to navigate within these levels of authority to ensure that they have a successful internship experience. One should also utilize the faculty supervisor as a liaison to the organizational structure.

ORGANIZATIONAL CULTURE

According to the Business Dictionary,[4] the definition of organization culture is the expectations that an organization has for employees. These expectations are based on values and behaviors that contribute to the unique social and psychological climate of an organization. Organizational culture is the engine that allows an organization to run efficiently or in other cases inefficiently. It is based on shared attitudes, beliefs, customs, written and unwritten rules that have been developed over time. It is an establishment of norms within the organization.

Quite often it is the "unwritten rules" that present challenges to the fieldwork/internship student. These unwritten rules are often difficult to navigate, particularly since the unwritten rules are exhibited arbitrarily. It is paramount that fieldwork/internship students be made aware of these potential pitfalls by the fieldwork supervisor. A good way to avoid improperly recognizing an agency's hierarchy is to have the fieldwork/internship student focus on the assigned duties of the job, required internship activities, and "stay clear" of "office politics," behaviors, and attitudes that are divisive and can be detrimental to the internship placement.

The focus of the internship is to apply theory to practice and to successfully complete the placement. Since power and information flow through people who have different personalities, it is best that the fieldwork/internship student share, with the faculty supervisor, everything that he or she experiences during their internship placement.

The formation of workplace climate has been categorized as structural, perceptual, or interactive.[20] The structural model states that the structure of the organization is the principle focus of workplace climate. The structural model should be clearly understood and poses little to no confusion of expectations since the structural component consists of established rules and procedures shown in the agency's policies and procedures. The structural model should be established at the time of the fieldwork/internship student's orientation to the agency.

In the perceptual view, workplace climate is seen as coming from an individual's perceptions of his or her work climate.[20] This model is solely based on how the person perceives the organization climate. Great variability exists with this model as the fieldwork/internship student is new to the agency and can only experience the work climate based on a short time frame.

The interactive model, which is another model that demonstrates variability among employees, suggests that workplace climate is the result of a group of individuals collectively interpreting their environment.[20] Like the perceptual view model, the interactive model will demonstrate variability among employees' personalities which can also present challenges to the fieldwork/internship student.

Again, communication between the fieldwork/internship student and faculty supervisor is crucial to make sure that the student correctly navigates the established expectations and does not inject incorrectly perceived actions that will present barriers to successful fieldwork outcomes. Quite often these hidden norms pose challenges to new employees and fieldwork/internship students to navigate. It is hope that the work climate will offer supportive environments that promote worker participation, free and open exchange of information, and constructive conflict resolution.[22] In some organizations this form of organizational culture is not clearly present, especially from the perception of the fieldwork/internship student. In this case, the faculty instructor will need to provide conflict resolution strategies and coping strategies to equip students to handle potential conflicts that may arise at the fieldwork site.

THE EFFECTS OF CONFLICT
IN THE WORK CLIMATE

Van de Vliert explains that the presence of conflict in an organization is perceived as having a negative impact on employees and the organization.[29] Furthermore, these results verify research assumptions that a negative work climate affects employees' or fieldwork/internship student's well-being.[1,11,13,14,22] From the perspective of these results, conflicts are seen as creating a negative work climate.

Furthermore, a perceived negative work climate leads to employees' feelings of burnout and in return can negatively affect how a fieldwork/internship student will be treated. The learning process can be significantly limited, and a negative perception of the discipline can become apparent because of conflicts within the organization. Additionally, the presence of conflicts in an organization leads to feelings of fatigue, emotional exhaustion, and physical and emotional burnout. Good conflict resolution management practice and good communication management are paramount and must be provided by the faculty supervisor.

WORK CLIMATE: ETHICS

Webster defines ethics as "a set of moral principles or values" and "the principles of conduct governing an individual or group."[31] Others say that these are *professional standards* of right/wrong behaviors which should be addressed by professionals within and out of session. An *Ethical climate* is the moral atmosphere of a social system, characterized by shared perceptions of right and wrong, as well as common assumptions about how moral concerns should be addressed.[30] Ethical climate in organizations, as a product of organizational culture, refers to the way in which an institution typically handles issues such as responsibility, accountability, communication, regulation, equity, trust, and the welfare of the persons that are receiving services.

It is important that fieldwork/internship students be adept at recognizing right and wrong ethical behavior and be able to appropriately address ethical dilemmas as well as understand that technical and ethical competencies are equally important in the success of an employee and fieldwork/internship student. Not practicing either one can quickly end tenure on a job as well as tenure at a fieldwork placement. Technical and ethical knowledge and skills should be learned prior to a student's start at an internship placement and it should be explored during the fieldwork/internship experience. The learning process should be demonstrated in a structured format that explains the six ethical principles (autonomy, beneficence, non-maleficence, justice, fidelity, and veracity) and appropriate ethical codes related to the student's specific field of practice. Likewise, ethical decision-making models should be introduced to prepare the fieldwork/internship student for possible ethical dilemmas at the internship site.

TABLE 1

ETHICAL PRINCIPLES

Ethical Principle	Definition
Autonomy	Value- desire to promote the freedom of others to make personal choices. Practitioner Behavior – Acting in a manner that respects consumers' freedom of choice. *Example:* Maintain confidentiality, right to privacy, obtains informed consent, etc.
Beneficence	Value - Desire to do well. Practitioner Behavior – Acting in a manner that promotes the growth and well-being of consumers. *Example:* Work within the limits of/maintain competence. Duty to protect/warn–not breeching confidentiality, involuntary hospitalization, initiating guardianship, termination & referral of consumers who are not benefiting from services.
Non-Maleficence	Value- Desire to prevent harm. Practitioner Behavior – Acting in a manner that does not cause harm to consumers or prevents harm to consumers. *Example:* Avoiding counseling or providing other services in areas where the practitioner is not competent.
Justice	Value- Desire to promote the fair treatment of people. Practitioners Behavior – Treating consumers fairly. *Example:* Providing same practices to consumers regardless of race, age, gender, culture, and disability. Advocating against discrimination.
Fidelity	Value- Desire to be true to one's commitments. Practitioner Behavior- Keeping promises or commitments to consumers, colleagues, and agencies, both stated and implied. *Example*: Loyalty to consumers; full professional disclosure; loyalty to colleagues and the profession; loyalty to employers; and keeping contracts, etc.

Veracity   Value – Desire to tell the truth, and it is grounded in
                            respect for persons and the ethical principle of autonomy.
                            Example: For a person to make fully rational choices, he
                            or she must have the information relevant to his or her
                            decision.

WORKPLACE BURNOUT

Burnout in the workplace was initially studied in the early 1970s within the human service sector. Work burnout has been defined as an inability to handle emotional stress at work or overuse of effort and resources that manifest feelings of failure and emotional and sometimes physical fatigue. Burnout can bring on depression which can affect nearly every aspect of the person's life. Worker burnout is a serious concern in human service organizations[18].

Emotionally burnt-out employees are dissatisfied with their jobs and are more likely to disrupt the learning opportunities of the fieldwork/internship student. Although the literature[4,9,20] addresses pathways to burnout and how to reduce burnout, there will be high likelihood that the fieldwork/internship student will be paired with an employee who demonstrates emotional burnout. In this situation, the faculty supervisor will need to quickly intervene to ensure that the student's perceived view of the internship placement is not negatively influenced. The faculty supervisor should not ignore this situation. It is important to use this situation as a teaching opportunity on how to recognize burnout and introduce ways that can prevent and reduce burnout. Quite often the person may feel that his or her stress was caused by the stressed employee, which can magnify the emotional stress, which can lead to burn out. The literature suggests that social support can reduce the impact of stress on a variety of outcomes including psychological well-being, job satisfaction and physical illness.[5]

PEER SUPPORT GROUP

Research on fieldwork/internships has mostly placed emphasis primarily on the benefits interns acquire from learning what the workplace is all about. Internships allow a fieldwork/internship student to reduce his or her fear and gather valuable information about the internship site. The internship site also provides the opportunity to preview specific job tasks and develop professional relationships with potential employers.

There are several advantages to a fieldwork/internship. Some disadvantages could involve students being exposed to negative workplace trends such as downsizing, low employee morale, and job insecurity, which could lead to fieldwork/internship students developing a pessimistic view of the workplace.[10] An added component that is needed during the internship experience is the use of support among other fieldwork/internship students, with the purposeful watch of the faculty supervisor.

Navigating agency policy and procedures; services rendered, and organizational culture (i.e., unwritten rules) of the workplace can be a daunting task for students. There may be situations where a student may feel confused and hesitant to discuss implications that can arise at the fieldwork site. The use of peers as support groups to assist each other to navigate the complex work climate can be very helpful and therapeutic.

BENEFITS OF A POSITIVE WORK CLIMATE

A healthy work climate allows employee or the fieldwork/internship student to implement a smoother organizational process, work attitudes, productivity, and outcomes. Effective leadership promotes a more positive work climate, which is, in turn, associated with more positive therapeutic alliance among employees.[2] Positive work attitudes among employees also direct the effects of climate on work performance and motivation.[23] Further, positive work climate influences employees' commitment to their organization and job satisfaction

Many fieldwork/internship programs represent a chance to experience a real-world work environment,[5,28] and students often view fieldworks/internships as the most credible means of obtaining information about the realities of today's workplace.[27] Indeed, students who have had fieldwork/internship experiences report higher levels of confidence toward obtaining a job upon graduation[7] and are more likely to be employed at graduation or to receive a job offer upon graduation, as compared to those who have not participated in a fieldwork/internship.[17] Research on fieldwork/internships to date has focused primarily on the benefits interns gain from learning firsthand what the workplace is like. Fieldwork/internships not only allow interns to reduce their uncertainty, they provide the opportunity to preview specific jobs and develop relationships with potential employers.[21]

CONCLUSION

Ultimately, a positive work climate will maximize learning opportunities for the fieldwork/internship student. The focal point of a positive fieldwork/internship placement is to have an opportunity to obtain valuable information about the workplace, and experience a "real-world" work environment.[6,25] It has been suggested that internships are the most credible means of obtaining information about the realities of today's workplace.[27]

DISCUSSION QUESTIONS

1. What is the function of an agency's policies and procedures?

2. What is the difference between a formal and informal work culture?

3. Why is knowledge of the chain of command important for fieldwork/internship students?

4. Compare and contrast the concepts of centralization and formalization.

5. What impact does conflict in the workplace have on employees?

6. How can conflict in the fieldwork/internship site influence the fieldwork/internship student?

REFERENCES

[1]Aghaei, N., Moshiri, K. & Shahrbanian, S. (2012). Relationship between organizational justice and job burnout in employees of Sport and Youth Head Office of Tehran. *Advanced Applied Science Research,* 3(4), 2438-2445.

[2]Aarons, G. A., Woodbridge, M., & Carmazzi, A. (2002, March). Examining leadership, organizational climate, and service quality in a children's system of care (pp. 15–18). Paper presented at the 15th Annual Research Conference. A System of Care for Children's Mental Health: Examining the Research Base, Tampa, FL.

[3]Boyas, J. & Wind, L. H. (2010). Employment-based social capital job stress and employee burnout: A public child welfare employee structural model. *Children and Youth Services Review,* 2, 380-388.

[4]Business Dicitionary.com Retrieved from http://www.businessdictionary.com/definition/organizational-culture.html

[5]Coco, M. (2000), Internships: a try before you buy arrangement, S.A.M. *Advanced Management Journal, 2,* 41.

[6]Cohen, S. & Wills, T. A. (1985). Stress, social support, and the buffering hypothesis. *Psychological Bulletin, 98*(2), 310-357.

[7]Cook, S. J., Parker, R. S. and Pettijohn, C.E. (2004), The perceptions of interns: a longitudinal case study, *Journal of Education for Business, 79,* 179-185.

[8]DePanfilis, D. & Zlotnik, J.L. (2008). Retention of front-line staff in child welfare: A systematic review of research. *Children and Youth Services Review, 30*(9), 995- 1008.

[9]Fonner, K. L. & Roloff, M.E. (200⁶). Effects of exposure to job insecurity on workplace expectations of interns in the United States and Australia. *International Journal of Organizational Analysis, 14*(3), 204-224.

[10]Glisson C, Durick M. (1988). Predictors of job satisfaction and organizational commitment in human service organizations. *Administrative Science Quarterly, 33*, 61–81.

[11]Greenberg, J. (1990). *Organizational justice: yesterday, today and tomorrow. Handbook of industrial and organizational psychology.* Chicago, IL: Rand McNally.

[12]Hage, J. & Aiken, M. (1967). *Relationship of centralization to other structural properties. Administrative Science Quarterly, 12,* 72-92.

[13]Hamama, L. (2012). Burnout in social workers treating children as related to demographic characteristics, work environment and social support. *Social Work Research, 36*(2), 113-125.

[14]Ivone, F. & Helenides, M. (2009). Burnout em professores universitarios: impacto de percepcoes de justica e comprometinento afetivo, Psicologia: Teoria e Pesquisa, Psic: *Teor.e Pesq.* 25(4),

[15]James, L. R., and A. P. Jones. (1976). Organizational structure: A Review of structural dimensions and their relationships with individual attitudes and behavior." *Organizational Behavior and Human Performance 16*, 74-113

[16]Katz, A. H. (1981). Self-help and mutual aid: An emerging social movement? *American Review of Sociology, 7,* 129-155.

[17]Knouse, S.B., Tanner, J.T. and Harris, E.W. (1999), The relation of college internships, college performance, and subsequent job opportunity. *Journal of Employment Counseling, 36,* 35-44.

[18]Lee, E., Esaki, N., Kim, J., Greene, R., Kirkland, K. & Mitchell-Herzfeld, S. (2013). Organizational climate and burnout among home visitors: Testing mediating effects of empowerment. *Children and Youth Services Review, 35,* 594-602

[19]Maslach, C., Schaufeli, W.B. & Leiter, M.P. (2001). Job burnout. *Annual Review of Psychology, 52*(1), 397.

[20]Moran, E. and Volkwein, J. (1992) The Cultural approach to the formation of organizational climate. *Human Relations, 45*(1) 19 – 47.

[21]Morris A, Bloom JR. (2002). Contextual factors affecting job satisfaction and organizational c commitment in community mental health centers undergoing system changes in the financing of care. *Mental Health Services Research, 4,* 71–83.

[22]Nordin, S. Md., Sivapalan, S., Bhattacharyya, E., Hashim, H., Wan Ahmad, W.F. & Abdullah, A. (2014). Organizational communication climate and conflict management: Communications management in an oil and gas company. *2nd World Conference on Business, Economics and Management (WCBEM 2013). Procedia Social and Behavioral Sciences,* 109, 1046-1058.

[23]Parker C.P., Baltes B. B., Young S. A., Huff J. W., Altmann R. A., Lacost H. A., Roberts J. E. (2003). Relationships between psychological climate perceptions and work outcomes: A meta-analytic review. *Journal of Organizational Behavior, 24,* 389–416.

[24]Pugh, D. S., D. J. Hickson, C. R. Hinings, and C. Turner. (1969). Dimensions of Organization Structure. *Administrative Science Quarterly 8*, 289-315

[25]Riordan & Beggs. (1987). Counselors and self-help groups. *Journal of Counseling Development, 65*(8), 427-429.

[26]Romero, C., Kalidas, M., Elledge, R., Chang, J., Liscum, K. R., & Friedman, L. C. (2006). Self-forgiveness, spirituality, and psychological adjustment in women with breast cancer. *Journal of Behavioral Medicine, 29*, 29–36.

[27]Scott, M.E. (1992), Internships add value to college recruitments. *Personnel Journal, 71,* 59-62.

[28]Taylor, S. (1988), Effects of college internships on individual participants. *Journal of Applied Psychology, 73*, 393-401.

[29]Van de Vliert, E. (1998). Conflict and conflict management. In P.D. Drenth, H. Thierry, & J. de Wollf (Eds.). *Handbook of work and organizational psychology, personnel psychology.* East Sussex Psychology Press Ltd.

[30]Victor, B., and Cullen, J.B. (1988). The organizational bases of ethical work climates. *Administrative Science Quarterly, 33*, 101-125.

[31]Webster Dictionary. (2019). Ethics. Retrieved from: https://www.merriam-webster.com/dictionary/ethic

PROFESSIONALISM

DENISE Y. LEWIS

CHAPTER DESCRIPTION

The purpose of this chapter is to provide students with an understanding of professionalism. The chapter will define the concept of professionalism. Discussion of the key concepts of professionalism will also be provided to aid the student in their professional practice. Readers will be provided with strategies to promote and engender professionalism in the workplace. Helpful resources about professionalism will also be provided to aid students in their growth and development as professionals. This information is essential during the internship/fieldwork process because it will assist students in becoming competent human services and rehabilitation professionals and leaders.

LEARNING OBJECTIVES

> ➤ To teach students the key components of professionalism.

> ➤ To teach students how to practice professionalism.

As students transition to their final semester in school, securing a fieldwork/internship can be a daunting task. Research by Koltz & Champe[11] states that "counselor education literature contends that becoming a professional counselor is a complex, developmental process that is not fully understood."[p.2] This sentiment is true and can be applied to all those working in the Human Services and Rehabilitation fields. The growth and learning that is necessary is ever evolving and is an ongoing process that many seek to embrace.

The shift from being a student that is regularly engaging in reading, writing, and discussing important topics such as how to provide specific services and work with a wide variety of consumers, to one that is actively involved in meeting with those consumers in a professional manner, is one that can be overwhelming for many students. It is important during this evolution that the fieldwork/internship student understands and establishes professionalism in every aspect of their work.

Professionalism is described as "students changing identification with the role of student to professional."[11 p.4] The main theme also describes a transition toward increased professional knowledge, behavior, and attitudes. Professionalism can also be described as gaining and maintaining a posture of leadership and direction that encompasses following the standards set forth by the human services and rehabilitation industry standards and guidelines.

The transition from a student to a professional is characterized as a time when numerous changes are taking place.[12 p.2] The fieldwork/internship experience brings not only the potential for geographic changes and increased income, but changes in responsibility and expectations for students as they prepare to join the workforce. The changes in professional identity must include "showing initiative and autonomy, rather than looking for direction and approval from others regarding the students' responsibilities and skills." [p.2] This will require the fieldwork/internship student to draw upon those skills they have learned through their program, as well as those they internally possess. It must also include managing relationships and boundaries, establishing and knowing limitations, and maintaining consistent professionalism in all areas. This can produce some uncertainty and disorientation, because the student is caught between the two worlds of being fully aware that they are still a student, while balancing the understanding that they are operating in a more professional role as a service provider.

KEY CONCEPTS OF PROFESSIONALISM

Kokemuller[10] outlines the key concepts of professionalism. They include appearance, accountability, competence, respectful communication, integrity, confidentiality, self-identification, record keeping, dual relationships, and sexual relationships. These concepts align with the responsibilities necessary to flourish in a fieldwork/internship setting. Let us now explore each concept in more detail.

APPEARANCE

First impressions are important, and your appearance is what people see when they meet you. Appearance helps set the stage as to whether a person believes they can relate to you, and if they believe you are someone who can be trusted.[10] Concerns such as "Is the intern well groomed?" and "Is the intern dressed appropriately for the setting?" are important in maintaining a professional image. If you appear to be over-dressed or under-dressed, you send a message that may be negative or positive. As discussed in the chapter on Work Climate, it is essential to ensure that you understand your internship/fieldwork environment and work setting, and your appearance should appropriately match the requirements of the setting.

If you are uncertain of what the appropriate attire for your fieldwork/internship site may be, just look around when you visit the site and see what the employees are wearing. It is also best practice to ensure that you ask your site supervisor what attire you should adorn. Additionally, you should also consult your university/faculty supervisor and program handbook to determine if your school has mandatory fieldwork/internship attire guidelines.

ACCOUNTABILITY

Accountability is defined as "the fact or condition of being accountable; responsibility."[17] Being a responsible and accountable service provider will challenge and empower the clients to be accountable as well.[10] Important aspects of accountability include knowing your limitations and your scope of practice, speaking up and accepting responsibility when something goes wrong, and seeking and accepting guidance and leadership from a supervisor in times of need. A high level of accountability perfectly aligns with the professional values and principles in the fields of human services and rehabilitation that are outlined in the codes of ethics presented by a variety of human service and rehabilitation governing bodies.

COMPETENCE

There are three types of competence; professional competence, functional competence, and cultural competence. Professional competence is the decision-making and thinking action behind the clinical skill.[4] Functional competence is the measurement of performing skilled acts in a controlled (i.e., laboratory or clinical) setting, and is a critical precursor for everyday functioning.[12]

Cultural competence is "a set of congruent behaviors, attitudes, and policies that come together in a system, agency, or among professionals and enable that system, agency, or those professionals to work effectively in cross-cultural situations."[5] It is also seen as "the ability of systems to provide care to patients with diverse values, beliefs, and behaviors, including tailoring delivery to meet patients' social, cultural, and linguistic needs."[3]

When working in their fieldwork/internship sites students will be called to demonstrate their competence in these key areas, which involves a mix of skills and confidence they possess that will enable them to work successfully with clients. It is important to remember that this does not mean you must do everything perfectly. It does mean, however, that you should be secure in your preparation and ability to work independently yet be willing and competent enough to ask for help when needed.

Often, students feel insecure and have self-doubt when entering a fieldwork/internship experience, thereby rendering them helpless when they come face to face with clients. It is important that students recognize their abilities and limitations at this stage of their training. Where they are limited, they must not exceed their abilities, and where they are strong, they must move forward self-assured in the skills they have acquired to this point. However, students should be mindful that their faculty instructor and their site supervisors are sources of information and support. These professionals hold a wealth of knowledge and they are eager and able to share this information to aid students in overcoming hurdles while learning.

RESPECTFUL COMMUNICATION

Respectful communication is necessary when working with colleagues and clients. This communication includes verbal and nonverbal communication, good eye contact, appropriate attending, and a general respect for all people. Sound and effective communication will enable both the intern and the client to relate to each other and move toward building good rapport. An expanded discussion on respectful and effective communication can be found in the chapter on Effective Communication.

INTEGRITY

Integrity is defined as "the consistency of an acting entity's words and actions."[16] Integrity is an essential characteristic for a professional. Being honest and transparent is the foundation of becoming a consummate professional. Students must demonstrate integrity throughout their tenure which will help minimize any ethical violations that could occur as a professional. For instance, a core professional value of the counseling profession is "safeguarding the integrity of the counselor–client relationship." This includes avoiding actions that cause harm and establishing a relationship in which the client is able to trust in the role maintained by the professional counselor."[P.10] The importance of operating with integrity is also included in the Certified Rehabilitation Counselor (CRC) Code of Ethics,[4] the National Organization of Human Services Ethical Standards,[15] the National Association for Alcohol and Drug Addiction Counselors (NAADAC) Code of Ethics,[13] and the National Association of Social Workers (NASW) Code of Ethics.[14] Each of these organizations recognize the importance of integrity for not only the counselor and the consumer, but for the profession as well.

In addition to the key concepts outlined above, there are several concepts that are specific to budding professionals/novice professionals, and students in the human service and rehabilitation fields. Concepts such as confidentiality, proper identification, record keeping, dual relationships, and sexual conduct are issues which students should be mindful of during their fieldwork/internship experiences. While these may seem very apparent to many, it is important that students are aware of them, as knowledge of these concepts will enable the student to function both professionally and ethically.

CONFIDENTIALITY

Confidentiality is guaranteed to the client by the service provider. Information disclosed during the helping process will be kept between the service provider and the client. There are two exceptions to confidentiality; if a client poses a threat to themselves or to someone else. When working in their fieldwork/internship site, students must be mindful to maintain the confidentiality of their clients. This includes everything from identifying information to case specific information such as diagnosis and service provision. When working in their fieldwork/internship site, students are not permitted to discuss any aspects of their work with clients with any outside sources unless the limits of confidentiality meet the requirements outlined in their licensing Code of Ethics or unless they have a signed consent form from the client/consumer.

As an example, Section B of the CRC Code of Ethics deals extensively with the issue of confidentiality.[4] There are specific guidelines that address respecting client rights, exceptions to the confidentiality standards, working with groups and families, and working with minors. Section 1.07 of the NASW Code of Ethics also discusses the importance of confidentiality for its professionals.[14] The language may slightly differ in each of the Codes; however, the nature of the regulations remains the same throughout all the professional Codes.

SELF-IDENTIFICATION

While working in the capacity as a fieldwork/internship student one is obligated to identify oneself as such while working at their fieldwork/internship site. Since students are at their fieldwork/internship site for a limited period, this can impact the work they do, the expectations from the clients and the site, and the treatment modalities they may want to implement. This important element will ensure the student is not misrepresenting themselves, their training and qualifications, and their abilities. This self-identification can be fulfilled with a simple verbal notification to clients and other service providers. The student can also wear a name badge that clearly identifies them as a fieldwork/internship student.

RECORD KEEPING

It is essential to ensure that all records are kept and maintained in a timely manner. Record keeping is important because it keeps tabs for every person who is seen and the services they are being provided. This develops a history, both past and present.[8] Each agency and organization have specific guidelines for maintaining client records, internship logs, or any other records they utilize, and guaranteeing these are done accurately and timely is important as a professional. It is necessary for the human services and rehabilitation professionals in training to become familiar with these specifics in order to ensure compliance.

DUAL RELATIONSHIPS

Students sometimes have a difficult time understanding the complexities of dual relationships with clients and coworkers they interact with in the work or fieldwork/internship setting. Section 1.06 of the NASW Code of Ethics,[14] as well as section A.6 of the 2014 ACA Code of Ethics[1] addresses relationships with both current and former clients and the potential for risk that can be associated with said relationships. While all professional organizations address these concerns, the guidelines may be somewhat ambiguous and seeking direction from the fieldwork/internship site and faculty supervisor is imperative in this area.

SEXUAL RELATIONSHIPS

While the guidelines around dual relationships with clients may be somewhat ambiguous, those that include sexual relationships with clients are not. Human services and rehabilitation professionals are not to engage in a sexual relationship with their clients, their client's family members, or their client's romantic partners, both current and former, per the specifics listed in each of the professional Code of Ethics. This is specifically addressed in Section A.5 of the 2014 ACA Code of Ethics,[1] Section A.5 of the CRC Code of Ethics,[4] and Section 1.09 of the NASW Code of Ethics.[14]

STRATEGIES FOR THE PRACTICE OF PROFESSIONALISM

Dr. Dorothy Firman[7] stresses the importance of remembering the "why" of the individual's reason for deciding to enter the field of counseling. Remaining focused on the "why" will help the student remain connected to their purpose, thereby helping them focus on the need for professionalism. This will be an important connection for students when the road seems difficult and they begin to lose motivation. This focus on the "why" is necessary for all those who choose to become human services and rehabilitation professionals as they work to be a guide for those they work with.

The fields of human services and rehabilitation can bring with it numerous challenges to overcome when working with individuals facing a variety of physical, emotional, social, economic and political challenges. As a service provider in these fields we have an obligation to employ effective strategies that will aid us in assisting our clients/consumers in accomplishing their goals and improve their quality of life. Strategies such as consultation, adhering to one's professional codes of ethics, and upholding one's professional responsibilities are all important factors in ensuring the counselor provides skilled and helpful services.

CONSULTATION

As defined in the chapter on Consultation and Collaboration, consultation is a form of indirect education and mental health service delivery involving a professional with specialized knowledge and skills (i.e. a consultant) working with another professional (i.e. a consultee) to support clients' needs.[6] Consultant roles may include that of advocate, expert, trainer/educator, collaborator, and other less common roles. However, consultants are considered "experts" in most situations.

An important resource to assist Human Services and Rehabilitation students in dealing with the challenges of the profession is the help you will find in seeking out other professionals and mentors. Asking for needed help and guidance from those persons who have worked or are working in the field will prove invaluable when trying to navigate the challenges associated with service provision.

Students should also remember to consult with their site supervisor, and/or their faculty if they need clarification regarding any questions they have concerning professionalism. As someone who is new to the fieldwork/internship experience, it may be difficult to understand how to proceed when faced with a difficult situation. Consultation with your supervisors will provide the guidance you need to deal with the challenges that may arise while working to serve the needs of your client/consumer.

PROFESSIONAL CODE OF ETHICS

Consulting the designated Code of Ethics will be imperative for human service and rehabilitation professionals when issues arise with which they may be uncertain as to how to address. The role of professionalism and ethical standards are intricately connected and seeking guidance in this manner will be helpful when determining how to proceed. In areas where the answer is unclear, the intern should seek guidance from the site supervisor. Please see the expanded discussion related to ethics provided later in this text.

CONCLUSION

It is important for the Human Services and Rehabilitation intern to be aware of the requirements of their site to ensure they are following the policies and procedures of the agency and to ensure that they are performing effectively and professionally. Students should work to ensure they are demonstrating professionalism in their appearance, level of accountability, competence, respectful communication, and integrity. Additionally, professionalism also requires Humans Services and Rehabilitation professionals to respect confidentiality, practice appropriate and ethical self-identification, and record keeping, while respecting client rights and avoiding dual relationships and sexual relationships with clients/consumers and those closely related to clients/consumers. Establishing and maintaining a sound understanding of these ideals will enable you to exhibit professionalism in your field of practice and it will help enrich the work that you do.

DISCUSSION QUESTIONS

1. Why is it important that counseling interns always maintain a level of professionalism during their tenure as an intern?

2. What should the counseling intern do when they are faced with an ethical issue they are not certain how to handle?

3. Why is it important that the Human Services and Rehabilitation intern have a good understanding of the appropriate Codes of Ethics?

4. Who are the most important resources for counseling interns in the internship setting?

5. What are the key concepts of professionalism?

REFERENCES

[1]American Counseling Association. (2014). *ACA Code of Ethics*. Alexandria, VA.: Author.

[2]Betancourt, J. R., Green, A. R., Carrillo, J. E., & Ananeh-Firempong, O. (2003). Defining cultural competence: A practical framework for addressing racial/ethnic disparities in health and health care. *Public Health Reports, 118*(4), 293–302.

[3]Bordes Edgar, V., Holder, N., Cox, D. R., & Suris, A. (2019). Competence in psychology board certification: Unlike a good wine, it does not get better with age. *Training and Education in Professional Psychology*.

[4]Commission on Rehabilitation Counselor Certification (CRCC). (2017). Code of professional ethics for rehabilitation counselors. Retrieved from: https://www.crccertification.com/code-of-ethics-3

[5]Cross, T. L., Bazron, B. J., Dennis, K. W. & Isaacs, M. R. (1989). Towards a culturally competent system of care: A Monograph on effective services for minority children who are severely emotionally disturbed. CASSP Technical Assistance Center, Georgetown University Child Development Center: Washington, D.C. Retrieved from: https://spu.edu/~/media/academics/school-of-education/Cultural%20Diversity/Towards%20a%20Culturally%20Compete

[6]Erchul, W. P., & Sheridan, S. P. (2014). Overview: The state of scientific research in school consultation (2nd ed.) In W. P. Erchul, & S. P. Sheridan, *Handbook of research in school consultation* (pp. 3-17). New York, New York: Routledge.

[7]Firman, D. (2009). Stepping up: Strategies for the new counselor. *Counseling with Confidence: From Pre-Service to Professional Practice*. Amherst, MA: The Synthesis Center Press.

[8]Griffith, R. (2015). Understanding the Code: keeping accurate records. *British Journal of Community Nursing, 20*(10), 511–514.

[9]Hazler, R., & Kottler J. (2005). The emerging professional counselor student dreams to professional realities (2nd ed.). Alexandria, VA: American Counseling Association.

[10]Kokemuller, Neil. (n.d.). Concepts of professionalism. Work - Chron.com. Retrieved from http://work.chron.com/concepts-professionalism-15156.html.

[11]Koltz, R., & Champe, J. (2010). A phenomenological case study: The transition of mental health counseling interns from students to professionals. Retrieved from http://counselingoutfitters.com/vistas/vistas10/Article_31.pdf

[12]Mausbach, B.T., Harvey, P.D., Pulver, A.E., Depp, C.A., Wolyniec, P.S., Thornquist, M.H., Patterson, T.L. (2010). Relationship of the brief UCSD Performance-based skills assessment (UPSA) to multiple indicators of functioning in people with schizophrenia and bipolar disorder. *Bipolar Disord, 12*(1), 45–55

[13]National Association for Alcohol and Drug Abuse Counselors (NAADAC): The Association for Addiction

[14]National Association of Social Workers. (2017). Code of ethics: Ethical Standards. Retrieved from: https://www.socialworkers.org/About/Ethics/Code-of-Ethics/Code-of-Ethics-English

[15]National Organization of Human Services (NOHS). (2015). Ethical Standards for Human Services Professional. Retrieved from: https://www.nationalhumanservices.org/ethical-standards-for-hs-professionals

[16]Palanski, M. E., & Yammarino, F. J. (2007). Integrity and leadership: Clearing the conceptual confusion. European Management Journal, 25([3]), 171–184.

[17]Webster Dictionary (2019). Accountability. Retrieved from: https://www.merriam-webster.com/dictionary/accountability

ETHICS AND ETHICAL DECISION-MAKING

MARY-ANNE M. JOSEPH

KAYLIN MOSS

CHRISTA A. MARTIN

CHAPTER DESCRIPTION

The purpose of this chapter is to provide the reader with an overview of ethics and ethical practices. This chapter will provide a definition of ethics and the ethical principles. Information will be provided about the code of ethics that governs a range of human service and rehabilitation internship/fieldwork students. Information will be provided about the ethical decision-making models and practical activities and mini case studies will be provided to aid readers in practicing ethical decision making. The chapter will also provide strategies and helpful hints for ethical practice and decision making. Helpful resources will be provided to enhance ethical knowledge and development.

LEARNING OBJECTIVES

1. To teach students the six ethical principles.

2. To assist students in developing a working knowledge of the ethical code of conduct that guides their professional practice.

3. Students will learn how to implement an ethical decision-making model.

Every day, human beings are faced with ethical decisions. Some may be considered minor, while others may pose a greater challenge. Ethical dilemmas arise in our daily lives while we are at home, school, work, and in other social environments. We often face ethical dilemmas in the following forms: Should I tell Randy I broke his drone? I did not study for this exam, and I can see Mia's paper. Should I just use her answers? I do not feel like seeing this client today, so maybe I will call in sick. Gail's boyfriend has been flirting with me. I wonder if I should ask him out. All these examples demonstrate how our ethical decision-making skills are tested on a regular basis in our day to day lives. Within these situations, we consider what to do and our final decision is often related to our ethics.

Ethics are a system of moral principles. More specifically, Neulicht, et al.,[22] define ethics as "referring to characteristics or customs, generally described how to evaluate life through a set of standards and how to regulate behavior." Weston[31 p. 1] indicates that ethics are concerned with how a person behaves while values relate to a person's beliefs and attitudes that guide how they behave.[23] There are many things that influence personal and moral values such as cultural views, observations of other people, and our own personal conclusions based on our experiences.[32] As we venture into this discussion about ethics, it is essential to clarify the difference between our ethical obligations and our legal obligations.

As previously discussed, ethics are a system of moral principles.[31,22] However, the law supersedes ethical guidelines and codes. Ethics and ethical obligations do vary from the law and legal requirements. Unlike ethics, law is "the system of rules that a particular country or community recognizes as regulating the actions of its members and may enforce by the imposition of penalties."[32] There are two sources of laws that govern our society: 1. laws that are passed by governmental bodies, and 2. laws that are made by courts. When posed with professional dilemmas, human services and rehabilitation professionals must first and foremost ask themselves what the requirements of the law are. It is essential for human service and rehabilitation professionals to note that the law *always* supersedes the ethical codes. More simply put, the law always trumps the given code of ethics.

ETHICAL PRINCIPLES
    Each profession follows a group of laws, ethical codes and principles, and policies that guide their ethical behavior. As such, it is essential for students to become familiar with the ethical principles and codes that guide the profession which they are joining. Accordingly, there are six ethical principles for which human service and rehabilitation professionals should make themselves familiar: autonomy, beneficence, non-maleficence, justice, fidelity, and veracity.[4,7,15] These ethical principles are viewed as central to the process of ethical decision-making within the helping professions.
    The first principle is autonomy, and it requires professionals to respect the rights of clients to be independent and have self-determination in their social and cultural environments.[5,9] This principle highlights the significance of allowing clients to make their own choices. As human services and rehabilitation professionals, it is necessary to foster independence among our clients. We do this by educating and providing them with the appropriate self-advocacy skills that will aide them in making independent and informed decisions.
    The second principle is beneficence. The principle of beneficence states that professionals have an obligation to do good when working with consumers with disabilities, and in doing so, human services and rehabilitation professionals are to contribute to the welfare of the client.[5,9] This principle is a guideline that emphasizes the need for professionals to act in the best interest of the client. In the spirit of doing good, as described under the ethical principle of beneficence, we come to the third ethical principle of non-maleficence. This principle calls for human services and rehabilitation professionals to do no harm. More specifically, rehabilitation professionals are to avoid engagement in any activity that may cause or result in any physical, psychological, or societal harm to their client.[1,5]
    The fourth ethical principle set forth is the ethical principle of justice. This ethical principle stipulates that professionals are to be fair in the treatment of all clients. Fifth is the ethical principle of fidelity, which calls human services and rehabilitation professionals to be faithful to their clients. In doing so, professionals are to keep their promises and honor the trust placed in them by

their clients.[5] The therapeutic alliance with the client is key to their successful accomplishment of service goals. Not upholding this principle can severely damage the working relationship and rapport built with a client. The sixth ethical principle is veracity. This principle requires professionals to be honest when working with their clients.

An additional principle that is often included in the discussion of ethical principles is confidentiality. Confidentiality is a guarantee to the client by the service provider that information disclosed during the helping process will be kept between the service provider and the client. There are two essential times when this confidentiality can be broken. When the client poses a threat to themselves or someone else, human services and rehabilitation professionals have a "Duty to Warn."[33 p. 125] More specifically, this is a "situation in which a helping professional must violate the confidentiality promised to a client to warn others that the client is a threat to self or others." The second instance in which confidentiality can be broken is when it is necessary to report child abuse and elder abuse.

CODES OF ETHICS

A code of professional ethics is an established set of professional guidelines that are intended to guide the behavior of professionals in a particular field or profession.[6,1,5,27] The code of ethics is in place to establish norms and expectations for professionals in order to minimize harm done to the client and the general public. When entering their field of specialty, professionals have an obligation to abide by their profession's code of ethics and the shared values that are replicated in that code.[10]

Human services and rehabilitation professionals serve a wide range of clientele, work with interdisciplinary team members, and serve in a variety of professional capacities. These may include but are not limited to: human services, case management, rehabilitation counseling, veterans rehabilitation, social work, vocational development, mental health services, independent living, addiction studies, recreational therapy, special education, parole & probation, assistive technology, and behavior support. As such, it is beneficial for them to make themselves familiar with the codes of ethics that guide these professional areas. In this section, we will provide a brief description of six codes of ethics that human services and rehabilitation professionals may encounter when working in the field depending on their area of expertise and/or specialty.

Commission on Certified Rehabilitation Counselors (CRCC) Code of Ethics. Rehabilitation professionals have a set of ethical guidelines called the CRCC Code of Ethics, which is intended to guide their professional behavior.[5] This code has been developed and set in place by the Commission on Certified Rehabilitation Counselors. The CRCC Code of Ethics consists of twelve sections (A-L), which address a wide range of issues including: *the counseling relationship* (Section A), *confidentiality and privileged communication* (Section

B), *privacy, advocacy and accessibility* (Section C), *professional responsibility* (Section D), *relationships with other professionals and employers* (Section E), *forensic services* (Section F), *assessment and evaluation* (Section G), *supervision, training, and teaching* (Section H), *research and publication* (Section I), *technology, social media, and distance counseling* (Section J), *business practices* (Section K), and *resolving ethical issues* (Section L).

　　The National Organization of Human Services (NHOS) Ethical Standards. In human services, there is a standard of conduct that professionals and educators are to follow in ethical decision-making.[21] The human services ethical standards consist of forty-four standards that are separated into seven areas, which address responsibility to: clients, colleagues, the profession, the public & society, employers, self, and students.

　　National Association for Alcohol and Drug Addiction Counselors (NAADAC). The NAADAC code of ethics is the accepted standard of conduct for professionals certified by the National Certification Commission for Addiction Professionals (NCC AP) who work in the area of addiction.[19] This standard of conduct consists of seven principles which address:

The counseling relationship (Principle 1),

Confidentiality and privileged communication (Principle II),

Professional responsibilities and workplace standards (Principle III),

Working in a culturally diverse world (Principle IV),

Assessment, evaluation, and interpretation (Principle V),

E-therapy, e-supervision, and social media (Principle VI),

Supervision and consultation (Principle VII),

Resolving ethical concerns (Principle VIII), and

Research and publication (Principle IX).

RECREATIONAL THERAPY

　　Recreational Therapists also have a set of codes that guide their professional behavior. The American therapeutic recreation association's code of ethics applies to all recreational therapy professionals.[2] This includes all certified therapeutic recreation specialists, recreational therapy assistants, and recreational therapy students. The recreation therapy codes of ethics have ten principles that are to be promoted and maintained in the professional setting. In this code of ethics, many of the principles addressed are in line with the six original ethical principles previously described in this chapter. These principles are:

Beneficence (Principle 1),

Non-maleficence (Principle 2),

Autonomy (Principle 3),

Justice (Principle 4),

Fidelity (Principle 5),

Veracity (Principle 6),

Informed consent (Principle 7),

Confidentiality & privacy (Principle 8),

Competence (Principle 9), and

Compliance with laws and regulations (Principe 10).

SOCIAL WORK

The National Association of Social Workers' code of ethics sets the standards for the profession. The code of ethics has six standards to follow that include:[20] *Social Workers' ethical responsibilities to clients* (Standard 1), *Social Workers' ethical responsibilities to colleagues* (Standard 2), *Social Workers' ethical responsibilities in practice settings* (Standard 3), *Social Workers' ethical responsibilities as professionals* (Standard 4), *Social Workers' ethical responsibilities to the social work profession* (Standard 5), and *Social Workers' ethical responsibilities to the broader society* (Standard 6).[20]

AMERICAN COUNSELING ASSOCIATION

The American Counseling Association's code of ethics has nine sections that guide the counseling professional's behavior.[1] These sections address the following areas: *the counseling relationship* (Section A), *confidentiality and privacy* (Section B), *professional responsibility* (Section C), *relationships with other professionals* (Section D), *evaluation, assessment, and interpretation* (Section E), *supervision, training, and teaching* (Section F), *research and publication* (Section G), *distance counseling, technology, and social media* (Section H), and *resolving ethical issues* (Section I).

It is noteworthy to indicate that the ACA code of ethics shares many similarities with the CRCC code of ethics, as both codes are quite similar in nature and structure.

ETHICAL DECISION MAKING

A variety of researchers have contributed to the development of ethical decision-making models over recent decades.[9,13,14,26,29] When making ethical decisions, these models should be actively utilized by human services and rehabilitation professionals. Since it would be cumbersome to discuss all the ethical models that have been presented by various researchers over the years, the authors have selected a single ethical decision-making model to review in this chapter. Wheeler & Bertram[32] developed an eight-step ethical decision-making model that they believe is important to progress through in resolving an ethical dilemma. The eight steps and their components are as follows:

DEFINE THE PROBLEM

The first step in dealing with an ethical dilemma is to identify the problem. Wheeler & Bertram[32] stated that a dilemma has two competing alternatives that have a positive and negative aspect. Essentially, there is an upside and a downside to every problem. When faced with an ethical dilemma, professionals should identify the pros and cons of the situation at hand, as well as their potential consequences.

IDENTIFY THE RELEVANT VARIABLES

The second step will be to identify all other aspects of the person that may be relevant in the situation.[32] This includes family, cultural background, age, gender, environmental influences, social life, etc. It is important that we look at an individual from a holistic perspective and consider everything about the person. Sometimes, what one may consider a problem may actually be a cultural norm.

For instance, Flo (Service Provider) may be concerned that Stacy (Client) is not being autonomous in her decision-making and is relying too much on the thoughts and ideas of her family members who do not support her service goals. Flo may begin to consider intervening between Stacy and her family to practice her ethical duty of beneficence. However, this may not be appropriate if Stacy comes from a collectivist family where they make decisions as a group based on what is best for the family, as opposed to what is best for the individual. In this case, Flo should consider the cultural background of the client and be mindful to respect Stacy's cultural values.

Alternatively, a service provider may encounter a situation that is indeed harmful to the client at which time they would proceed to the next step of the ethical decision-making model. For instance, perhaps a member of Stacy's family appears to be abusive. Stacy reports to Flo that she cannot move forward with her service plan because it would make her husband very angry. She explains that she does not want to make him angry because he gets very aggressive with her and their children when he is angry. This information would lead Flo to the third step in the ethical decision-making model.

REVIEW ETHICAL CODES, INSTITUTIONAL POLICY, & THE LAW

The third step will be to review your code of ethics, your company's or institution's policy pertaining to the issue, and what the state and federal laws are regarding the issue at hand.[23] With the information Flo has received from Stacy regarding her husband, it would be appropriate for Flo to find out what her ethical code, the company's policy, and the law state in respect to the potential abuse of a client by a family member. Additionally, Stacy indicated that there were children involved; therefore, Flo needs to identify what the law states concerning abuse of children. Domestic violence and child abuse are serious offenses that are addressed by the law throughout the United States. It is noteworthy to indicate that human services professionals are mandated by law to report signs of child abuse as previously discussed in this chapter.

BE AWARE OF PERSONAL INFLUENCES

It is essential that the service provider ensure that he/she is not letting personal feelings regarding the dilemma obstruct their ability to make a sound ethical decision.[32] It is always beneficial to take the time to reflect on how personal values and viewpoints could have an influence or impact our decision-making process. At this step of the ethical decision-making process, it is important for Flo to assess her own biases. Perhaps it would be helpful for Flo to ask herself if she is being biased about the situation because she has previously been in an abusive relationship. Whether or not biases are at play, it would be appropriate to move to the next step of the model, since consultation will help Flo explore the situation more thoroughly.

PROFESSIONAL CONSULTATION

Being able to seek outside help from supervisors, colleagues, and a national board can be helpful in bringing insight and different perspectives.[32] As previously stated, consultation will help Flo explore the situation to a greater extent. During consultation, she can seek out the advice, knowledge, experience, and perspective of other professionals that can assist her in making a more effective ethical decision as she works to help Stacy. As the age-old adage says, "two heads are better than one."

ENUMERATE OPTIONS AND CONSEQUENCES

After proceeding through the above-mentioned steps, it is time to consider options for action.[32] In considering options for action, it is also necessary to assess the benefits and consequences of each option for action. To respect the client's right to autonomy, the service provider should make a concerted effort to ensure that the client is involved in the decision-making process regarding the ethical dilemma. However, if the situation does not require the client's participation, or the client's participation in the decision-making process is not going to be appropriate, they may not be included in this process by the service provider.

After defining the problem, identifying the relevant variables, reviewing her ethical codes, institutional policy, and the law, identifying and addressing her personal influences, and consulting with another appropriate professional(s), it is now time for Flo to explore her options for action. Flo should ask herself some things first. Here are a few examples: Should I report the potential child abuse to Child Protective Services? If I report the potential abuse to Child Protective Services, what are the pros and cons of this action? Is there a better way to address my concern about potential child abuse?

DECIDE AND TAKE ACTION

Now it is time to act! In this step of the ethical decision-making process, the service provider decides based on all the information gathered.[32] At this point, Flo will make a final decision whether to report the potential child abuse to Child Protective Services and act on that decision.

DOCUMENT DECISION

Upon proceeding through the ethical decision-making process, it is vital that the service provider document the ethical dilemma and the decisions they have made.[32] The steps that were taken to address the dilemma should be documented in the client's case file. Documentation of the ethical dilemma is at the end of the process because it is essential that human services and rehabilitation professionals explore their concerns and verify the validity of these concerns prior to placing the information into the client's file. It is essential to note that misunderstandings and miscommunications occur; therefore, it is essential that sufficient and adequate research be conducted in order to ensure that the client is being properly represented and assisted.

STRATEGIES FOR ETHICAL PRACTICES & THINGS TO CONSIDER

It is critical that human services and rehabilitation service providers always remain professional and ethical. Oramas[23] presented six best practices for ethical decision-making. The first one is supervision and consultation. Oramas[18] posited that frequently seeking professional supervision and consultation to address complex issues is one of the best methods of ethical decision-making to adopt as a young professional.[18]

The second-best practice for ethical decision-making presented by Oramas is ethical reflection. This is the practice of reflecting upon one's morals and values when determining the best course of action regarding an ethical decision.[12,32] As previously mentioned, human services and rehabilitation professionals must be careful not to let personal morals and values influence their ethical decisions.

The third best practice for ethical decision-making is self-awareness.[23] Ethical decision-making goes beyond implementing laws, rules, and codes. Human services and rehabilitation professionals would do well to consider the cognitive and emotional aspects of ethical decision-making. They must work diligently to ensure that their emotions and personal opinions do not obstruct their ability to make effective ethical decisions.[24,17]

Fourth is the assessment and maintenance of core principles, values, and qualities.[23] By striving to achieve our profession's core principles, human services and rehabilitation professionals can lessen the risks of engaging in unethical behaviors.[12] Certain personality traits such as empathy, being open minded, and modeling can aid professionals to be more effective in the implementation of their ethical decision-making skills.[12,23]

The fifth and sixth best practices for the engagement in effective ethical decision-making skills is cultural competence and working with the LGBTQ+ community.[23] Cultural competence is defined as "the capacity to draw effectively upon cultural knowledge, awareness, sensitivity, and skillful actions in order to relate appropriately to, and work effectively with, others from different cultural backgrounds."[25] There are four dimensions of culture competence: cultural knowledge, cultural awareness, cultural sensitivity, and cultural action. When working with minorities and individuals who are a part of the LGBTQ+ community, it is vital that human services and rehabilitation professionals are aware of their beliefs and attitudes about gender, sexuality, and sexual orientation to ensure that we do not have a negative impact on the people we serve.[11]

CONCLUSION

Ethical issues arise on a routine basis; therefore, it is essential that human services and rehabilitation professionals are well equipped to manage these challenges. These professionals have a responsibility to ensure that they are knowledgeable about their ethical principles and codes as set forth by their governing bodies. Additionally, human service and rehabilitation professionals should seek out opportunities to enhance their knowledge on the implementation of ethical decision-making models to ensure they engage in the appropriate courses of actions when they are faced with an ethical dilemma.

DISCUSSION QUESTIONS

1. What constitutes an ethical dilemma?

2. Explain the difference between ethical and legal obligations for professionals.

3. Give a working example of each of the six core ethical principles discussed.

4. When can the ethical principle of confidentiality be broken?

5. Compare and contrast the six codes of ethics presented that human services and rehabilitation professionals may encounter.

6. Identify your potential profession's code of ethics and describe how you might apply those ethical standards in practice.

7. Explore and reflect on your own biases. What personal biases do you possess that could possibly influence the provision of client services?

8. Describe an example of an ethical dilemma and show how you would progress through Wheeler & Bertram's[32] eight-step ethical decision-making model to resolve it.

9. Which strategies for ethical practice are the most and least beneficial in your ethical decision-making process? Why?

10. Provide an example of how you can improve your cultural competency for each of the four given dimensions.

DESCRIPTIVE CASE STUDIES

Students can utilize the case scenarios below to practice navigating through the ethical decision-making model previously discussed in this chapter.

CASE STUDY #1

Selwyn is a 34-year-old male client with a seizure disorder who is recovering from a recent stroke, which has left him with moderate to severe issues with his ambulation and mobility. Selwyn has a bachelor's degree in Communications/Journalism with previous radio broadcasting experience and switchboard operation. His driver's license is currently suspended due to recent seizure activity and he cannot be medically cleared for at least another six months to be reinstated. Despite his limitations, Selwyn has been driving around the community to engage in a variety of work-related events. While he finds this challenging, Selwyn does not want his disability to limit his career.

CASE STUDY #2

Ann Marie is a 22-year-old female who is working as an intern at a local nursing home facility where she has been working for the last two months. While working at the agency Ann Marie has been training under the direct supervision of Lawrence who has been teaching her how to work with the clients, document her interactions, and submit records for Medicare billing. In recent weeks, a few incidents have had Ann Marie concerned.

Ann Marie works at the nursing home along with Earl who is another student in her class. Ann Marie noticed that Earl was rarely at the nursing home, and she wondered how he was acquiring his hours to complete the internship. While in class one day, Earl presented a case study that was based on one of Ann Marie's clients at the nursing home, which Earl had not worked with in the past. The following week, Ann Marie walked into the classroom to find Earl completing his log sheets at which time she saw him sign Lawrence's name to the form.

CASE STUDY #3

Ruby is a 23-year-old male-to-female transgender client who lives in a rural community and works at a local supermarket. She experienced intense bullying at the high school once she came out as a member of the LGBTQ+ community. She has a history of substance and alcohol abuse. Ruby is currently participating in a sobriety and recovery program, as well as receiving mental health counseling in conjunction with the services you provide.

You reside in the same rural area and have recently noticed Ruby's vehicle parked in front of a local bar. Since then, you have overheard someone in your place of worship saying that they too have noticed your recent observation. At Ruby's next appointment, she states that everything is going well with her sobriety and that her mental health counseling has been very therapeutic. However, she also mentions that she is still struggling with her depression and addiction.

CASE STUDY #4

Maxine is a 16-year-old female client who has a disability and receiving Social Security benefits. She is currently participating in Pre-Employment Transition Services (Pre-ETS) from one of your vendors that is working with the school district. Maxine's father has stated that he does not want her involved in community-based work experiences because it may have an impact on her "check." He does not believe she can, nor does he want her to, work.

Maxine is excited about doing a job shadowing at a local veterinarian clinic. She loves being with animals and thinks this may be a great place to work one day. Although she does not want to become a veterinarian, she does like the idea of being employed in some capacity within this field of practice. The vendor tells Maxine that she will not be going on their planned community outing to job shadow. She calls you not understanding why they told her she could not participate as anticipated.

CASE STUDY #5

Allen is a 42-year-old male Iraqi War Veteran with quadriplegia due to a C-7 spinal cord injury. He is being referred to you for further assistance from the VA Hospital where he has received a broad range of human and rehabilitation services since being honorably discharged. After meeting with him to determine eligibility for your services, you decide to send him for additional assessment and evaluation before making him a client. The vocational evaluation report comes back indicating that he is interested in working outdoors with his hands and has an aptitude for scientific and skilled professional areas of work. His psychological assessment report shows a diagnosis of Seasonal Affective Disorder.

When meeting with Allen as a new client, he explains that he would either like to go to school to learn a trade skill or go directly into employment. He has his high school diploma, and he did quite well in school. However, he does not think college is right for him and dislikes academics. Allen will require extensive assistive technology and reasonable accommodations in either route he chooses. You feel that college is the best option for him.

CASE STUDY #6

Sierra is a 15-year-old female client who has epilepsy and ADHD. She has difficulty focusing on homework and gets distracted easily. Sierra also has trouble communicating with other people. In the last year or so Sierra's biological mother and stepfather separated, and they were homeless during that time but now are in a stable condition. Sierra wants to become a nutritionist or a sports psychologist and is currently participating in community-based work experiences to help develop the appropriate skills needed. During our session, Sierra mentions that she is being sexually abused by a family member and does not want to tell her mom about it out of fear of being called a liar. Sierra has been experiencing deep sadness and her seizures have increased because of this issue. Sierra is not motivated to continue her community-based work experience opportunities.

CASE EXPLORATION QUESTIONS:

1. What is the problem or potential ethical dilemma?

2. What are the relevant variables in this case?

3. What does your profession's ethical codes state regarding the potential ethical issue?

4. What does your institutional or company's policy state about the potential ethical issue?

5. What does the law state regarding the potential ethical issue?

6. Which of your personal influences has the potential to impact your perception of the potential ethical issue?

7. Identify three professionals who you can consult about the ethical issue and discuss why each person would be an appropriate consultant for this potential ethical dilemma.

8. What would be your potential options for action in this case if you were the service provider?

REFERENCES

[1]American Counseling Association. (2005). ACA code of ethics. Alexandria, VA: Author.

[2]American Therapeutic Recreation Association. (2018). Guidelines for the Ethical Practice of Recreational Therapy. Retrieved from: https://www.atra-online.com/page/Ethics

[3]Ancona, D. (2012). Sensemaking: Framing and Acting in the Unknown. In S. Snook, N. Nohria & R. Khurana (Eds.), *The Handbook for Teaching Leadership: Knowing, Doing, and Being* (pp. 1-19). Thousand Oaks, CA: SAGE Publications.

[4]Beauchamp, T. L., & Childress, J. F. (2012). *Principles of biomedical ethics (7th ed.).* New York, NY: Oxford: University Press.

[5]Commission on Rehabilitation Counselor Certification (CRCC). (2017). Code of professional ethics for rehabilitation counselors. Retrieved from: https://www.crccertification.com/code-of-ethics-3

[6]Corey, G., Schneider, Corey, M., & Callanan, P. (2007). *Issues and ethics in the helping professions. (7th Ed.).* Belmont, CA: Thomson Higher Education.

[7]Coughlin, S. (2008). How many principles for public health ethics? *The Open Public Health Journal, 1*, 8–16.

[8]Forester-Miller, H., & Davis, T. E. (2016). Practitioner's guide to ethical decision making (Rev. ed.). Retrieved from http://www.counseling.org/docs/default-source/ethics/practioner's-guide-toethical-decision-making.pdf

[9]Forester-Miller, H., & Rubenstein, R. L. (1992). Group counseling: Ethics and professional issues. In D. Capuzzi & D. R. Gross (Eds.), *Introduction to group counseling* (2nd ed., pp. 307–323). Denver, CO: Love.

[10]Francis, P. C., & Dugger, S. M. (2014). Professionalism, ethics, and value-based conflicts in counseling: An Introduction to the special section. *Journal of Counseling & Development, 92*(2), 131-134.

[11]Ginicola, M., Filmore, J., & Smith, C. (2017). Developing Competence in Working with LGBTQI+ Communities: Awareness, Knowledge, Skills, and Action. In M. Ginicola, J. Filmore, & C. Smith. (Eds.), *Affirmative Counseling With LGBTQI+ People* (pp. 1-20). Alexandria, VA.: American Counseling Association.

[12]Granello, D., & Young, E. (2012). *Counseling Today: Foundations of Professional Identity*. Upper Saddle River, N.J. : Pearson

[13]Haas, L. J., & Malouf, J. L. (1989). *Keeping up the good work: A practitioner's guide to mental health ethics*. Sarasota, FL: Professional Resource Exchange.

[14]Kitchener, K. S., & Anderson, S. K. (2011). *Foundations of ethical practice, research, and teaching in psychology and counseling (2nd ed.)*. New York, NY: Routledge.

[15]Kitchener, K. S. (1984). Intuition, critical evaluation and ethical principles: The foundation for ethical decisions in counseling psychology. *Counseling Psychologist, 12*, 43–55.

[16]Lambie, G. W., Ieva, K. P., Mullen, P. R., & Hayes, B. G. (2011). Ego development, ethical decision-making, and legal and ethical knowledge in counselors. *Journal of Adult Development, 18*, 50-59. [17]

[17]Manning, S. S. (2003*). Ethical leadership in human services: A multi-dimensional approach*. Boston: Pearson Education Inc

[18]McAuliffe, D., & Sudbery, J. (2005). 'Who do I tell?' *Journal of Social Work*, 5(1), 21-43. doi:10.1177/1568017305051362

[19]National Association for Alcohol and Drug Abuse Counselors (NAADAC): The Association for addiction professionals. (2016). NAADAC/NCC AP Code of Ethics. Retrieved from https://www.naadac.org/code-of-ethics

[20]National Association of Social Workers. (2017). Code of ethics: Ethical standards. Retrieved from: https://www.socialworkers.org/About/Ethics/Code-of-Ethics/Code-of-Ethics-English

[21]National Organization of Human Services (NOHS). (2015). Ethical standards for human services professional. Retrieved from: https://www.nationalhumanservices.org/ethical-standards-for-hs-professionals

[22]Neulicht, A. T., McQuade, L. J. & Chapman, C. A. (2010). *The CRCC desk reference on professional ethics: A Guide for rehabilitation counselors*. Athens, Georgia: Elliot & Fitzpatrick.

[23]Oramas, J. E. (2017). Counseling ethics: Overview of challenges, responsibilities and recommended practices. *Journal of Multidisciplinary Research (1947-2900), 9*(3), 47–58.

[24]Pawlukewicz, J., & Ondrus, S. (2013). Ethical Dilemmas: The Use of applied scenarios in the helping professions. *Journal of Social Work Values & Ethics, 10*(1), 2.

[25]Sperry, L. (2012). Cultural competence: A Primer. *Journal of Individual Psychology, 68*(4), 310–320.

[26]Stadler, H. A. (1986). Making hard choices: Clarifying controversial ethical issues. *Counseling and Human Development, 19*, 1–10.

[27]Tarvydas, V. & Cottone, R. R. (2000). The code of ethics for professional rehabilitation counselors: What we have and what we need. *Rehabilitation Counseling Bulletin, 43*(4), 188-196.

[28]Van Hoose, W. H. (1986). Ethical principles in counseling. *Journal of Counseling & Development, 65*(3), 168-171.

[29]Van Hoose, W. H., & Paradise, L. V. (1979). *Ethics in counseling and psychotherapy: Perspectives in issues and decision making.* Cranston, RI: Carroll.

[30]Weick, K. (1995). Sensemaking in organizations. Beverly Hills, CA: Sage.

[31]Weston, A. (2008). *A 21st century ethical toolbox (2nd ed.).* New York, NY: Oxford University Press.

[32]Wheeler, A. M., & Bertram, B. (2015). *The counselor and the law: a guide to legal and ethical practice.* Alexandria, VA: American Counseling Association

[33]Woodside, M.; McClam, T. (2013) *Generalist case management: A Method of human service delivery (4th Ed).* Brooks/Cole Cengage Learning, Belmont, CA.15

SELF-CARE

MARY-ANNE M. JOSEPH
SHAYNA HOBSON
CHRISTAN HORTON

CHAPTER DESCRIPTION

This chapter will provide a working definition of self-care for rehabilitation and human services internship/fieldwork students. It will also provide a brief description of eight categories of self-care. Students will be provided with clear strategies for implementing self-care in each category. Additionally, students will be presented with resources for building a self-care wheel and guidelines for updating the wheel as needed as they progress in their profession. This chapter will also provide key resources that students can explore as they further engage in the practice of self-care.

OBJECTIVES

1. Students will learn the meaning and importance of self-care.

2. Students will become familiar with eight types of self-care.

3. Students will learn strategies for implementing self-care in the eight self-care areas discussed in this chapter.

4. Students will learn how to utilize a self-care wheel and make a continual plan for self-care.

INTRODUCTION

Self-care "is the practice of activities that mature people initiate and perform independently within a time frame to promote and maintain personal well-being, healthful functioning and continuing development throughout life."[16 p.525] Additionally, "self-care is described as the application of a range of activities with the goal being 'well-functioning'," which is described as "the enduring quality in one's professional functioning over time and in the face of professional and personal stressors."[9 p.5] Further, self-care is a responsibility to care for the overall health and the wellbeing of oneself. It is essential that young professionals are taught the importance of self-care during their educational training. This will ensure that these young professionals are prepared to implement effective self-care strategies daily and minimize the impact of fatigue and burnout.

In the fields of rehabilitation and human services where professionals strive to serve the needs of others, the practice of self-care is synonymous with success. These professionals are responsible for providing safe, high quality services to a wide range of consumers across a variety of disciplines. It is important that rehabilitation and human service professionals learn and practice self-care because the work that these professionals do is both emotionally and physically exhausting.[16]

Exhaustion can lead to fatigue, which can in turn have a negative impact on service provision. When human service and rehabilitation professionals are fatigued, the services they provide to consumers can be compromised, thus it is essential that these professionals actively engage in self-care.[16] Self-care should be viewed as a core competency for rehabilitation and human service professionals. It has been said that "self-care is not an indulgence. It is an essential component of prevention of distress, burnout, and impairment. It should not be considered as something 'extra' or 'nice to do if you have the time' but as an essential part of our professional identities."[3 p.603] Simply put, self-care is an essential professional activity for promoting ethical practice.[3]

It is noteworthy to indicate that working as a rehabilitation and human service professional can be rewarding. However, overtime the professionals working with these consumers will experience significant challenges and stressors. This includes things such as, relationship endings and empathy fatigue. Relationship endings or termination is the ending of the therapeutic relationship. Termination is indeed a pivotal phase for a client as well as the professional and may create strong feelings of fear.[23] With respect to termination, it is important for the professional to encourage the client to identify positive feelings during this process as a practice of independence, autonomy, and therapeutic gains.[23] Empathy fatigue occurs when an individual encounters an emotional or physical state of exhaustion due to the constant exposure to their client's illness, trauma experiences, or disability/condition.[30] Challenges and stressors associated with the service rehabilitation and human service provides highlights the need for these young professionals to learn how to practice effective self-care, because without it they are "taking a risk of becoming impaired by not having effective ways of coping and resources to help with the stress."[6 p.15]

Self-care is also an important practice for students who are in the fieldwork, internship and/or practicum stage of their education training program.[21] Self-care should be a key component of professional development for novice professionals. Learning the importance of self-care at an early point in one's career can have a potentially lasting impact on their professional success and professional longevity. More specifically, the practice of self-care may lead to greater job engagement and compassion satisfaction, enhanced self-care, and improved patient care and satisfaction.[24] During this stage of training, it is important for students to gain hands-on experience working with consumers, but also learn how to cope with the challenges of assisting with the management of the burdens, hardships, and disadvantages experienced by consumers. We must be mindful that when "self-care is not performed regularly it is easy to slip in behaviors that are not professional."[18]

It is essential to consider compounding factors that highlight the need to learn effective self-care strategies while engaging in the internship/fieldwork process. Often, students are exposed to a significant number of stressors that may impact their success both inside and outside of the classroom. Factors such as living away from home, heavy workloads, and unhealthy lifestyles may increase students stress levels and hamper their success both inside and outside of the classroom.[16]

Additionally, many minority students often have heavier workloads than their more privileged peers. Minority students are often juggling a fulltime academic schedule and full-time or part-time employment, while attempting to engage in an internship/fieldwork experience. Such a burdensome workload can be detrimental to your success. As a student, it is important to practice self-care. This sets the stage for your practice of self-care as a professional. While racing to the ultimate finish line of "graduation," students often engage in a rigorous level of activity which often leads to burnout prior to graduation. Therefore, the development of self-care practices early in one's career has the potential to lead to the implementation of ongoing behaviors that can last throughout your career.[4]

CATEGORIES OF SELF-CARE

Over time, researchers have developed a wide range of self-care categories. These categories have included, but are not limited to, personal, social, environmental, physical, emotional, psychological, intellectual, cultural, spiritual, sexual, physiological, professional, occupational, vocational, academic, and financial. This chapter focuses on the self-care areas that the authors deemed most relevant to students. In this section we will briefly describe eight self-care categories and discuss how you can practice self-care in these areas of your life.

PERSONAL SELF-CARE

The personal self-care refers to strategies for taking better care of oneself.[24] Students should engage in active efforts to achieve a balance between their professional and personal lives.[4] Who do you know that practices effective self-care? Consider looking to your peers, family, faculty, and supervisors as role models for self-care. Building relationships with others who actively practice effective self-care can aid you in the development of connections and relationships which you can use to promote professional wellness throughout your career.[4]

Personal self-care activities can include things such as the outlining of long- and short-term goals, making a vision board, pursuing a hobby, cleaning your environment, mindfulness, meditation, tai chi, massage, exercise classes, walks, and a healthy diet.[4] Consult your faculty and student affairs administrators to determine if any of these activities are available at your institution. These activities offer various levels of reflection, relaxation, and planning that can assist you in developing a clear picture of and purpose for your life.

Outlining the long- and short-term goals that you have for your life can help to motivate you, give you structure, and provide a source of meaning.[7] A vision board is a "collage of images that represent the things an individual wants out of his or her life."[8 p.1] Creating a vision board gives you the opportunity to think about the things that are important to you and develop a positive mindset. Additionally, engaging in hobbies is therapeutic, and can help you to release the stressor of the day.

Your environment includes your home, your office, and any other space where you work and live. Keeping your environment clean and organized can help your life and mind. In combination with keeping a calm and clear mind is the art of mindfulness. Mindfulness meditation is described as placing consistent and intentionally focused awareness on the present moment.[5] In mindfulness, you experience things in their natural form without judgmental labels of moral, immoral, correct, or wrong. Mindfulness meditation can help you gain a sense of peace and calmness within the mind and the benefits of fewer distractions. Mindfulness is known to improve quality of life along with biological outcomes across various populations.[5] Tai chi is an additional technique for personal self-care. Tai chi is a mind-body exercise that combines meditation. Tai chi can help enhance psychosocial well-being and manage depression and anxiety.[40] Exercise classes, such as yoga, aerobics, Zumba, and weightlifting can help you improve mood and anxiety.[17] Walks can be therapeutic and help with psychological stress. You can take this time to focus on the present moment and what you see around you. A healthy diet is important because it can help reduce health risk behaviors.[1] Research has shown that a healthy diet can reduce the development of conditions such as diabetes, high blood pressure, stroke, cancer, and asthma.[29]

SOCIAL SELF-CARE

Social self-care involves addressing one's social needs. Albert Bandura stated that "human health is a social matter, not just an individual one."[2 p.143] As such, we must engage in social systems. Active involvement in social systems promotes human health and wellbeing.[2] This is further supported by the notion that human beings cannot be fully understood outside of their environment. Oftentimes when the environment is not well, neither is the person in the environment. In order to improve your self-care, you must engage your social self.

There are two components of the social self: friendship and love.[19] Research has demonstrated that friendships and intimate relationships have a positive impact on the quality of one's life, while self-isolation is correlated with poor health. More specifically, social support and engagement have been found to positively impact physical, mental and social health. Enhancing the quality of your social self can be accomplished through the active practice of social self-care. Practicing social self-care ensures that we effectively meet the basic human needs for companionship, intimacy, belonging, and self-affirmation.

It is important to note that social self-care and physical self-care have a reciprocal relationship.[11] When a person is in good physical health, they are more likely to engage in social activities, and likewise when a person practices active social self-care they tend to strive for physical health so they can remain engaged in their social systems.

Supportive social networks have been shown to enhance health regardless of stress.[11] These networks also provide individuals with a means of accessing new contacts and solving problems through increased access to information. Specific social self-care activities may include; getting coffee with friends, attending a theatre production at your institution, attending an athletic event on campus, and/or volunteering at a community agency such as a school or a center for independent living, joining a student organization, joining a community organization, getting actively involved in your religious organization (i.e. church, mosque, synagogue, temple, etc.).

PHYSICAL SELF-CARE

The physical practice of self-care can help prevent physical and mental breakdowns caused by stress. Research has shown a positive relationship between regular physical activity/exercise and physical and psychological well-being.[33] It can enhance a person's self-esteem, psychological balance, positive attitude, and a healthy personality. Physical self-care activities can include; nature walks, taking the stairs, working out in the campus gym, taking fitness classes, and healthy eating habits.[33]

EMOTIONAL SELF-CARE

Emotional self-care is inextricably linked to emotional intelligence, which is described as "a concept including perception, expression and control of emotions, self-control and empathy, communication, conflict resolution process, conscience, and perhaps many more."[15 p.118] Additionally, emotional intelligence is also described as one's ability to carry out three primary task:

➢ understand one's own feelings,

➢ listen to the feelings of others and empathize with those feelings, and

➢ the ability to express one's own emotions in a productive manner.[10]

In order to carry out these tasks, one needs to be proficient in the following skills; the ability to control impulse, minimize impatience, regulate mood, prevent frustration, have empathy, and hope for self.[22] More simply, the primary feature of emotional Intelligence is self-knowledge. Self-knowledge helps us to observe our feelings, recognize them, identify or name those feelings and express them in a productive and effective manner. Emotional self-care activities can include; positive affirmations,[13] laugher, read a leisure or self-help book, watching a movie, journaling, engaging in therapy and/or a self-help group.

SPIRITUAL SELF-CARE

The practice of spiritual self-care focuses on the connection of the mind, body, and spirit. Spiritual self-care consists of practices that encourage overall well-being in both health and illness. The concept places emphasis on individual experiences, morals, and religious roots which originate from a combination of faith and emotions.[37] Spiritual well-being is an assertion of life in relationship with God, the self, others, the community, and the environment that nurtures and celebrates wholeness. People who appreciate spiritual well-being tend to feel alive, purposeful, and satisfied.[5] Moreover, studies have suggested that spirituality is the essence of human beings and plays a vital role in people's lives.[39] Addressing the spiritual dimension of care makes a considerable difference in physical and psychosocial outcome. Nursing study shows the positive effects of spirituality on health, well-being, and satisfaction.[12,34,26] Spiritual self-care activities can include; meditation, self-reflection, finding and engaging in a spiritual community, and practicing prayer, yoga, and/or Tai Chi.

ACADEMIC SELF-CARE

While pursuing their academic goals students are to be mindful of the stressors that can be caused by the pressures of academia. While in the academic arena students are presented with a safe environment to engage their stressors and develop effective self-care strategies to manage their workload and balance the needs of their personal lives. Moreover, students who are training to serve in the fields of human services and rehabilitation have a great need to learn how to practice self-care in academia as their self-care skills will transfer into their practice in the field.

Self-care is a useful complement to the professional training for those preparing to work in the fields of human services and rehabilitation.[28] For instance, Mindfulness-Based Stress Reduction (MBSR) was found to reduce stress, negative affect, anxiety, and significantly increase positive affect and self-compassion. The practice of academic self-care can involve the practice of smart and effective timelines for completing assignments, developing an appropriate and effective study schedule, developing an effective and appropriate sleeping and eating schedule. These simple self-care practices can improve students' academic effectiveness and success. These academic self-care practices will certainly translate into the workforce.

PROFESSIONAL SELF-CARE

Over time, research has highlighted the fact that human service clinicians experience distress and grief in response to the challenges and stressors that are faced by their clients.[24] These emotional stressors have the potential to compromise the professional well-being of rehabilitation and human service professionals in training. As previously stated in this chapter unexamined emotions may lead to burnout, moral distress, compassion fatigue, and poor service decisions which can adversely affect service provision. A primary means of combating stress and burnout is the engagement in self-care activities to promote and maintain professional well-being.

Becoming an active member of an academic student club or organization can help you to build relationships with peers and develop a professional network with peers. Developing communication and management skills, and attending professional conferences can allow you opportunities to network with seasoned professionals, build professional relationships with peers and more experienced professionals. This is beneficial to you because it can expand your opportunities for resources as well as employment.

FINANCIAL SELF CARE

A primary stressor that has been identified among college students is personal finances. More specifically, college students often express concerns about having enough money for regular expenses, repaying student loans, the cost of education, and finding a job after graduation.[14,36] You may find yourself relating to some of the abovementioned concerns as well as the following statement. Over time, it has been found that financial stress has been associated with academic failure, health issues, and negative financial practices. Therefore, it would be prudent for you as a student to learn how to practice effective financial self-care to minimize these stressors and live a more financially stable and satisfying life.

Financial self-care activities may include; making a monthly and yearly budget, planning to get out of debt, take a financial literacy course, meeting with a financial advisor and planning for retirement. Everyone should have a budget. Whether you are getting a monthly stipend from your university or parent, or if you are working, it is best practice to develop and operate from a working budget so you can account for your money and ensure that you are not spending your money in a wasteful manner or going into debt.

You may be young and think you have plenty of time to prepare for retirement, however, it is never too early to begin planning for retirement. The earlier you begin planning for retirement, the more money you will be able to secure, and the earlier you will be able to retire. Different means of preparing for retirement can be investing in a managed mutual fund, retirement accounts, 401k, pension funds, etc. It is no longer realistic to depend on the government for retirement. Additionally, in their recognition of the need for employees to practice financial self-care, some employers have provided resources for financial planning (i.e. retirement, tax services, college savings for children) and peer support to assist those experiencing distress.[27]

SELF-CARE WHEEL

A self-care wheel is an organizational tool that can help you to determine how you are progressing towards the achievement of your self-care goals. The wheel can also be used as a tool to help you revise old goals and implement new goals that will assist you in practicing self-care in a holistic manner. Witmer and Sweeney developed the original Wheel of Wellness model in 1992 based on Individual Psychology in the early 1990s.[31] Following an extensive review of theory and research across disciplines, they identified several characteristics that correlated positively with healthy living, quality of life, and longevity. A self-care wheel typically consists of six to eight components. These components include but are not limited to personal, social, physical, emotional, spiritual, professional, and financial.

When using the self-care wheel, you would first fill in the section of the wheel with new activities you would like to try on your self-care journey. Secondly, you would rate yourself on each activity using a scale that measures from one to ten, with ten being representative of the highest level of accomplishment and practice in the self-care area and one being representative of no accomplishment or self-care practice in that area. Thirdly, you would identify and list strategies and activities you can engage in to improve your practice of self-care in the designated area of your life. Finally, you would implement your strategies and activities.

Please note that self-care is a continual process, which requires us to revisit our accomplishments, practices, and shortcomings on a routine basis. While it is best practice to engage in self-care daily, we may need to build in reminders to ensure that we are accomplishing our goals. Additionally, it may be appropriate to post your self-care wheel some place where you can see it daily and plan to review and possibly revise your self-care wheel every three to six months.

Upon reviewing a wide range of self-care wheels, the authors believed that the needs of students warranted the development of a somewhat different self-care wheel. The modified self-care wheel presented below is intended to address the needs of students and young professionals. If this wheel does not suit your self-care needs, we have also provided a blank wheel which you can format independently based on your self-care needs.

Below is a blank Self-Care Wheel that you would use. Fill in the section of the wheel with new activities you would like to try on your Self-care journey. Rate yourself from 1-10. With 10 being the highest in the area that you feel is in need of more work.

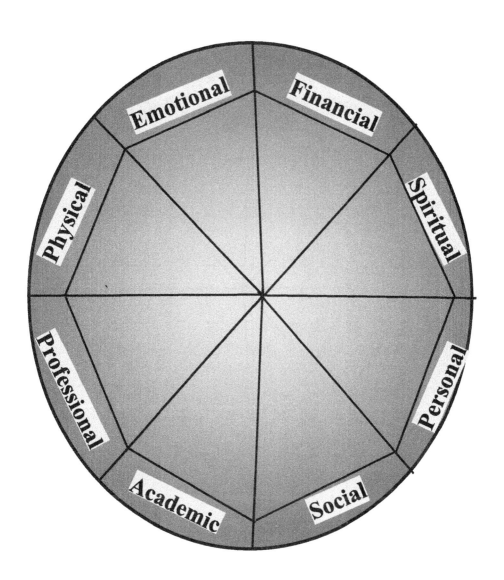

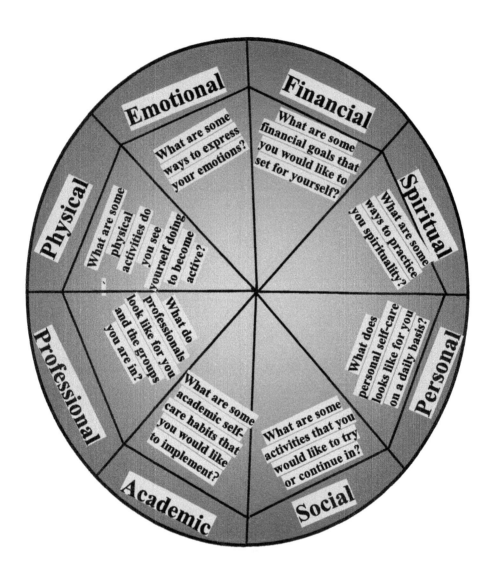

CONCLUSION

Self-care will be a vital component of the work you will do as a rehabilitation and/or human services professional. While coping with the everyday challenges of serving minorities from underserved communities and lower socioeconomic background you will be exposed to multitudes of stressors that can lead to burnout and compassion fatigue. Engaging in everyday self-care activities is an effective means of managing the stressors related to serving the needs of others. The routine practice of self-care as a student will further prepare you to effectively implement these practices while serving in your career field. Take a few moments and consider the instructions given by flight attendants on an airplane. Prior to takeoff, their instructions are to place your own oxygen mask on prior to assisting others.

"Self-care is not selfish. You cannot serve from an empty vessel"
Eleanor Brown

DISCUSSION QUESTIONS

1. Why is the practice of self-care important for Human Service and Rehabilitation Professionals?

2. How can a lack of self-care impact a professional?

3. List three ways in which you can practice professional self-care. Discuss exactly how each can help you.

4. List three ways in which you can practice social self-care. Discuss exactly how each can help you.

5. List three ways in which you can practice financial self-care. Discuss exactly how each can help you.

6. Describe spiritual self-care and discuss why this type of self-care is important.

7. Describe personal self-care and discuss why this type of self-care is important.

8. Describe academic self-care and discuss why this type of self-care is important.

9. What is the purpose of a self-care wheel and how can it benefit a fieldwork/internship student?

CASE STUDIES

CASE STUDY 1
Claire, Academic Self-Care

Claire is a 22-year-old rehabilitation and human services student in her junior year of undergraduate studies. Being a first-generation college student, Claire vowed to never allow her grades to slip to avoid the likelihood of academic probation, or worse, the loss of financial aid. Claire is a huge source of support for her family, and often works long hours to provide them financial assistance. Claire attends school full-time maintaining 15 credit hours and must sustain certain employment hours to ensure her personal basic needs are met. Midway through Claire's final semester of her junior year, Claire noticed that she is becoming extremely tired during the day and finds herself falling asleep during class. Due to the demand of daily responsibilities, Claire skips meals and barely maintains a healthy diet. Claire is becoming forgetful of class assignments, pertinent due dates, and tests. Claire no longer attends study group sessions due to feeling like there is not enough time in the day. Additionally, Claire is becoming agitated at work and has been placed on a performance plan due to managerial concerns regarding productivity.

Claire is approaching her senior year and must take steps to identify an internship location that is flexible with her work schedule. This is quite a conundrum, as internship placement deadlines are approaching and there is no confirmed location for a site. Significant to note, Claire is in jeopardy of losing her job. Claire is overwhelmed and unsure of her career trajectory due to not having adequate time to truly research areas of interest within the rehabilitation field. Claire expressed in class that she never has time for herself, grades are beginning to slip, feels like the weight of the world is on her shoulders, and she has no idea of what she will do after graduation. Claire is worried about her school, work, and life balance and doesn't want these behaviors to translate into her internship.

Think about each question below: Pair with a partner to discuss ideas:

1. Given what you know about Claire's situation, what are some ways Claire can implement academic self-care into her daily routine?

2. Does this case study have implications for other areas of self-care (e.g., emotional, physical, social)?

3. Share overall experiences as a large group discussion.

CASE STUDY 2

Dylan, Professional Self-Care

Dylan is in his last semester of undergraduate studies as a social work major. Dylan is currently completing his internship with a local mental health agency as a case manager intern. Dylan enjoys the practical experiences he is receiving, but often overextends by filling in other roles for the agency. Dylan's internship site is a high traffic area for clients, many of whom are "high risk". Due to Dylan's impressive work ethic and interaction with the clients, the "high risk" cases are typically assigned to Dylan's caseload. The direct supervisor and other staff members are consistently busy with client concerns. This limits Dylan's access to seasoned professionals at the site. Dylan receives the minimum amount of supervision and support required. Dylan has expressed the need for more supervision and feels that a stronger provider network may support him with navigating such an intense line of work. Dylan wants to pursue a future in mental health but is nervous due to his recent feelings of burnout.

Dylan does a great job taking theory to practice by placing emphasis on the concepts learned within the classroom to best support clients served at the site. As a result of recent client encounters, one specific term resonates strongly with Dylan. That term is vicarious trauma. Dylan feels he may struggle with "taking on" client's trauma and furthermore wants to avoid such behaviors. Dylan reported to both the university and site supervisors his difficulty with creating clear boundaries between work and home. Often, clients call Dylan's cell-phone afterhours to express concerns. Dylan's co-workers and university professors describe him as an empathetic and genuine individual with a "heart of gold" and compassion for his clients. Dylan expressed feelings of burnout and is now concerned about his future in the field after graduation. Dylan is confident that he will be successful as a mental health professional but questions his ability to be effective due to the feelings of extreme overload. Dylan was offered a job at the current site to become permanent after graduation. Dylan wonders if linking with other professionals in the field will help create a sense of homeostasis to enhance service within the field.

Pair with a partner to discuss your response to the questions below:

1. Given what you know about Dylan, describe a few strategies that would be beneficial for Dylan to incorporate into his daily routine to enhance professional self-care.

2. Does this case study have implications for other areas of self-care (e.g., emotional, financial, social)?

CASE STUDY 3
Crystal, Social Self-Care

Crystal is a Therapeutic Recreation student who received a paid practicum opportunity in an unfamiliar location within her current state. By accepting the practicum, Crystal was expected to relocate to fully complete the duties, responsibilities, and expectations of the job. While the move was tough, Crystal enjoys working at the local assisted living facility to support individuals with a variety of illnesses and/or chronic conditions through recreation and other activity-based interventions. Due to the unfamiliarity of the area, the practicum experience is now the center of her life, leaving no room for peer interaction. While her role at the facility is fulfilling, Crystal is having a hard time making meaningful connections with other individuals. Fellow peers back at the university, as well as the current practicum site, have a keen interest in Crystal because of her pleasant personality and helpful disposition.

Crystal receives invites to participate in extra-curricular activities and other outings to increase social interaction and networking with other professionals, but she consistently declines due to her devotion to the practicum site and the perception that it is best to keep busy in this unfamiliar part of the state. Crystal reported feelings of loneliness and has the desire for companionship. Crystal doesn't want her quality of life to decline nor does she want to look back over her life with regret. Family and other peers have tried to explain to Crystal that she needs an outlet to debrief and detach from the stressors of work and life in general. Crystal often desires to connect with others but is unsure how to move beyond her perception that it is best to stay focused on work. Crystal understands that having a social network can influence positive peer relationships which has the potential to translate into the workplace and future careers.

Pair with a partner to discuss your responses to the following questions:

1. Given what you know about Crystal, describe a few strategies that would be beneficial to incorporate into her daily/weekly/monthly routine to enhance social self-care.

2. Does this case study have implications for other areas of self-care (e.g., emotional, financial, physical)?

CASE STUDY 4
Derrick, Personal Self-Care

Derrick, a gerontology scholar, a single parent of two teenagers, and caregiver for his aging parents. In conjunction with Derrick's familial roles, he is a full-time student striving to complete his internship. Derrick is family oriented and wants to best support them in reaching their goals. While obtaining family goals is important, Derrick also wants to accomplish his personal goal of earning his bachelor's degree. For many years, Derrick has placed completing his degree on hold to care for his parents. While the family wants nothing more than to see Derrick's dreams come true, carrying out those aspirations were constantly deferred. Derrick tries to maintain a healthy balance between school and home, but often becomes frustrated due to his family obligations. To maintain his GPA and service to the department, Derrick finds time to attend study groups and conducts other scholarly activity.

Derrick's peer group is becoming concerned due to obvious agitation during study sessions. By consistently managing familial responsibilities and school expectations, Derrick rarely has time for self. Engaging in self-care activities is obsolete and Derrick is beginning to feel resentment. He lacks meaningful relationships outside of his family or has no time for a companion. On many occasions Derrick has considered talking with his academic advisor about potentially "sitting out" a semester or the entire year. He enjoys the work exposure at the internship site but is losing self-confidence. Derrick is so accustomed to taking care of others, he has negated the significance of personal self-care. Derrick is at an impasse as he is in desperate need to enhance his quality of life in order to persevere towards his ultimate goal.

Pair with a partner to discuss your responses to the following questions:

1. Given what you know about Derrick, describe a few strategies that would be beneficial to incorporate into his daily/weekly/monthly routine to enhance personal self-care.

2. Does this case study have implications for other areas of self-care (e.g., emotional, social, physical)?

REFERENCES

[1]Adriaanse, M. A., Vinkers, C. D. W., De Ridder, D. T. D., Hox, J. J., & De Wit, J. B. F. (2011). Do implementation intentions help to eat a healthy diet? A systematic review and meta-analysis of the empirical evidence. *Appetite, 56*(1), 183–193. https://doi-org.proxy.library.ohio.edu/10.1016/j.appet.2010.10.012

[2]Bandura, A. (2004). Health promotion by social cognitive means. *Health education & behavior, 31*(2), 143-164.

[3]Barnett, J. E., Johnston, L. C., & Hillard, D. (2006). Psychotherapist wellness as an ethical imperative. In L. VandeCreek & J. B. Allen (Eds.), *Innovations in clinical practice: Focus on health and wellness* (pp. 257–271). Sarasota, FL: Professional Resources Press.

[4]Barnett, J. E., & Cooper, N. (2009). Creating a culture of self-care. Clinical Psychology: *Science and Practice, 16*(1), 16-20.

[5]Bauer-Wu, S. (2010). Mindfulness meditation. *Oncology Nurse Edition, 24*(10), 36-40.

[6]Brownlee, E. (2016). How do counsellors view and practice self-care. *Healthcare Counselling & Psychotherapy Journal,* 16(2), 15-17.

[7]Bühler, J. L., Weidmann, R., Nikitin, J., & Grob, A. (2019). A closer look at life goals across adulthood: Applying a developmental perspective to content, dynamics, and outcomes of goal importance and goal attainability. *European Journal of Personality.* https://doi-org.proxy.library.ohio.edu/10.1002/per.2194

[8]Burton, L., & Lent, J. (2016). The use of vision boards as a therapeutic intervention. *Journal of Creativity in Mental Health, 11*(1), 1-14.

[9]Coster, J.S. & Schwebel, M. (1997). Well-functioning in professional psychologists. *Professional Psychology: Research and Practice, 28,* 5-13.

[10]Goleman, D. (1998). *Working with emotional intelligence.* New York: Bantam Books

[11]Hibbard, J. H., & Greene, J. (2013). What the evidence shows about patient activation: better health outcomes and care experiences; fewer data on costs. *Health affairs, 32*(2), 207-214.

[12]Jenkins, M. L., Wikoff, K., Amankwaa, L. & Trent, B. (2009). Nursing the spirit. *Nursing Management, 8,* 29-36.

[13]Lannin, D. G., Guyll, M., Vogel, D. L., & Madon, S. (2013). Reducing the stigma associated with seeking psychotherapy through self-affirmation. *Journal of Counseling Psychology, 60*(4), 508–519. https://doi-org.proxy.library.ohio.edu/10.1037/a0033789m

[14]Lim, H., Heckman, S., Montalto, C., & Letkiewicz, J. (2014). Financial stress, self-efficacy, and financial help-seeking behavior of college students. *Journal of Financial Counseling and Planning, 25*(2), 148-160.

[15]Loannidou, F., & Konstantikaki, V. (2008). Empathy and emotional intelligence: What is it really about? *International Journal of Caring Sciences, 1*(3), 118.

[17]MacRae, N., & Strout, K. (2015). Self-care project for faculty and staff of future health care professionals: Case report. *Work, 52*(3), 525-531.

[18]Mikkelsen, K., Stojanovska, L., Polenakovic, M., Bosevski, M., & Apostolopoulos, V. (2017). Exercise and mental health. *Maturitas, 106*, 48–56. https://doi-org.proxy.library.ohio.edu/10.1016/j.maturitas.2017.09.003

[19]Miller, R. A., Jones, V. A., Reddick, R. J., Lowe, T., Franks Flunder, B., Hogan, K., & Rosal, A. I. (2018). Educating through microaggressions: Self-care for diversity educators. *Journal of Student Affairs Research and Practice, 55*(1), 14-26.

[20]Myers, J. E., & Sweeney, T. J. (2004). The Indivisible Self: An Evidence-Based Model of Wellness. Journal of Individual Psychology, *60*(3), 234-245.

[21]Myers, J. E., Sweeney, T. J., & Witmer, J. M. (2000). The wheel of wellness counseling for wellness: A holistic model for treatment planning. *Journal of Counseling & Development, 78*(3), 251-266.

[22]Nelson, J. R., Hall, B. S., Anderson, J. L., Birtles, C., & Hemming, L. (2018). Self–compassion as self-care: A Simple and effective tool for counselor educators and counseling students. *Journal of Creativity in Mental Health, 13*(1), 121-133.

[23]Petrides, K. V., & Furnham, A. (2000). On the Dimensional Structure of Emotional Intelligence. *Personality and Individual Differences, 29*, 313-320.

[24]Roe, D., Dekel, R., Harel, G., Fenning, S., & Fenning, S. (2006). Clients' feelings during termination of psychodynamically oriented psychotherapy. *Bulletin of the Menninger Clinic, 70*(1), 68-81.

[25]Sanchez-Reilly, S., Morrison, L. J., Carey, E., Bernacki, R., O'Neill, L., Kapo, J., Periyakoil, V. S., & Thomas, J. (2013). Caring for oneself to care for others: physicians and their self-care. *The Journal of Supportive Oncology, 11*(2), 75-81.

[26]Self-Care Wheel, English. Created by Olga Phoenix. Copyright @ 2013 Olga Phoenix, All Rights Reserved.

[27]Seymour, B. (2009). What do nursing students understand by spirituality and spiritual care? Scott *Journal of Healthcare Chaplain. 12*, 38-46.

[28]Shanafelt, T. D., Lightner, D. J., Conley, C. R., Petrou, S. P., Richardson, J. W., Schroeder, P. J., & Brown, W. A. (2017). An organization model to assist individual physicians, scientists, and senior health care administrators with personal and professional needs. In Mayo Clinic Proceedings, 92 (11), 1688-1696).

[29]Shapiro, S. L., Brown, K. W., & Biegel, G. M. (2007). Teaching self-care to caregivers: Effects of mindfulness-based stress reduction on the mental health of therapists in training. *Training and education in professional psychology*, 1(2), 105.

[30]Shepherd, J., Harden, A., Rees, R., Brunton, G., Garcia, J., Oliver, S., Oakley, A. (2006). Young people and healthy eating: A systematic review of research on barriers and facilitators. *Health Education Research, 21*(2), 239-257.

[21]Stebnicki, M. A. (2007). Empathy fatigue: Healing the mind, body, and spirit of professional counselors. *American Journal of Psychiatric Rehabilitation, 10*(4), 317-338.

[32]Sweeney, T. J. (1998). *Adlerian counseling: A practitioners approach (4th ed.)*. Philadelphia: Taylor & Francis.

[33]Sweeney, T. J., & Witmer, J. M. (1991). Beyond social interest: Striving toward optimum health and wellness. *Individual Psychology, 47*, 527-540.

[34]Teixeira, P. J., Carraça, E. V., Markland, D., Silva, M. N., & Ryan, R. M. (2012). Exercise, physical activity, and self-determination theory: a systematic review. *International Journal of Behavioral Nutrition and Physical activity, 9*(1), 78.

[35]Tiew, L. H. & Drury V. (2012). Singapore nursing students' perceptions and attitudes about spirituality and spiritual care in practice: A qualitative study. *Journal of Holistic Nursing, 30*, 160-169.

[36]Tomasso, C. S., Beltrame, I. L. & Lucchetti, G. (2011). Knowledge and attitudes of nursing professors and students concerning the interface between spirituality, religiosity and health. *Review of Latin American Enfermagem, 19*, 1205-1213.

[37]Trombitas, K. (2012). Financial stress: An everyday reality for college students. Inceptia. Retrieved from: https://www.inceptia.org/PDF/Inceptia_FinancialStress_whitepaper.pdf

[38]White, Mary Louise, "Spirituality and spiritual self-care: Expanding self-care deficit nursing theory" (2010).Wayne State University Dissertations. Paper 191.

[39]Witmer, J. M., & Sweeney, T. J. (1992). A holistic model for wellness and prevention over the lifespan. Journal of Counseling and Development, 71, 140-148.

[40]Wu, L. F., Liao, Y. C. & Yeh, D. C. (2012). Nursing student perceptions of spirituality and spiritual care. *Journal of Nursing Research, 20*, 219-278.

[41]Zheng Guohua, Zhenyu Xiong, Xin Zheng, Junzhe Li, Tingjin Duan, Dalu Qi, Lidian Chen. (2017). Subjective perceived impact of Tai Chi training on physical and mental health among community older adults at risk for ischemic stroke: a qualitative study. *BMC Complementary & Alternative Medicine, 17*, 1–7. https://doi-org.proxy.library.ohio.edu/10.1186/s12906-017-1694-3

RÉSUMÉ DEVELOPMENT

PHILLIP D. LEWIS

DEAMBER L. JOHNSON

BERNADETTE WILLIAMS-YORK

CHAPTER DESCRIPTION

The purpose of this chapter is to teach readers how to build an effective résumé in preparation for employment. This chapter will provide information about effective and efficient résumé building. Information regarding cover letter development and the selection of appropriate references will also be discussed. Strategies for résumé, cover letter, reference, and letters of recommendation profiles will be provided to aid novice professionals in effectively marketing themselves in the world of work. Helpful resources for résumé and profile development and maintenance will also be provided.

OBJECTIVES

After reading this chapter, you should be able to:

1. Construct an effective cover letter.

2. Develop an effective résumé.

3. Distinguish the differences between various types of résumés.

4. Understand how to write a résumé that reflects one's personal strengths and abilities.

5. Discuss the importance of discretion and disability disclosure on a résumé.

6. Develop a list of effective professional references.

7. Draft a letter of recommendation.

While fieldwork/internship experiences are experimental in nature and provide students with an opportunity to learn and grow as professionals, these opportunities also serve as work experience. Thus, when students are preparing to engage in their internship/fieldwork experience, one of the first things students need to ensure they have is an effective résumé. This résumé should be accompanied by supporting documents such as a cover letter, letters of recommendation, references and/or transcripts, and other résumé related documents. In this chapter, we will explore the effective means of compiling these documents and preparing for the job application process.

WHAT IS A RÉSUMÉ?

A résumé is a brief document that typically is used when seeking gainful competitive employment. Merriam Webster specifically defines a résumé as a set of accomplishments.[6] The résumé summarizes any previous civic services, education, skills, training, employment history, professional affiliations, organizational involvement, awards or recognitions, and relevant volunteer experiences that are usually related to a one's qualifications for a job. Résumés often highlight your transition from high school, to college, to work, or from career to career, that showcases all your abilities, accomplishments, and experiences. The purpose of a résumé is to get you in the door for an interview with the least amount of restrictions.

Résumés can be formulated to your own personal and unique style. However, do not try to be too creative. Try to stay consistent with the use of font, graphics, and color. A professionally developed résumé is preferably in black ink. On the other hand, allowing individuality in your résumé just may make your résumé stand out from other competitors. When creating a résumé, it is best to have a well thought out strategy on how you are going to display all your various experiences in a confident manner. Job seeking is very competitive, so your résumé needs to be as persuasive and flawless as possible. Many recruiters seek the smallest mistakes to discredit your skills and interest in the job.

TYPES OF RÉSUMÉS

According to the Purdue Writing Lab, depending on the type of job you are applying for, different résumé formats may apply. The four traditional types of résumés include: chronological, functional, combination, or targeted. Chronological résumés are the most commonly used format. When using this format, you will list in order your most recent job and qualifications. If you have a strong work history, this format is for you!

Functional résumés focus on your skills and experiences.[3] This résumé is great for people who are transitioning from college into the workforce, individuals with little to no work experience, people changing careers, or job seekers with gaps between employments.

Combination résumés focus on detailed information of your skills and experiences while using the chronological listing of work history. This format is great for highlighting one's abilities and expertise.[3] Remember, there is a difference between the minimum required qualifications for a job and the preferred qualifications, so do not be afraid to apply even if you do not meet all the preferred qualifications for the position.

Targeted résumés focus on a specific position that you are applying for in order to highlight your specific skills and experiences that are relevant to the job for which you are applying.[8] This allows your potential future employer to better see if you are a good candidate for the position. You do not have to be the most qualified person for the position, but you do want to be the most qualified person that applies!

There are also non-traditional résumé formats, such as visual résumés. This type of résumé utilizes pictures and/or a video of the job seeker performing specific tasks. If an employer can see and visualize a qualified candidate doing an essential function of the job, it can help eliminate attitudinal barriers to employment and reduce stigma. Visual résumés are extremely useful for individuals with disabilities, especially when they may have a need for supported or customized employment. These types of résumés are not currently as common as others.

In the case of a person seeking employment with the Federal Government, your résumé will be non-traditional, too. When creating a federal résumé, it may be many pages longer than a traditional résumé. It is extremely important to highlight as much detail as possible to make sure you are given appropriate credit for job skills and functions. The more detail the better in this case. If it is not on your résumé, then it does not exist. You not only want to make sure you are meeting the minimum requirements of the position, but you are documenting any additional relevant experience you may have had in the past or currently. This will directly impact the pay grade and pay rate you can receive upon an offer and acceptance of employment with the Federal Government.

RÉSUMÉ CONTENT

All résumés must include your contact information (i.e., your name, address, telephone number, and email address). This is vital information for your future employer to have because without the correct contact information you may miss the opportunity for employment if the employer is unable to contact you. Throughout your work experience, you will need to update your résumé. At times you may also need to tailor fit the contents of your résumé to match the objectives of the position you are applying for. It is a living document, and it is meant to be amended as needed and per the position of interest.

Your résumé is a one-time shot for you to captivate the attention of your potential employer and interest them to invite you for an interview. The résumé is what sells you on paper and gets your foot in the door; the interview is what sells you in-person and gets you the job offer. Employers will usually take, at most, only thirty-five seconds to look at your résumé before deciding whether they may be interested in hiring you.[7] To ensure that you will make it past that initial screening, you should design your résumé in such a way that employers can read the document easily and process information quickly. One way to do this is to employ the conventional format of a résumé. Since employers know how résumés work and where to locate certain information the conventional formatting will provide them with ease of access to your information.

Designing your résumé can be a challenge and requires you to take a closer look at how readers read this type of document. Consistent formatting is key to drawing the person's eyes where they need to go, especially when a cursory review is done so quickly. Your job title is more important than where you worked. Your experience is more important than your education. The dates of your employment history should be formatted consistently. Stay away from "fancy" or small fonts. Do not decrease your font size because you are trying to condense your résumé to one page. Smaller fonts can make your resume difficult to read, which may in turn frustrate the employer, which may not work in your favor.

It is acceptable to have a two-page résumé. It is also appropriate to have your résumé printed front and back. Depending on the industry and profession, it may be acceptable for your résumé to be longer than two pages. Some jobs may require the submission of a curricula vita. In the case of a non-traditional Federal résumé, it could be upward of twelve pages for some people.

Be sure to proofread your résumé for grammar and spelling errors and if it is possible, allow time for an unbiased observer (i.e., someone else) to critique your work.[7] You cannot trust spell-check! You must thoroughly proofread this document with a fine-toothed comb! Reading it aloud can assist in picking up on spelling and grammar errors. Not checking your work before you submit it for consideration can be a quick way to end up in the "trash" pile!

As stated previously, when creating a résumé, you want to separate yourself from other competitors. Your résumé needs to be so great that your employer would want to invite you for an interview. Here are some important tips that can be useful when developing your résumé:

➢ *Make a List.* Produce a master list of dates (if you can remember) of your jobs, skills, accomplishments, volunteer activities, professional affiliations, organizational involvement, of everything you have done and give detailed information on each. If you cannot remember, try reviewing your tax papers, W2s, Social Security information, or other records to gather missing information about your work history.

➢ *Headings.* A well-organized résumé will have clear and concise title headings, that includes the information you would like to highlight. Headings on a résumé include things such as: education, work experience, awards, extracurricular activities, professional affiliations, volunteer experience, skills, certifications, licenses, languages spoken, special skills, etc.

➢ *List Accomplishments.* List and describe all experiences and extracurricular activities in detail.

➢ M*odify Information.* Create your résumé in a snapshot where employers can identify you as the best candidate for that position. Make sure to keep your résumé organized, concise, and detailed.

➢ *Have Your Résumé Critiqued.* Proofread every single word and allow someone else to review your work as well. Always remember that two heads are better than one!

RÉSUMÉ TIPS FOR PEOPLE WITH DISABILITIES

In general, you do not want to disclose your disability on the resume. However, sometimes this is not always possible. For example, if you use a video phone for communication, this is typically going to be listed as your contact number and so indicated. Unfortunately, the ugly truth remains. Potential employers may not be knowledgeable about disability and this may result in unintended discrimination against you. Remember, the goal of a résumé is to highlight your skills and qualifications to ultimately get an interview and become employed. You want to reduce the risk of discrimination as much as possible. Again, it is the résumé that sells you on paper and gets you the interview; the interview is what sells you in person and gets you the job offer.

The goal is to market yourself to the best of your ability with both your résumé and interview. If there has been a significant gap in your employment, creating a functional résumé may be more effective for you to highlight your skills. If you have a disability, upon disclosure, you are protected under the Americans with Disabilities Act.[2,4] If employers have over 15 employees, they must abide by all the rules and regulations of the law and 2008 amendment of the Americans with Disabilities Act. You should also take time to familiarize yourself with your state's laws regarding reasonable accommodations in the workplace.

If you do not have a visible disability and do not require a reasonable accommodation, it is advisable not to disclose your disability until post-offer or not at all. You do not have to disclose your disability to employers, but if you want to be protected under the Americans with Disabilities Act as a qualified individual with a disability and/or receive a reasonable accommodation, you need to be prepared to do so. It is much harder to prove discrimination during the application and hiring process than it is once you've been hired. If you feel you or a client is being discriminated against, remember to keep an accurate chronological record of events. Documentation is key in these cases.

COVER LETTER, REFERENCES & RECOMMENDATIONS

In line with the previous discussion regarding types of résumés and their content, we will now discuss the documents that generally accompany a résumé. When applying for a job, you will find that many employers request a cover letter, a list of professional references. and even letters of recommendation. In some cases, additional documentation such as academic transcripts, personal philosophies, and statements are requested. Therefore, prior to beginning your application and job search process, it is wise to gather the necessary materials to ensure full completion of your application.

CONSTRUCTING AN EFFECTIVE COVER LETTER

The purpose of your cover letter is to succinctly summarize your qualifications and fit for the desired position.[1] It is a very important part of the process and one you should spend some time thinking about and drafting. If you are a recent graduate or have only a few years of work experience, then you should aim to keep your cover letter to no more than one page. Why? Because the person reading the cover letter wants to be able to quickly decide as to whether you are a good candidate for this position.

Your grammar, spelling and punctuation must be impeccable, so please read your letter several times and have at least one person proofread it as well before you submit it. Remember, the first impression that the hiring manager or supervisor will have of you will be the one you create through your cover letter. Therefore, it must be free of any typos or grammatical errors. In addition, it is very important to use professional language and not slang or jargon. Most likely, the people reading and evaluating your letter are older and more experienced than you are and will expect you to present yourself as a professional.

The first paragraph is your introduction; therefore, you need to convey your enthusiasm for the position and clearly state the job title and company.[1] If you know the name of the individual who will be making the hiring decision, then please use it. However, if you are in doubt as to whether you should address the person by their first name, then error on the side of caution and use an official title such as, Mr, Ms. or Dr. Please see the example below:

Dear Mr. _____ :

I am very excited to submit my application for the position of _____ at ABC company. I feel my experience and qualifications uniquely qualify me for this position and I am confident that I can make a substantial and immediate contribution to your company.

In the second paragraph, go into more detail about your work experience and qualifications for the position. It is very important to tailor your cover letter to match the qualifications and experience that are mentioned in the position advertisement/posting.[1] In fact, it is strongly advised that you have a copy of the position ad right in front of you when you draft your cover letter. In this second paragraph, start by writing your major qualification for the position and, if you can, give an example of what you have already done either through your work or volunteer experience that showcases your expertise in this area.

For example, my work experience over the last several years has been concentrated in developing my customer service skills and motivating clients to engage in healthy behaviors. As a Patient Client Technician, I assisted licensed health care providers in greeting patients, assisting them with paperwork, answering any questions they had about the services, and teaching them home exercise programs. I received excellent annual evaluations and was awarded Employee of the Month three times during the time I worked at XYZ Company.

If you have had more than one job or position that highlights your skills and expertise, please add those in this paragraph. The more detail and specifics you can add, the better. If you just vaguely mention that you're qualified for the position, your letter will lack any real conviction and may not convey that you are the ideal candidate. You should leave no doubt in the hiring manager's mind about your fit for the job.[1] It is your responsibility to make it easy for them to "see" you in the position. You do that by clearly linking your education and experience to what they have advertised that they are looking for. Remember, this position description was likely carefully drafted by several people and approved and revised by several levels up the chain before it was posted. Therefore, every word in the job posting needs to be taken seriously and addressed by you in the cover letter. Any omissions to key qualifications may disqualify you from moving to the next level.

Under no circumstances should you lie or exaggerate your experience or qualifications. Your honesty and integrity are non-negotiable and if you compromise on this in your cover letter, you may doom yourself for this employer and possibly future opportunities as well. What you may not know now, but will soon discover, is that your professional field is small, and everybody knows everybody. If they do not, then they know someone who knows that person. Seven degrees of separation is true in the human service and rehabilitation professions. Do not make the mistake of thinking you can fudge a little on your résumé or cover letter. It will come back to haunt you.

In your third or final paragraph, you should reiterate your enthusiasm for the job and your confidence that you are the ideal candidate for the position. Also, in closing, this is your last opportunity to convey to the hiring manager that your experience and qualifications are perfectly suited for this position. Finally, you want to exude confidence that you will move to the next step and fully expect to hear from them soon regarding this. See the example below:

In closing, I am very excited about this opportunity and feel confident that I am the ideal candidate for the position of _____ in ABC Company. As my résumé will attest, my experience and qualifications are a perfect match for this position, and I believe I will make an immediate contribution to your company. I look forward to hearing from you soon regarding the next step. Please feel free to contact me for an interview on my cell at _____ or by email at _____. Thank you for this opportunity.

In closing your letter, remain professional and use a simple word like "sincerely." Type your full name and any credentials that you have after your name, leaving space for your signature. Some companies will accept an electronic signature, and some want an original signature. Find out which one is acceptable for the position for which you are applying. Remember, after you complete your letter, proofread it several times before asking one or two other people whom you trust and respect to give you their feedback and to proofread. This step cannot be skipped. Once you hit the submit button, you cannot take it back, so make sure that it is perfect before you decide to send it.

PROFESSIONAL REFERENCES & LETTERS OF RECOMMENDATION
When you have completed the construction of your résumé and cover letter, it is wise to then turn your efforts to the development of a list of professional references. Under the "References" section of your résumé it is best to write "Available upon request." You should have an established list of professional references. Be sure to format your reference list with the use of the same fonts, headers, and other formatting you use for your résumé.

This list should include five professionals whom you have asked to serve as your professional references. This should satisfy the needs of varying employers. Your professional references can include professors, internship/fieldwork site supervisors, work study supervisors, student organization advisors, work supervisors, and co-workers. Avoid using friends and family members as references--employers tend to require professional references who can speak to your skills and work ethic in a non-biased manner.

Your list should contain the name, professional title, place of employment, telephone number (office and cellular phones if approved by your reference), office address, and professional email address.

Name:	John Doe
Title:	Assistant Professor
Institution:	Scholar University
Address:	1500 Scholar Avenue
	Los Angeles, CA 90009
Telephone:	555-555-5555 Office
	333-333-3333 Cellular
Email Address:	johndoe@scholar.edu

This will be the information employers will utilize to contact your references.
Please use caution and courtesy when selecting your professional references. Note that no one is required to serve as your professional reference, and you should avoid listing someone as a reference prior to asking them if they will serve as your professional reference. When someone agrees to serve as your professional reference, they are indicating that they have confidence in your abilities, and they are staking their reputation on your abilities as a young

professional. Your performance on the job will have an impact on their reputation as a professional and a reputable source as a reference for employers and other potential employees.

Employers often require written letters of recommendation to be submitted during the application process. You can request such letters from some or all five professionals you have listed on your reference page. When asking individuals for letters of recommendation or support:

Ask early. People take writing letters of support and recommendation seriously. Completion of a letter will take some time. Allow ample time for those you request to provide you with a letter. It is crucial that you remember that you are not entitled to a letter of recommendation and that you understand the magnitude of your request.

Basically, you are asking an individual, whether it be a professor or former supervisor to put the name of the organization they represent and their very own professional reputation at risk. Therefore, the request must be afforded the attention warranted. Also, it is appropriate to schedule an appointment to discuss your request in person. You may also send a professional email requesting a letter. Make sure to include due dates, so that the individual will be able to make an informed decision about their ability to complete the request. It is appropriate to provide a minimum of three weeks for the letter to be completed. As you approach the third week, if the letter has not been completed or received by you or the organization, it is appropriate to send a "gentle" reminder. It is critical to ensure that the letter is received by the deadline.

Start with someone who knows you well in a variety of contexts. The more the individual knows about you, the better. Otherwise, you run the risk of either receiving a "generic" letter of reference that is less impactful to prospective internship supervisors, or a denial of the request. The more detailed the information provided in the letter, the more it helps to paint a picture of who you are as a candidate.

It is also beneficial to include a resume or transcript. Include a brief description of the position and organization, as well as contact information for the prospective site supervisor. When forwarding supplemental information, you should ensure that it is complete and that you are not just sending parts of the document. This will limit unnecessary emails and will avoid frustration and confusion to the individual writing the letter.

Remember to express gratitude. Make sure that you contact the individual by phone or email to say thank you. This gesture goes a long way. Also, follow up to let the individual know the outcome of their efforts.

If you use an email when requesting a letter of recommendation, ensure that your email contains the following information: a greeting, a formal request for a letter of recommendation, the title of the position(s) for which you are applying, the name of the agency where you are seeking employment, the name of the contact person who is to receive the letter, the contact information for the person who is to receive the letter, and the due date of the letter. It is also best practice to attach a copy of the position description and a copy of your résumé to the email. Below is a sample email requesting a letter of recommendation:

Dear Mr. Doe

I hope this email finds you well. I am writing to ask if you are willing and able to write a letter of recommendation. I am applying for a Rehabilitation Specialist position with the Department of Rehabilitation in Los Angeles. If you are able to assist me you can send the letter to Jane Doe, the Unit Manager at janedoe@deptrehab.org. For your convenience I have attached a copy of the position description and my résumé. I have also taken the liberty of drafting a letter of recommendation that you may use if you prefer.

I look forward to hearing from you. Thank you for your time and consideration of my request.

Respectfully,
Jasmine Doe

If possible, it is also a good idea to draft a letter of recommendation and include it in your email. This can help them complete your letter in a more efficient manner. You know yourself and your strengths better than anyone, so you could be more effective at crafting an effective letter. If they decide to use your draft letter, your recommender can simply edit it. A letter of recommendation should begin with a paragraph that explains the recommender's identity, how and for how long the recommender knows the applicant, and a note that positively highlights the applicant's character.

Dear Jane Doe,

My name is John Doe and I am writing this letter in support of Jasmine Doe's application for the Rehabilitation Specialist position. Over the last two years, I have had the honor of serving as Jasmine's professor here at Scholar University. In the time that I have known Jasmine I have found her to be an outstanding student.

The second and third paragraphs of the letter discusses the applicant's skills and accomplishments. This section is one of the reasons why the person who is recommending you for a position should be familiar with your skills and abilities. In this section of the letter, the recommender is selling you as an applicant and telling the employer why they should hire you. The second paragraph can focus on your skills as a student.

As she prepares to graduate from Scholar University, Jasmine holds a 3.5 GPA. In the classroom, Jasmine demonstrates outstanding oral and written communication skills. Her work is always organized, well researched, creative, and exemplary. She is a motivated student and hard worker who is always consistent and dependable. In addition to her performance in the classroom, Jasmine is a leader among her peers as she serves as a member of the Student Government Association and as the Treasurer of the Human Services Club.

The third paragraph can be used to highlight the applicants service in the community as well as their employment experience. Once listed, it is a good idea to briefly discuss the work the applicant did in these positions and use key words that are used in the job posting. This will further highlight the applicant's suitability for the position.

Jasmine is also actively involved in her community. She serves as a volunteer at the American Red Cross and the Boys and Girls Club where she works to _____

Once the applicant's skills, abilities, and experiences have been highlighted, the letter can be ended with confidence, support, and an invitation for contact if needed.

It is without reservation that I recommend Ms. Jasmine Doe for the Rehabilitation Specialist position at the Department of Rehabilitation. It is my belief that Jasmine will make an outstanding member of your team. Please feel free to contact me if you have any questions.

It is essential to note that employers may request additional documents besides the traditional résumé, cover letter, references, and letters of recommendation. Depending on the type of job for which you are applying other documents may include academic transcripts, personal statements/ philosophy, samples of your work or portfolio, writing samples, etc. You will get a better sense of what documents you will need to submit once you have filled out a few applications for the type of position you are seeking. All employers vary, and some may require documents others deem unnecessary, just as some may require a résumé and cover letter and others may require an application, cover letter, résumé, and more. Always expect the unexpected and be prepared.

CONCLUSION

A job seeker must decide which résumé format will best compliment the employer or the job itself. A résumé is a brief document that summarizes your qualifications and fitness for a job of interest. The ultimate purpose of a résumé is to get you in the door for an interview. Research has shown that it takes an average of ten interviews to receive one job offer, so your résumé needs to be as persuasive as possible to get your foot in the door.

CHAPTER QUESTIONS

1. List and describe one traditional and one non-traditional résumé format. Discuss when it is appropriate to use each; a traditional versus non-traditional résumé.

2. When and why is it necessary to disclose disability-related information in the hiring process?

3. List and describe the varying types of résumés described in the chapter.

4. Why is it important to write a cover letter?

5. What are the components of a good cover letter?

REFERENCES

[1]Addams, L., & Woodbury, D., (2009). Teaching job search written and oral communication skills through an integrated approach. *American Journal of Business Education, 2*(4), 13-18.

[2]Americans With Disabilities Act of 1990, Pub. L. No. 101-336, 104 Stat. 328 (1990).

[3]Crosby, O. (2009). Résumés, applications, and cover letters. *Occupational Outlook Quarterly, 53*(2), 18–29.Dispenza, F., Kumar, A., Standish, J., Norris, S., & Procter, J. (2018). Disability and sexual orientation disclosure on employment interview ratings: An analogue study. *Rehabilitation Counseling Bulletin, 61*(4), 244–255. https://doi-org.proxy.library.ohio.edu/10.1177/0034355217725888

[4]Gouvier, W. D., Sytsma-Jordan, S., & Mayville, S. (2003). Patterns of discrimination in hiring job applicants with disabilities: The role of disability type, job complexity, and public contact. *Rehabilitation Psychology, 48*(3), 175-181.

[5]Merriam Webster (2019). Résumé. Retrieve from: https://www.merriam-webster.com/dictionary/résumé

[6]Purdue Writing Lab. (n.d.). Résumé design. Retrieved from
   https://owl.purdue.edu/owl/job_search_writing/résumés_and_vitas/résumé_
   design.html

[7]Wendleton, K. (2014). *Packaging yourself: The targeted résumé.* Cengage
   Learning. Retrieved from https://search-ebscohost-
   com.proxy.library.ohio.edu/login.aspx?direct=true&db=cat00572a&AN=ali
   ce.b5734150&site=eds-live&scope=site

JOB SEARCH & INTERVIEW PREPARATION

BERNADETTE WILLIAMS-YORK

CHAPTER DESCRIPTION

The purpose of this chapter is to provide readers with information about job search and interview preparation. This chapter will provide information about effective and efficient job search and interview preparation strategies to aid novice professionals in effectively marketing themselves in the world of work. Information about employer preferences and hiring practices will be included to aid readers in catering to the needs of the employer to enhance their potential for successful employment. This chapter will also provide readers with practical activities and resources that are geared towards the development and enhancement of job search and interview skills development. Resources for continued growth and development will also be provided.

OBJECTIVES

1. Students will learn how to prepare themselves for a job interview.

2. Students will explore and practice answering key interview questions.

3. Students will learn how to conduct an effective job search.

4. Students will be presented with job search resources to aid them in expanding the vocational search.

INTRODUCTION

So, you want a job? Well, get ready for some work to find it, because the process of job hunting is a job in and of itself. Do not underestimate the amount of time, thought, and preparation that will go into this process. Is it worth it? Yes! The time and effort you put into your job search can potentially reward you for many years to come in the areas of your financial success, job satisfaction, and overall wellbeing. Remember, on average, we spend the bulk of our waking hours working to earn a living and that much time should be spent doing something you love and that rewards you in terms of finances and a sense of accomplishment and fulfillment.

So, what is the first thing you should do when you decide to enter the job market? The first thing you should do is take an inventory of yourself. Do you know who you are? What are your strengths and weaknesses? What do you really enjoy doing and what things you cannot stand doing? Are you a people person or do you prefer working alone or behind a computer? Are you an introvert or extrovert? If you are not clear on who you are and what excites you, stop now and spend some time exploring the answers to the questions above.

It's that important. Please see the *Designing Your Life* resource at the end of this chapter for some guidance in getting to know yourself better and getting clear on what type of work will bring you joy and satisfaction. After all, who wants to work at a job they hate? Get clear on what your values are: is money the most important thing to you? Are you willing to sacrifice everything else to make a lot of money? Or does making a difference resonate with you? What drives you and what excites you? Chances are if you're excited about something, you probably enjoy doing it and will be good at doing it. This step cannot be skipped.

STRATEGIES FOR JOB SEARCH & APPLICATION

Ok, now that you're clear on who you are, what excites you and have taken a thorough inventory of your strengths and weaknesses, what next? The next step is to clearly articulate on paper who you are and what you have done in the past that highlights your strengths and accomplishments. In other words, it's time to draft your resume and cover letter. Again, please understand that how you "look" on paper is critically important and not to be underestimated. Especially, in this age of technology and electronic communication, many young people have short circuited their writing skills in lieu of texting and instant messaging. Unfortunately, employers still expect job applicants to present themselves effectively in writing and communicate their qualifications and skills for the desired position. The resume and cover letter are your chance to sell yourself even before the potential employer ever meets you in person. The resume and cover letter are the first line of screening and if you don't make it past this initial screening, you will never move on to the next step in the process. So, how do you write a compelling cover letter and resume? Let's take it step by step:

STEP 1: PREPARING YOUR RESUME
Please refer to the previous Chapter on Resume Development for detailed instruction on preparing your resume. Your resume represents who you are on paper and, therefore, it is critical that you construct a resume that is accurate, concise, and comprehensive. This cannot be understated. Once your resume is constructed and has been reviewed by at least two other trusted friends/ colleagues, you are ready to construct your cover letter.

STEP 2: REVIEW/REVISE YOUR SOCIAL MEDIA PAGES
Make it a point to view all your social media pages with a critical eye BEFORE you apply for any positions. Employers often check the social media pages of applicants to get a sense of who they are prior to extending an invitation for an interview. Be careful what you post on your social media

pages. Remove anything that you would be embarrassed to have a future employer see. Change your username to something that is clean and professional. Remove any photos that are revealing a lot of skin or where you are in questionable poses. Your job is to eliminate any material that may cast a negative light on you. More detail on this topic is also provided in the previous chapter.

STEP 3: PREPARING YOUR COVER LETTER

The purpose of your cover letter is to succinctly summarize your qualifications and fit for the desired position.[2] It is a very important part of the process and one you should spend some time thinking about and drafting. If you are a recent graduate or have only a few years of work experience, then you should aim to keep your cover letter to no more than one page. Why? Because the person reading the cover letter wants to be able to quickly decide whether you are a good candidate for this position. The previous chapter also provides more detailed instruction on how to compile an effective cover letter. Assuming all goes well, and your cover letter and resume do their job, you will impress the hiring manager and be asked to move on to the next step – an interview.

THE INTERVIEW

The job interview is still the most common selection method that most employers use to select potential employees.[7] A job interview is your opportunity to promote yourself as the best candidate for the advertised position. It is also the employer's opportunity to find the best available candidate for the job. Therefore, it is a two-way street and usually, if you've been granted an interview, then you have made it through the first level of screening which is your cover letter and resume. At this point, both you and the prospective employer feel that a potential "fit" may be likely.[1]

Unlike in years past, job interviews can occur in multiple formats: phone interview, videoconferencing (i.e. Skype), in-person. Many companies have adopted the practice of conducting phone or videoconferencing interviews first, either as a cost-saving measure or to expedite the hiring process. Depending upon the company, you may be required to participate in two or more interviews before a hiring decision is made. Again, your best strategy is to be prepared.

In this section, we will delve deeper into effective strategies to nail your job interview, but first let's clarify the goals of the interview process - from your perspective as the potential new hire. The goal of the interview process from the employer's perspective is to attract and hire the best candidate for the position that will ultimately become an outstanding employee[1].

GOALS FOR INTERVIEWS

Clearly, your goal of any job interview is to impress the interviewer(s) and get a job offer. With that said, listed below are smaller goals or objectives that you need to achieve in order to assure your success in landing the job of your dreams:

Goal 1: Obtain working knowledge of the company. As soon as you decide to accept an offer to interview for a position, it is time to start doing some research on the company. Take advantage of the internet as your primary source to learn as much about the company as possible. This may take some time if the company is well-respected and has been in business for a long time. It's likely that they have a team of professionals who regularly update the company website with information about the company's mission, values, goals, strategic plan, major initiatives, key personnel, employee handbook, policies and procedures, current news, employee biographies, and much more. You get the idea.

There is a host of information waiting for you to discover and absorb. You should make it your mission to become an expert on the company website and regularly peruse it up until your interview day. The more background information you have on the company, the more confident you will feel on interview day. There's also another benefit to doing your homework on the company website–you get to discover if the company and the position are really a good fit for you. Do your values sync with those of the company? Does the overall mission and vision of the company excite you? Do you agree with the company's philosophy regarding work/life balance and employee rights? Does their benefit plan allow you ample time off? Sick leave? Medical coverage? The more you can learn about the company and the position before your interview, the more you can advocate for your fit for the position during the interview.[8]

Goal 2: Present yourself effectively, highlighting your strengths and fit for the job. You should know your resume "cold," like the back of your hand. Review Chapter 9 again for tips on constructing your resume and review it again and again. Once you are comfortable with everything you have written in your resume, it is your job to "sell" yourself to the prospective employer. So how do you sell yourself? Try thinking of yourself as a product to be marketed. Think of all the advertisements and television commercials you have seen over the years. What about you stands out in a positive way? Highlight that! Are you an excellent writer, speaker, communicator? Are you good with numbers, organization, details? Are you a people person? Do you have an exceptional work record? Have you received excellent evaluations from your fieldwork supervisors or clinical instructors? Have you been recognized as an up and coming leader in your field? Now, think about how all these attributes align with the job you are interviewing for.

Read the job announcement/posting again. Be sure to emphasize those qualities, attributes, strengths, and accomplishments that are mentioned in the required qualifications section of the job description.[2] If you have additional strengths that are considered "desirable" but not "required," please make sure you highlight those and mention them during your interview. It is your job to listen for any question that may allow you to do so. We will discuss potential questions later in this section and how you might effectively respond to them.

Goal 3: Relax and feel comfortable knowing you are well-prepared. If you are the type of person who waits until the last minute to do everything and were able to cram the night before an exam in college, please read this section carefully. Waiting until the night before your interview to start getting things together will not work. In order to be ready for your interview, you must begin to prepare at least 1-2 weeks in advance. In fact, as soon as you are granted an interview, that is the time to begin preparing. If you are given options as to days and times you want to interview, try to schedule your interview at least one week out so that you can prepare adequately. Also, ideally, schedule your interview in the morning if you are given the option of morning and afternoon slots. You want to be fresh and alert, not worn out or tired from other activities you have engaged in prior to your interview. Assuming you have 1-2 weeks to prepare for your interview, the next section presents an outline of what you should be doing as the big day approaches.

PRACTICAL ACTIVITIES/STRATEGIES FOR INTERVIEW PREPARATION

1-2 WEEKS BEFORE INTERVIEW DAY

1. *Know your resume in detail.* Review it. Double check for typos/errors. Again, this cannot be emphasized enough. It's also a good idea to bring a copy of your resume with you to the interview. The interviewers may have a copy of it themselves, but it may not be the most updated version, or you may want to share it with others. In any event, be sure the copy you bring is spotless and carry it in a portfolio or folder to protect it from any mishaps.

2. *Select the suit/clothes* you will wear for your interview and try them on in advance. Your clothes must be polished and professional.[5] Remember, you have been trained as a professional and you must convey that you are serious, have good judgement, and can be trusted. The clothes you wear will either help to make that impression or distract from your intended impression.

Choose a dark colored suit if you want to be safe and secure that you are appropriately dressed. If the suit is new, hang it up so that it will be free of wrinkles until you put it on the day of your interview. If it is one you already own, check it for stains, rips, or loose threads. Dry clean or take it to a tailor, if necessary.

Ladies *choose your hairstyle, nail color and jewelry carefully.* This is not the time to show how fashionable you are. Keep everything simple and classic. Your hair should be clean, colored, and cut in a flattering style that does not draw unnecessary attention. Nail color should be neutral or light colored. No glitter or embellishments, please. If you do not wear nail color, be sure your nails are cut short and manicured. This goes for the men as well. Impeccable grooming is a must. If you can spring for it, consider having your teeth whitened or do it yourself with an over the counter product (if this is a safe method for you). Everyone responds to a great smile and a great smile starts with clean, white teeth. This is especially important if you smoke cigarettes or cigars. In addition, ladies, a good, sensible pair of shoes with a 1-2-inch heel will be your best choice, not 4-inch heels that you have to struggle to walk in. Everyone needs to check their shoes for scuffs, worn heels or dull shine. Polish them or get the heels repaired, if necessary. If you do not own a pair of appropriate shoes, buy a pair or borrow them from a friend. If they are new, wear them around the house for a few days so that they will give a little and be comfortable on your interview day. There's nothing worse than pretending your feet do not hurt from shoes that are too tight and this can be distracting during your interview. Again, do not neglect the importance of the impression your entire outfit will make on those interviewing you, including your shoes.

If you are a smoker, avoid smoking prior to your interview. Your interviewer may find cigarette odor offensive and you do not want to bias them against you. In fact, in many workplaces, smoking is prohibited and frowned upon by those in the healthcare or counseling fields where many human services and rehabilitation professionals work. To be on the safe side, abstain from smoking the day of your interview.

3. *Research the company.* If it helps, assume that you have been given a homework assignment. Your assignment is to research the company that you are interviewing with to find out as much as possible about who they are in preparation for your interview.[1] Approach this assignment as though you are being graded and you want to get an A. Today, everything is available for anyone who has a computer or cell phone with internet access. Go to the company website and thoroughly

read each page. Do you know someone who currently works for the company or used to work for the company? Call them and have a conversation about what it was like to work there. What thing does the current or former employee like about the company? What do they dislike? Why did the person who is no longer working there leave? Who are the key decision makers and which people will you be interacting with? Again, the more you can find out about the company before your interview, the better prepared you'll be to ask and answer questions on your big day.

4. *Research the position; know the salary range.* Ok, now that you have a clear idea of the company, what they stand for, and what it's like to work for them, you are even more excited about the prospect of working there. If that is the case for you, then apply that same attitude of approaching your research as a graded assignment to learning as much as you can about the position that you are applying for. Is it an entry level position or one that requires previous experience?

    The job announcement and posting should provide you with a lot of the information you need but check out other resources as well. If you know someone who is working in the same position as you are, even if it is with a different company, talk to them and find out the day to day responsibilities of their job. Ask them what an appropriate salary range might be. Talk to your professors or others who may be able to share with you their experience in jobs they have had that are like what you are trying to acquire. Be sure to network at conferences and professional meetings in person or online to glean as much information as you can about your desired position.

5. *Find out as much as you can about the people who will be interviewing you.* If you can, find out the name(s) and position(s) of the people who will be interviewing you. Google them to learn as much as you can about who they are, what they have accomplished in their professional career, how long they have been with the company, etc. If they have published anything or presented at a professional conference, try to locate the publication or presentation so that you can read or watch it. Being able to genuinely show an interest in the person interviewing you by referring to their previous work, will undoubtedly leave a good impression on them. Remember, your interviewer is a human being, and everyone likes to think that the work they've done is important and by you commenting on this it will set you apart.

    If you can find out a little about their personal life, this may help if your interview includes lunch or dinner. Are they married? Single? Do they have pets? Are they from another state? Are they a vegetarian or vegan? Again, your purpose in learning more about your interviewer is to be able to engage them in light conversation and show that you are the type of person who can converse about a variety of things without being intrusive or demanding. You may discover that you and the interviewer have several things in common that may make you believe that you will be a good fit for the company.

6. *Anticipate questions (potential interview questions).* One very important way to prepare for your interview is to anticipate the questions you may be asked during your interview. The more potential questions you can think through and draft an answer to, the less anxious you will be when your big day arrives. You can find examples of commonly asked questions on the internet, but here is a sampling on ones you should prepare for:

➢ Tell me a little about yourself.

➢ What are three strengths and three weaknesses?

➢ What attracted you to this job? This company?

➢ Why do you believe you are the best candidate for this job?

➢ Tell me about a time when you faced a challenge and how you dealt with it.

➢ How do you manage stress?

➢ What are your career goals in the next 5 years? 10 years?

➢ What are you passionate about?

➢ What do you consider to be your greatest accomplishment?

These are just a few of the potential questions an interviewer may ask you.[4] Be prepared for other open-ended questions that are aimed at assessing how you have performed in the past in certain situations. Employers know that past behavior is the greatest predictor of future performance, so you can be certain that you will be asked questions that open with the following stems: Give me an example of … Describe a situation when… Walk me through when… Think of a time when… Tell me about the most… Here are three specific examples:

➢ Give me an example of how you dealt with a conflict between two people in your life, either personal or professional.

➢ Describe a situation when an angry client/patient or family member approached you.

> Walk me through an example of what you've done when a client/patient has said they do not want to participate in the service provision process.

7. *Practice, practice, practice.* Again, the more you go over your resume and practice answering some potential interview questions, the more prepared you will feel when your interview day arrives. Participating in a mock interview is also a valuable method of gaining meaningful insights into your interview strengths and weaknesses.[2] In addition, saying out loud your responses will give you the opportunity to revise them until they feel natural to you. You do not want to sound robotic or rehearsed. It is important to infuse your answers with your own style and personality so that the interviewer will be impressed with your ease and self-confidence.

1-3 DAYS BEFORE INTERVIEW DAY

Drive to the location prior to the interview day to make sure you know where you're going, how long it will take to get there, and where to park. You do not want to leave it up to chance regarding how long it will take you to get to the place you will be interviewing, therefore, take the time to make the drive. Being late is not an option. Arrive early, if possible. Call ahead to ask about parking, security checks, bus or subway routes, etc.

Write down at least three questions to ask during or at the end of the interview process. Asking good questions shows the interviewer that you are interested in the position and provides you with valuable information. Here are five questions that are often asked at the end of interviews and why each is important:

> What do you like most about working for this company?
> *Why?* They will tell you what they value most, and you can see if you value the same thing.

> Can you give me examples of how I would collaborate with my manager?
> *Why?* Their response will tell you how staff members are used and allow you to think about how you can showcase your skills to your manager.

> What are the first priorities for this position?
> *Why?* Their response will help you know what to focus on if you get the job and how to make a good first impression.

> What are the challenges of this position?
> *Why?* Their response will let you know what you are facing if you should get the job. If they don't list any challenges, then be very suspicious. What are they hiding? Every job has challenges and

their non-response may indicate a lack of transparency and honesty.

➤ What have past employees done to succeed in this role? *Why?* Their response will give you an idea of how the company measures success.

NIGHT BEFORE INTERVIEW DAY

On the night before your interview day, hopefully you will be excited and filled with anticipation. You may also feel a little nervous or anxious, which is understandable. After all, a lot is riding on tomorrow. What are some strategies you can employ to ease the nerves and assure you rock your interview? Simply put, relax and take it easy. Set aside the suit/clothes you have decided to wear, including your shoes and accessories. Print out a clean copy of your resume and place it in your portfolio.

Then engage in whatever self-care activities you have found successful in the past to relax and wind down. Some suggestions are: Take a walk outdoors, practice yoga, Thai chi, or meditation, listen to music, dance to your favorite tune, watch a funny movie, workout or exercise, play catch with your dog, etc. Finally, go to bed early and get a good night's sleep. Adequate sleep, which is 7-8 hours, will show on your face and nourish your brain to function at its optimal level. To ensure restful sleep, avoid caffeine in the evening, sleep in a dark cool room and do not check your smartphone for at least one hour before bed.

INTERVIEW DAY: YOUR WINNING ATTITUDE

By this day you will have practiced and rehearsed potential questions and answers in front of the mirror and or participated in a mock interview with friends, colleagues, or classmates. You have proofread your resume and cover letter several times and consulted at least two other trusted people for their feedback. You know what is in your resume and you have highlighted your strengths in your cover letter. Now, the big day has arrived. Today is your interview for the job you really want. How do you conduct yourself during the interview to impress your prospective employer? Below is a list of qualities and behaviors you should try to clearly demonstrate with everyone whom you come into contact with during your interview day.[8] They may seem common sense and self-explanatory, but are very important to assure you get the job offer:

➤ *Honesty/sincerity:* Simply put, be honest and do not lie about your work history or education. You must portray yourself as someone with integrity and strong ethics.

➤ *Enthusiasm/positivity:* Act like you are excited about the possibility of working for the company. Be positive. Do not bad mouth your former or present employer or supervisor. Speak and act as though you are the best candidate for the position.

➤ *Smile/friendly demeanor:* Now that you have had your teeth whitened and polished, show off your smile. Make sure you are smiling with your whole face, meaning that your eyes also reflect your joy. Try to engage your interviewer and anyone you encounter with pleasant conversation. Respond to questions in a conversational tone, not as though you're being interrogated. Be professional but have fun.

➤ *Eye contact/body language:* In the United States, making eye contact with others, conveys your interest and sincerity. Be sure to make eye contact with anyone you have a conversation with. Also, be aware of the message your body language is sending including your handshake. Make sure your handshake is firm and you make eye contact as you extend your hand.[5] Posture is important. Sit up straight, but not stiffly. Stand erect and walk with a quick pace. Avoid slumping, slouching, or dragging your feet.

➤ *Professionalism:* Conduct yourself with the utmost professionalism. Do not chew gum or eat messy foods if your interview is over a meal. Don't use slang or jargon and speak in complete sentences. Address everyone by their title and don't be overly familiar unless specifically requested to do so. Again, arrive early and look impeccable.

➤ *Flexibility:* Life happens, and it is important for you to show that you can roll with the punches without getting bent out of shape. If your interviewer is late or needs to reschedule, be gracious. If you find out once you arrive that you will not have time for a lunch break, don't complain. If someone forgets your name or a detail about your resume, take it in stride.

➤ *Appreciation/Gratitude:* Mind your manners. Say thank you and please as often as you can. Remember, you have been granted an interview and people have set aside valuable time in their schedules to interview you. Show your appreciation by respecting their time and following up your interview with a thank you note or email.

➤ *Confidence:* Throughout your interview, everything you do and say must convey your self-confidence. Don't be shy about promoting yourself and your accomplishments. This is the time to brag about any professional accolades you have received or milestones you have achieved. Your confidence will be a combination of your good posture, articulate speech, and your professional conduct. If you begin to feel anxious, take a couple of deep breaths and relax. You got this!

THINGS TO AVOID DISCUSSING
DURING YOUR INTERVIEW

RELIGION

Although you may consider your faith to be a foundational part of who you are, do not initiate discussions regarding your religious beliefs during your interview. Not everyone is likely to share your beliefs or engage in similar practices, so refrain from these discussions. It is okay to quietly bow your head and say grace if your interview is over a meal but be discreet about it and do not ask others to join in with you.

POLITICS

In today's climate, this topic is strictly off limits during your interview. Many have strong opinions regarding their political views and any discussion of current politics can ignite negative emotions or comments that polarize those in earshot. You do not want your political affiliation to enter any decision regarding your fitness for the job.

MONEY

Questions about your starting salary should not be posed early in the interview process. Only after you have been offered a position, should you start negotiating a salary and benefit package. Asking salary questions too early may convey to the employer that you are more interested in the money you'll make than you are about the position itself.

ALCOHOL/DRUG USE

Your use of alcohol, recreational, or pharmaceutical drugs is not something you want to discuss during your interview. In fact, although your interviewer may offer you a glass of wine during a dinner interview, your best bet is to decline so that you can be fully alert and attentive. Remember, even over lunch or dinner, you are being assessed and you don't want to say or do anything that may cast a negative light on you.[7]

PROTECTED AREAS

It is illegal for a prospective employer to ask about your marital status, so you should feel no compulsion to share this personal information during your interview. Sharing it may work against you in some cases, i.e., where all your co-workers are married and you're not. Unless you are married/partnered and your spouse/partner's hiring at the same company is a condition of your employment, you can wait until you are hired to share this information with your employer[3].

Sexual preference and identity should not be discussed during an interview. Again, this is a protected status and your prospective employer cannot legally ask you about your sexual preference or gender identity. For obvious reasons, this information is highly personal and should not be a topic of discussion during your interview. In addition, please refrain from asking about anybody else's sexual preference or gender identity even if it appears that your interviewer is liberal and open minded.

Disability is another protected status, and your prospective employer cannot legally ask you about your disability status. For obvious reasons, this information is highly personal and should not be a topic of discussion during your interview. In addition, please be mindful that you may disclose your disability with the employer if you so choose, however, research still shows that employers still tend to exhibit bias towards persons with disabilities and this may impact your ability to get the job.[6,3]

In addition to the above-mentioned areas, there are several other topics that employers are mandated to refrain from asking job applicants. These other areas include but are not limited to; age, race, nationality, religion, and marital status. Fieldwork/internship students would do well to research these and other restricted areas to ensure their rights are not being violated when they are engaging in the job application and interview process

CONCLUSION

In conclusion, taking the time to assess one's personal preference for employment is only the first step in the process toward acquiring gainful employment. In the job search journey students will need to develop an effective cover letter and resume, as well as fine tune their social media profile. Once these tasks have been accomplished and an employer or employers have found your paper profile intriguing, then it is time to engage in the interview process.

In this chapter the author has provided goals for the interview that can be actively followed by the job seeker. Things such as learning about the company, highlighting your skills and being comfortable with your skills will help prepare any job seeker to engage in an effective interview. As noted it is essential that you begin your process of preparation for an interview early to ensure that you are thoroughly prepared for the experience.

The detailed task of preparing for an interview deserves careful attention and dedication if successful employment is the final goal of the interviewee. As you embark upon this journey, please note that there will be hurdles, however the goal at the end of the day is to try, try again. Do not be discourage if you do not get the position. Simply assess your performance and continue to improve your skills and self-presentation.

DISCUSSION QUESTIONS

1. What is an interview and what purpose does it serve?

2. When should you begin preparing for your interview? What are specific actions you can take to assure you are prepared for it?

3. What attire is considered most appropriate for a job interview?

4. What topics should you avoid discussing during your interview?

5. How can you make a good impression on your interviewer during and after your interview?

HELPFUL RESOURCES

HELPFUL RESOURCES FOR JOB SEARCH

1. *Designing Your Life: How to Build a Well-lived Joyful Life* by Bill Burnett & Dave Evans. 2016. Knopf Publishing.

2. *Step-By-Step Guide for a Successful Job Search* by Allison Doyle. www.thebalancecareers.com/jobsearch

3. *How to Work Your Social Network to Find Jobs* by Joshua Brockman.
a. www.npr.org/templates/story/story.php?storyId=

4. Private Notes of a Headhunter: Proven Job Search and Interviewing Techniques for College Students & Recent Grads by Kenneth A. Heinzel. 2013. Pythian House Publishing

5. *Getting Hired in a Tough Market* by R. Anne Hull, MEd www.apa.org/careers/resources/job-seekers/hired-tough-market.aspx

HELPFUL RESOURCES FOR INTERVIEW PREPARATION

1. *Managing Anxiety Around Interviews* by Konjit V. Page www.apa.org/gradpsych/2009/03/corner.aspx

2. Get That Job! The Quick & Complete Guide to a Winning Interview by Kelley & Orville Pierson. Plovercrest Press, 2017.

3. *The Guide to Successful Interviewing* by Allison Doyle. www.thebalancecareers.com/winning-interview-skills-2061350

4. *Job Interview Preparation: The Ultimate Guide* by Anita Bruzzese www.livecareer.com/career/advice/interview/job-interview-preparation

REFERENCES

[1]Acikgoz, Y, (2019). Employee recruitment and job search: Towards a multi-level integration. *Human Resource Management Review, 29*, 1-13.

[2]Addams, L., & Woodbury, D., (2009). Teaching job search written and oral communication skills through an integrated approach. *American Journal of Business Education, 2*(4), 13-18.

[3]Bell, A. H. (2000). Avoiding the Snakepit of Illegal Interview Questions. Stained Glass: Quarterly of the Stained-Glass Association of America, *95*(3), 226. Retrieved from https://search-ebscohost-com.proxy.library.ohio.edu/login.aspx?direct=true&db=oih&AN=34543707&site=eds-live&scope=site

[4]Blazevich, R., & Alcisto, T. (2017). Amazing Interview Questions: 44 Tough Job Interview Questions with 88 Winning Answers. Dallas, TX: Signal Tower Publishing.

[5]Chaplin, W.F., Phillips, J.B., Clanton, N.R., & Stein, J.L., (2000). Handshaking, gender, personality, and first impressions. *Journal of Personality and Social Psychology, 79*(1), 110-117.

[6]Lassman, F., Henderson, R. C., Dockery, L., Clement, S., Murray, J., Bonnington, O., ... Thornicroft, G. (2015). How does a decision aid help people decide whether to disclose a mental health problem to employers? Qualitative interview study. *Journal of Occupational Rehabilitation, 25*(2), 403–411. https://doi-org.proxy.library.ohio.edu/10.1007/s10926-014-9550-5

[7]Tews, M.J., Stafford, K., & Michel, J.W., (2019). Interview etiquette and hiring outcomes. *International Journal of Selection & Assessment.* 1-12. https://doi.org/10.1111/ijsa.12228.

[8]Wilhelmy, A., Kleinmann, M., Melchers, K.G., Konig, C.J., & Truxillo, D.M., (2016). How and why do interviewers try to make impressions on applicants? A qualitative study. *Journal of Applied Psychology. 101*(3), 313-332.

LICENSE & CERTIFICATION

CARMELA DRAKE

CHAPTER DESCRIPTION

The purpose of this chapter is to provide the reader with information about licensure and certification in the fields of human services and rehabilitation. This chapter will discuss the purpose and benefit of rehabilitation and human service field licensures and certifications. Students will also be provided with information about licensures and certification for which they qualify as well as information about the preparation and application process for such certifications and licensures.

OBJECTIVES

1. Students will be exposed to a variety of license and certifications for which they may be qualified.

2. Students will acquire basic knowledge regarding license and certification requirements.

3. Student will learn how to navigate the license and certification application process.

According to the United States Department of Treasury,[12] "more than one-quarter of U.S. workers now require a license to do their jobs. Approximately 73%) of healthcare and technical workers had a license in 2016.[25] Carefully designed and implemented licensure standards can provide high quality services and improve health and safety standards. Licensing and certification can offer important health and safety benefits and consumer protections. Licensing and certification can provide individuals with clear professional development and training guidelines as well as marketability in the workforce.

Evidence of licensure requirements for working professionals date as far back as the 1800s. For instance, by the end of the 19th century, more than half of the states required license in the medical professions and allied fields.[19] By the 1970s different fields in human services began to develop commissions to create standards of licensure and certification for professionals. In 1974, the Commission of Rehabilitation Counselor Certification (CRCC) was officially incorporated and began to certify rehabilitation counselors.[16] Four years later, the Association of Social Work Boards (ASWB), formally the American Association of State Social Work Boards (AASWB), was founded and five years later offered its first licensure examination.[4] Virginia became the first state to license counselors in 1976.[19] The first certification examination for addiction medicine was administered in 1983 in the state of California.[34] As years progressed, there were an increasing number of professional organizations developed that have also created credentialing programs to preserve and promote their career fields.

DEFINING LICENSE AND CERTIFICATION

License and certification are considered specific types of credentials. For a professional to obtain such credentials, they must undergo a specific credential process in order to be recognized as earning a license and/or certification. Credentialing is a process used to designate an individual, a program, an institutional, or a product having met an established set of standards as well as recognized as being qualified to perform the designated role or function.[15] Licensure and certification show that an individual possesses specific knowledge and skills to perform a job. Those credentials are typically earned after one has completed higher education. In some cases, one can become licensed or certified in a professional area after they have gained practical experience through an internship, residency, or time on the job. Earning a license or certification requires an individual to meet a specific set of standards and pass a competency examination. Once obtained, the license and certification are only valid for a prescribed period of time and must be renewed. In general, the intent for licensure and certification is to:

> ➢ Safeguard public health and safety,

> ➢ Protect consumers by guaranteeing minimum educational requirements and industry oversight,

> ➢ Support career development and pathways for licensed workers and enhanced professionalism for licensed and certified workers,

> ➢ Step in when competitive market forces fail to achieve desired outcome.[15]

At times, these credentialing terms are used interchangeably; however, there are distinctive differences in the way the terms are defined.

Licensure is a state's grant of legal authority to practice a profession within a designated scope of practice. Most U.S. states require individuals to meet minimum standards of practice to work in various disciplines in human services (i.e., social work, addictions treatment, etc.). The professional must be able to demonstrate practice competencies and adherence to a code of professional ethics, and this can be accomplished through state licensure.

Certification is defined as a voluntary process but may be required in order to practice in certain states. Certification is often provided by a non-governmental organization. This type of credential is created by professional groups to convey the specialty area in which the professional can perform services.[29] Like licensure, certification provides the professional with the opportunity to demonstrate professional competencies. The National Commission for Certifying Agencies (NCCA)[24] defined three hallmarks of certification:

> ➤ Voluntary process,

> ➤ By a private organization,

> ➤ For the purpose of informing the public of those individuals who have successfully completed the certification which proves their ability to perform their professional competency.

It is important to understand the difference between certification (professional/personnel), certificates of participation, and assessment-based certificate programs. Professional/personnel certification is what has been described earlier in this section. The focus is on validating knowledge, skills and/or competencies.

Certificates of participation acknowledge the individuals' presence at an education/training or event and in some cases their active participation in the event. Assessment-based certificate programs focus on building knowledge, skills, or competencies.[14] Most individuals that complete an assessment-based certificate program are seeking to correct areas of deficiencies in order to be validated through the credentialing process to obtain licensure and/or certification.

Licensure and certification are forms of credentials that allow professionals to ensure the public that they are knowledgeable, competent, and skilled in the area that they will be providing services. Possessing one or both credentials allows the professional to be marketable and protect the consumer who is receiving the services.

WHY IS LICENSURE AND CERTIFICATION NEEDED?

As stated in the previous section, licensure and certification provides security for consumers in the competencies of the professionals from whom they seek services. Licensing and certification can provide recourse for consumers when practitioners fail to safely or adequately deliver services. In addition to providing consumer protection, it also ensures quality of service by the professional through regulation of their code of ethics as well as stringent continuing education requirements.

Licensing and certification provide professionals with additional endorsements in specific specializations. The process to obtain licensing and certification validates that the professional met rigorous standards of knowledge and experience in the specialty area.[33] Because it is time-limited, licensure and certification also promote continuing education among those professionals who possess the credentials.

There is a demand for demonstrated positive outcome from policy makers and funding sources for agencies to use proven evidence-based interventions employed by properly trained professionals.[33] These funding sources are often government grants and insurance carriers. Both funding sources will request evidence of the individual's competency in providing specific services. This evidence can be provided through the professionals earned credentials.

In order to be an insurance provider of specific services, the professional must be able to provide the insurance company with copies of current license and/or certification reflecting one has the skill set and knowledge to provide hands-on care. Regarding Medicaid providers, depending on the state in which the professional is seeking to provide services, there may be very specific requirements associated with who is eligible to provide care.[18] In many cases, the individual who is often deemed eligible to provide care is the individual who possesses specific state licensure and/or certification to work in that state. For example, autism insurance legislation reform across the United States mandates insurance carriers to cover autism related services and stipulate applied behavior analysis (ABA) services to be reimbursable expenses.[13]

In several states, licensure has presumably been driven in part by insurance companies wanting mechanisms in place to be able to identify competent providers. Licensure and certification boards are established to monitor behaviors of their professionals.[26] This added security for the insurance carriers ensures that the individuals who possess specific credentials should conduct and provide services in a professional and ethical manner.

Each licensure and certification credential were developed by a professional organization that has also created, amended, and published a set of code of ethics that their professionals must follow. The credentialing association articulates a professional code of ethics and conduct that certified and licensed individuals use to guide professional practice.[1] Those codes of ethics assist the professional in upholding standards of practice when providing services to the consumer. The professional is expected to follow the code of ethics and often are required to participate in yearly professional development or continuing education activities that address the code of ethics and ethical decision making. When the credentialed professional's behavior violates the professional ethics, the organization adjudicates claims against the professional using those codes of professional ethics and conduct.[1] Please see the chapter on Ethics and Ethical Decision Making for more discussion regarding professional codes of ethics.

Credentialing boards and associations ensure that professionals meet the requirements for certification and recertification and one of those requirements involve continuing education.[26] Continuing education can be completed by the professional through professional development activities. Professional development is training activities that enhance the skills and understanding of the individuals, and often the development is required for professional recertification and license renewal.[2]

Lastly, possessing licensure and/or certification is an asset toward marketability. One should consider options within the profession for improving marketability.[1] Obtaining credentials in a specialty area will allow professionals to improve their marketability. Davenport[11] noted that credentialing increases the professional's marketability and employers as well as consumers view professionals with credentials as having more of a competitive edge. Credentialing also demonstrates the professional's commitment to the profession and career. For both individuals and organizations, certification enhances the acquisition of relevant skills, and allows for differentiation in the market.[11]

PREPARING AND APPLYING FOR LICENSURE AND CERTIFICATION

Before beginning an undergraduate program, it is beneficial for students to conduct some preliminary research into the options that are available to assist in meeting their career goals. Many undergraduate programs such as recreational therapy, social work, and education have licensure and/or certification requirements that must be satisfied prior to the conferring of the degree. Other license and certifications require that the individual satisfy requirements after one has received their bachelor's degree. It will be important to learn all that is required prior to pursuing vocational goals.

Tarvydas, Hartley, and Gerald[29] have provided several tips that professionals should consider when preparing for licensure and certification:

> ➢ Research requirements by contacting the licensure or certification board,

> ➢ Complete a spare application as a trial run to educate yourself on the application process,

> ➢ Maintain specific and detailed training records and professional experiences,

> ➢ Seek and maintain malpractice insurance,

> ➢ Research requirements for any state you plan to be employed.

These tips can help to prepare professionals for the licensure and/or certification process while improving their chance of successful acquisition of the licensure or certification which they seek to enhance their marketability and skill level.

It is essential to note that the 10th amendment to the Constitution of the United States grants each state the right to regulate professional practices.[18] Standards for professional practice, to include licensure and certification requirements, will differ in each state unless the certification is a national certification; hence, it is imperative for professionals to research all the information regarding licensure and certification requirements for the state in which they plan to be employed.

HELPFUL RESOURCES

The following list, with brief descriptions, provides some of the certifications and licenses that are available to individuals who have earned a Bachelor of Science or arts degree or higher in a human service, rehabilitation, behavioral, or social services field:

Human Services Board-Certified Practitioner (HS-BCP). Applicants are required to have an associate or higher conferred degree in human services or a related field. A qualifying degree must be from a regionally accredited college or university, or a state-approved community or junior college. Applicants for the HS-BCP must verify 350 hours of postgraduate human services work experience.[6] For more information regarding educational requirements and the application process, visit the following link: https://www.cce-global.org/HSBCP.

Board Certified Case Manager (CCM). Applicants are required to have a baccalaureate or master's degree from a health or human services field. Applicants for the CCM must verify 24-months, fulltime case management experience. To learn more about eligibility and the application process, visit the following link: https://ccmcertification.org/get-certified/certification

Qualified Intellectual Development Professionals (QIDP). Applicants seeking this certification must meet the federal definition of a QIDP. The federal definition states that the professional must have at least a year of experience and possess at least a Bachelor of Science degree in a human services field.[27] In addition to meeting the federal definition, the individual must complete an additional year of experience, a stringent certification program, and become a member of the National Association of Qualified Developmental Disabilities Professional (NAQ). To learn about this certification and application process, visit the following link: https://naq.memberclicks.net/apply-now.

Board Certified Assistant Behavior Analyst (BCaBA). This is an undergraduate level certification in behavioral analysis. Individuals who seek this certification make use of applied behavior techniques to teach individuals more effective ways of behaving and making changes to social consequences of existing behavior.[5] This certification also requires the completion of verified coursework to include applied behavior analysis, ethical and professional conduct, and research methods as well as supervised experience before applying for the examination.[5] To obtain additional information, visit the following link: https://www.bacb.com/bcaba/bcaba-requirements/.

Board Certified Behavioral Analyst (BCBA). This is a graduate level certification in behavioral analysis. Individuals who seek this certification make use of applied behavior techniques to teach individuals more effective ways of behaving and make changes to social consequences. This certification also offers a doctoral level (BCBA-D). To obtain additional information, visit the following link: https://www.bacb.com/bcba/bcba-option-1/

National Certification Commission for Addictions Professionals (NCC AP). The NCC AP offers several different certifications in the addictions field across different educational levels. The National Certified Addictions Counselor-Level II(NCAC-II) is an addictions certification requiring the applicant to have at least an undergraduate degree in the field of addiction studies or human services related field. The applicant is also required to complete a prescribed number of supervised work experiences before taking the examination. The individual must possess a state level certification prior to applying for the national-level certification. NCC AP also offers the National Certified Adolescent Addictions Counselor (NCAAC) and the Nicotine Dependence Specialist (NDS) certifications which requires a minimum of a bachelor's degree. To learn more, visit the following link: https://www.naadac.org/certification.

Board Certified Coach (BCC). The applicant interested in pursuing this certification must possess at least a bachelor's degree in any field of study or a higher degree. The applicant can focus on one of the following four specialty areas: executive, corporate, business, leadership coach; health and wellness coach; career coach; and personal life coach. Training towards BCC certification must be completed using a Center for Credentialing and Education (CCE) approved board certified coach training program. To learn more, visit the following link: https://www.cceglobal.org/Credentialing/BCC/Requirements.

Certified Autism Specialist (CAS). Applicants seeking this certification must have a master's degree or higher in special education, education psychology, psychology, human development, social work, occupational therapy, physical therapy, or closely related field. The applicant must also have two years of work experience working with individuals with autism, complete 14 hours of continuing education related to autism, and pass a competency examination. International Board of Credentialing and Continuing Education Standards provides CAS and other certifications such as the Board-Certified Cognitive Specialist (BCCS). The BCCS also shares the same requirements to obtain the certification as CAS. For more information, visit the following link: https://ibcces.org.

Licensed Professional Counselor (LPC). This is a graduate level licensure that requires the applicant to have earned a master's degree or higher in counseling from an accredited institution, that includes an internship and coursework on human behavior and development, counseling strategies, ethical practice, and other knowledge areas.[3] In addition to coursework, the applicant must also complete 3,000 hours of post-master's degree supervision in clinical experience, passage of NCE or similar state recognized exam, and adherence to the code of ethics. To learn more about specific requirements for your state, visit the following link: https://www.counseling.org/knowledge-center/licensure-requirements/state-professional-counselor-licensure-boards

Certified Rehabilitation Counselors (CRC). The applicant interested in pursuing this certification must possess at least a master's in rehabilitation counselor or a master's in clinical rehabilitation counseling from an accredited institution that included a 600 hours internship supervised by a professional or faculty member with a CRC.[10] The applicant must also pass the certification examination. For more information, visit the following website https://www.crccertification.com/filebin/pdf/CRCCertificationGuide.pdf.

PROFESSIONAL ORGANIZATIONS

Joining professional organizations provides valuable resources for the professional and the student pursuing a degree in a specific profession. Students are especially encouraged to join professional organizations. In most cases, student membership rates are less than the rates of professional membership. For instance, NAADAC[21] and NOHS[22] provide a discounted rate for students that is almost half the amount of the practitioner rate. Membership in these organizations affords professionals and students the unparalleled networking opportunities with colleagues, mentors, and experts in their field of specialty.[28]

Professional organizations provide regular communication to its membership. Members are provided with consistent dissemination of professional knowledge through the solicitation of scholarly manuscripts[17] and communication updates on new legislative rulings and advancements in technology that effect the profession.[28]

In addition to networking and communication, professional organizations provide professional development opportunities at a discounted price for financially active members. In some cases, the professional organization may provide continuing education units or contact hours for free or at discounted rates.[17] Lastly, membership also provides great resources for finding the latest jobs in the field.[28]

The following is a list of a few commonly joined professional organizations in the behavior and social sciences fields:

➢ National Organization for Human Services (NOHS): http://www.nationalhumanservices.org/

➢ American Public Human Services Association (APHSA): http://www.aphsa.org/Home/home_news.asp (*Site includes links to 10 other affiliate organizations).

➢ National Human Services Assembly (NHSA): http://www.nassembly.org/

> National Association of Social Workers (NASW):
  http://www.naswdc.org/

> American Counseling Association (ACA): http://www.counseling.org/

> California Association for Alcohol/Drug Educators (CAADE):
  http://caade.org/

> National Independent Living Association (NILA):
  http://www.nilausa.org/

> NAADAC, the Association for Addiction Professionals:
  https://www.naadac.org/

> National Rehabilitation Association
  (NRA):https://www.nationalrehab.org/

> The National Association of Qualified Intellectual Disabilities
  Professional (QIDP): https://www.qddp.org/

CONCLUSION and
BRIEF DESCRIPTIVE DISCUSSION

The attainment of the appropriate licensure and certification can have a positive impact on one's employability and marketability. Becoming certified and/or licensed in your area of practice highlights your skills as a professional and indicates that you are among the best of the best in your field. To summarize the discussion of this chapter the author has provided a brief description of how the acquisition of licensure and/or certification is directly connected to the world of work and services provision for our clients/consumers.

DESCRIPTIVE DISCUSSION

"Employers, colleagues and policymakers interested in improving health care delivery know the value of board certification." [9] In the area of mental health, there has been a move to encourage providers to also incorporate evidence based case management services to eliminate duplication of services, expand access to needed services, and to improve the lives of clients. [9] States in the southeastern United States have attempted to incorporate a statewide case management certification to satisfy this need to better serve clients receiving mental health services. With the increase in individuals with the credential of certified case management (CCM) the southeast region is also seeking to employ individuals with this credential in their mental health agencies.

In the State of Alabama, agencies that have state certification to be substance use disorder treatment or prevention services providers must employ professionals who also have substance use disorders (SUDs) or prevention certification. The professional can be employed and provide services within the agency under supervision; however, they must obtain at least their SUD certification, prevention certification, or licensure within two years of employment in order to continue to be employed with any state certified agencies. The investment in obtaining certification equates to job security.

As an employer, it is always a plus to see the applicant hold several certifications in the area of services that are provided within their agency. Often, several good applicants resume will be submitted for a vacancy, but there are several things that will be considered to find the absolute best candidate for the available position. Does the candidate possess a current CPR/First Aid certification? Do they currently possess certifications in behavioral analyst, prevention, and or addictions treatment? As an employer, the applicant's involvement in professional organizations can also tell a story about the individual's commitment to the profession. The agency is always looking to market and the best way to market is through professional organizations. The more involvement their employees have, the more visible the agencies name is at different annual meetings and conferences. The applicant that possesses the certifications and is active in professional organizations is usually the applicant that gets extended the invitation for employment.

The illustrations highlight the importance and applicability of licensure and certification acquisition in the fields of human services and rehabilitation. Obtaining the appropriate licensures and/or certification in your area of specialty is essentially the same as stamping a seal of approval on your resume. It is an official means of letting employers know that you have been adequately trained to work with their consumer populations. Additionally, your dedication to that licensure or certification indicates that you maintain a level of integrity and you recognized and abide by a specific code of ethical conduct. All students should take the time to explore the licensure and certifications that will enhance their marketability in their specific field of practice.

DISCUSSION QUESTIONS

1. What is the general intent for licensure and certification?

2. Discuss the significant differences between licensure and certification?

3. Explain the importance of license and/or certification and its relationship to insurance carriers.

4. How does possessing a licensure or certification allow one to be marketable in their career field?

5. Given the license and/or certification resources provided, what are the minimum requirements for obtaining the credentials?

REFERENCES

[1]Adams, P.S., Brauer, R.C., Kares, B., Bresnahan, T.F., & Murphy, H. (2004). Professional certification: It's value to SH&E practitioners and the profession. *Professional Safety, 49*(2), 26-37.

[2]Altshauld, J. W. (2005). Certification, credentialing, licensure, competencies, and the like: Issues confronting the field of evaluation. The Canadian *Journal of Program Evaluation, 20*(2), 151-168

[3]American Counseling Association (2011). Who are licensed professional counselors? Retrieved from, https://www.counseling.org/PublicPolicy/WhoAreLPCs.pdf.

[4]Association of Social Work Boards (2018). History, Retrieved from https://www.aswb.org/about/history/

[5]Behavior Analyst Certification Board (2018). BCaBA requirements. Retrieved from, https://www.bacb.com/bcaba/bcaba-requirements/

[6]Center for Credentialing and Education (2016). Human services board-certified practitioner (HS-BCP): Application requirements. Retrieved from, https://www.cce-global.org/Credentialing/HSBCP/Requirements.

[7]Center for Credentialing and Education (2016). Board certified coach (BCC): Requirements. Retrieved from, https://www.cce-global.org/Credentialing/BCC/Requirements.

[8]Commission for Case Manager Certification (2018). CCM eligibility at a glance. Retrieved from, https://ccmcertification.org/get-certified/certification/ccmr-eligibility-glance.

[9]Commission for Case Manager Certification (2018). Policy positions. Retrieved from, https://ccmcertification.org/about-ccmc/differences-between-certified-case-managers-and-case-managers/policy-positions.

[10]Commission on Rehabilitation Counselor Certification (CRCC) (2018). Eligibility requirements. Retrieved from, https://www.crccertification.com/eligibility-requirements

[11]Davenport, R. (2006). Credentialing and Certification. *T+D, 60*(5), 60–61. Retrieved from http://search.ebscohost.com.ezproxy.lib.alasu.edu/login.aspx?direct=true&db=aph&AN=21543998&site=ehost-live

[12]Department of the Treasury Office of Economic Policy (2015). Occupational licensing: A framework for policymakers. 2015. Retrieved from, https://obamawhitehouse.archives.gov/sites/default/files/docs/licensing_report_final_nonembargo.pdf.

[13]Guercio, J. M., & Murray, W. J. (2014). Licensure for behavior analysts: The path to responsible and cooperative action. *Behavioral Interventions, 29*(3), 225–240. https://doi-org.ezproxy.lib.alasu.edu/10.1002/bin.1388

[14]Institute for Credentialing Excellence (2012). About us. Retrieved from, http://www.credentialingexcellence.org/p/cm/ld/fid=32

[15]Institute for Credentialing Excellence (2012). Certificate v. certification. Retrieved from, http://www.credentialingexcellence.org/p/cm/ld/fid=4

[16]Leah, M, & Holt, E. (1993). Certification in rehabilitation counseling: History and process. Rehabilitation Counseling Bulletin, 37(2), 71.

[17]Matthews, J.H. (2012). Role of professional organizations in advocating the nursing profession. The Online Journal of Issues in Nursing, 17(1), Retrieved from, http://ojin.nursingworld.org/MainMenuCategories/ANAMarketplace/ANA Periodicals/OJIN/TableofContents/Vol-17-2012/No1-Jan-2012/Professional-Organizations-and-Advocating.html.

[18]Miller, J. E. (2014). How to Become a Medicaid Mental Health Provider? Alexandria, VA: American Mental Health Counselors Association.

[19]Moore, Thomas G (1961). The purpose of licensing. *Journal of Law & Economics, 90,* 112Shallcross, L. (2009). Counseling profession reaches the big 5-0. Counseling Today, Retrieved from https://ct.counseling.org/2009/12/counseling-profession-reaches-the-big-5-0/

[20]NAADAC, The National Association for Addiction Professionals (2018). National certification commission for addiction professionals (NCC AP): Certifications. Retrieved from, https://www.naadac.org/assets/2416/ncc_ap_credentials_matrix_07-15-2016.pdf

[21]NAADAC, The National Association for Addiction Professionals (2018). Membership dues. Retrieved from, https://www.naadac.org/membership-dues.

[22]National Organization of Human Services (NOHS) (nd). Membership: Join now. Retrieved from, https://www.nationalhumanservices.org/join-now

[23]National Conference of State Legislators (2017). The state of occupational licensing: Research, state policies, and trends. Occupational licensing: Assessing state policy and practice. Retrieved from http://www.ncsl.org

[24]NCCA Standards for Accreditation of certification programs (2002). Retrieved from, http://www.credentialingexcellence.org/p/cm/ld/fid=66

[25]Shallcross, L. (2009). Counseling profession reaches the big 5-0. Counseling Today, Retrieved from, https://ct.counseling.org/2009/12/counseling-profession-reaches-the-big-5-0/

[26]Simons, L., Haas, D., Mossella, J., Young, J., & Toth, P. (2017). The value of certification in the era of licensure: An exploratory study of professional identity. Development in Alcohol & Drug Professionals, Alcoholism Treatment Quarterly, 35(2), 130-150.

[27]State of California Department of Development Services (2018). Qualified intellectual developmental disabilities (QIDP) requirements. Retrieved from, https://www.dds.ca.gov/ICF/QIDPRequirements.cfm.

[28]Santiago, A.C. (2018). The benefits of joining professional associations. Retrieved from, https://www.verywellhealth.com/professional-association-1736065.

[29]Tarvydas, V. M., Hartley, M. T., & Gerald, M. (2016). What practitioners need to know about professional credentialing. In I. Marini & M. A. Stebnicki (Eds.), The professional counselor's desk reference., 2nd ed. (pp. 17–22). New York, NY: Springer Publishing Co.

[30]The National Association of QIDPs. Certification program, Retrieved from https://www.qddp.org/about-the-program

[31]Torepy, E. (2016). Will I need license or certification for my job? Career Outlook, U.S. Bureau of Labor Statistics, Retrieved from https://www.bls.gov/careeroutlook/2016/article/will-i-need-a-license-or-certification.htm

[32]U.S. Department of Labor, Bureau of Labor Statistics (2017). 2016 Data on certification and licenses. Retrieved from https://www.bls.gov/cps/certifications-and-licenses.htm.

[34]Van Houtte, E. (2010). Validating certification in a recovery focused mental health systems. *Psychiatric Rehabilitation Journal, 33*(3), 242-243.

[35]White, W. (nd). Significant events in the history of addiction treatment and recovery in America. Retrieved from, http://www.williamwhitepapers.com/pr/AddictionTreatment&RecoveryInAmerica.pdf

WHAT'S NEXT?
TAKING YOUR CAREER
TO THE NEXT STEP

SABRINA HARRIS TAYLOR

CHAPTER DESCRIPTION

The purpose of this chapter is to assist readers in exploring their vocational and education options upon completion of their undergraduate rehabilitation degree. This chapter will provide readers with information about progressing in to graduate education. Information about varying types of graduate study options will be provided. Discussion about program specifics, requirements, and qualities will be included to assist readers in learning the best means of assessing a graduate studies program to determine the best match for their needs. This chapter will also provide information concerning the application process for graduate studies programs and graduate studies program resources.

LEARNING OBJECTIVES

1. To assist readers in exploring their vocational and education options upon completion of their undergraduate rehabilitation degree.

2. To teach readers how to select a graduate studies program based on their specific educational and professional needs.

3. To assist readers in learning the best means of assessing a graduate studies program to determine the best match for their needs.

4. To educate readers about the application process for graduate studies programs.

GRADUATE SCHOOL?

In 1860, Milton Bradley created a board game called the Game of Life. The modern-day version requires players to select whether they are going to attend college or get a job. Depending upon the choice, the player's life will be impacted by their initial decision.

The Game of Life is an accurate reflection of the decisions all college students make when nearing the end of their undergraduate degree. Students often ask themselves, "should I go left, or should I go right?" Many factors determine a student's decision to attend graduate school such as finances, family, location, and support. Support is key. In 2002, 17 percent of undergraduate college students were first generation college students. Those numbers spiked to 34 percent between 2011 and 2012.

Students living in rural areas may not have exposure or access to college summer enrichment programs, learning camps, or college preparatory programs to prepare for college. Therefore, many students are not fully equipped to make educated decisions about college due to lack of awareness.[15]

To fill in the gap, let us discuss graduate school. What is graduate school? Berkeley University defines graduate school as an advanced program of study that focuses on a specific academic discipline or profession.[3] Undergraduate human services and rehabilitation students have many options as it relates to obtaining advanced training. Later in this chapter you will learn how to select a graduate training program that fits your professional goals.

Students often wonder how graduate school is different from an undergraduate degree training program. First, graduate school is designed to make students experts in their chosen profession. Academic coursework is more rigorous and often designed using a cohort model. More university programs are converting to the cohort model in which students enter graduate degree programs and are placed in a cohort. Cohorts are designed for students to begin a program together and graduate together. Universities have discovered using a cohort format promotes in-class interactions, group cohesiveness, increases student retention, and provides an opportunity to serve as resources for one another.[11]

Students enrolled in graduate school often have the option of enrolling part-time or full-time. In traditional undergraduate training programs, students must enroll in 12 credit hours to be considered full time and six credit hours to be considered part time. At the graduate level, 9 credit hours is full time and less than 9 credits is part time.

Graduate schools offer post-baccalaureate programs, master's degrees, and doctoral degrees. Post-baccalaureate programs are designed for students to obtain a second bachelor's degree or a second entry degree. In order to obtain admittance into a post-baccalaureate program, candidates must have a bachelor's degree. Examples of post-baccalaureate degree programs include obtaining licensure as a teacher, obtaining certificates, and/or obtaining a second degree such as in nursing.

Master's degrees include many fields of study. Some master's degree programs are designed for students to progress to a doctoral degree while others are designed to be a terminal degree into the profession. For instance, persons who have obtained a master's degree in rehabilitation counseling are eligible to obtain certification as a Certified Rehabilitation Counselor (CRC).

The CRC certification can only be obtained by individuals who have a master's or doctoral degree in rehabilitation counseling or a master's in a counseling degree that included coursework in rehabilitation counseling. Persons who receive CRC certification have a marketable credential that leads to job placement, job advancement, salary advancement, and private referrals[6]

In order to provide services to consumers and bill insurance providers, it is important to become licensed. Social workers, counselors, recreational therapists, and addictions counselors must be licensed in their state in order to practice and bill insurance providers. Each state has various requirements in order to obtain licensure and it is best to check with your state to review licensure requirements. Also, it is important to attend accredited graduate programs.

The National Association of Social Workers provides a list of accredited graduate programs in the United States at www.socialworkers.org. The Council on Social Work Education accredits baccalaureate and master's degree social work programs. By attending an accredited social work program, social work students are eligible to sit for certification or licensure in the field of social work after graduation.

Human services programs are accredited by the Council for Standards in Human Service Education (CSHSE). Associate, baccalaureate, and master's degree programs accredited by CSHSE ensures students receive quality instruction and a robust curriculum grounded in theory and knowledge that develops and promotes competent human services professionals.[8]

Recreational therapy programs are accredited by the Commission on Accreditation of Recreational Therapy Education (CARTE). Recreational therapists provide treatment to consumers that is designed to restore and rehabilitate an individual's level of functioning and independence by promoting health and wellness and reducing or eliminating limitations caused by a chronic medical condition or disability.[5]

After achieving a master's degree, a select few decide to apply to a doctoral program. It can take up to seven years for a person to obtain a doctoral degree. A doctoral degree is an advanced level degree that afford individuals with the expertise to teach in a university setting, conduct research, or work in senior level positions. If you decide to begin a master's or doctoral program, there are various factors you must consider.

GRADUATE SCHOOL IS A HUGE COMMITMENT

Before you begin graduate school, you must ask yourself, is this the best time for me to pursue a graduate degree. Graduate school requires students to complete rigorous coursework, conduct research, attend professional conferences, complete exit exams, and complete practicums and clinical internships. Prior to applying to a graduate program, you must consider your personal obligations. Applicants are encouraged to have conversations with their family about how graduate school will impact daily routines and family outings. Having support from family and friends is paramount for success in a graduate program.

Attending graduate school is a full-time job and must be treated as such. Masters training programs are shorter in length and usually takes two-three years to complete. Doctoral training programs may take up to 7 years to complete. Graduate school is more than just attending class and submitting assignments. Graduate students spend at least twenty hours a week doing assignments, conducting research, and studying for exams. When students begin clinical internships, graduate school will require students to work more than forty hours a week while obtaining internship hours, completing assignments, studying, and conducting research. Due to these demands, students often must make hard choices when it comes to employment. Many students work full time while attending college.

Graduate school will require you to have a flexible schedule and it may cause you to have to change jobs or reduce work hours. Fortunately, some graduate programs offer funding such as scholarships, fellowships, teaching/research assistant positions, or even campus employment to offset financial costs. We will discuss more in the next section.

HAVE A FINANCIAL PLAN

Depending on your selected program, graduate school may take three to seven years to complete. Prior to applying to a graduate program, assess your current financial situation. How much money do you need to pay your bills and cover personal expenses while enrolled in college?

Do you need to find a more flexible job so you can meet the demands of school and take care of your personal financial obligations? Sometimes, it makes more sense to work and save a nest egg before beginning a graduate program. Meeting with a financial advisor or taking budgeting classes is a smart move before taking on a huge financial endeavor such as graduate school.

Many churches offer free budgeting classes. You may also learn how to get out of debt using Dave Ramsey's snowballing technique.[14] You can purchase the Dave Ramsey series or go to your local library and check out his books on getting out of debt and the snowball method. The Budgetnista is another free resource developed by Tiffany Aliche on how to get out of debt and develop a budget.[1] She has many free resources on her webpage, Facebook, and Instagram account. Also, YNAB (You Need a Budget) is a popular app that is used to help people create a budget and plan for their financial future. There is a fee associated with this service. Links to these resources are included in the resource section of this chapter.

After assessing your financial needs, apply for federal financial aid through the Free Application for Federal Student Aid (FASFA). Contact program coordinators at the university you intend to apply and ask if the department offers scholarships or fellowships. Many government, private, and non-profit agencies offer scholarships to students majoring in counseling.

HOLIDAY & SEASONAL BREAKS

Throughout the school year, universities have scheduled breaks for holidays, spring break, and summer break. However, the demands of graduate school will often require students to continue working over a break period due to research study requirements, clinical internships, and presentations at local and/or national conferences. It is important students take that into consideration when planning vacations and events that could interfere with meeting the demands of graduate school. Remember, graduate school is not permanent, and you will get your life back soon.

NETWORKING: KEY TO SUCCESS

Everyone dreams of being successful in their chosen profession and achieving their professional goals. Graduate programs realize this and create opportunities for students to reach those goals. Faculty often encourage students to present at local and national conferences.

In doctoral programs, students are often matched with faculty based on their research interests and conduct research with their faculty advisor. Once the data has been collected and analyzed, faculty often invite students to attend professional conferences and present research.

Professional conferences may be held locally or nationally and can last up to five days. Students must be able to arrange for childcare, time off from work, and take care of personal affairs in order to attend. National Conferences such as the National Rehabilitation Association and the National Association of Social Workers, offers student mixers for students to meet and interact with faculty, scholars, peers, and other counseling professionals in the field. Employers often attend these conferences and may even conduct interviews on the spot. Therefore, it is important for students to have their resumes available and research conference attendees prior to attending.

At the end of 2018, there were 783 master's-level rehabilitation counseling programs accredited by the Council for Accreditation of Counseling & Related Educational Programs. CACREP is an accrediting body that accredits master's and doctoral degree programs in counseling within the United States and internationally. The Council of Social Work Education has 540 accredited baccalaureate degree programs and 290 master's degree programs in the United States. The Council for Standards in Human Service Education currently accredits 51 Associate level and bachelor degree human services programs. Lastly, there are six accredited recreational therapy programs accredited by the Commission on Accreditation of Allied Health Education programs.

Your academic training has equipped you with the ability to assist consumers/clients to improve their lives and to live as independently as possible through evaluation, counseling, employment, training, social support, social services, independent living services, etc. Having this training makes you special and receiving training from an accredited program guarantees to the public that you are competent in your field.

If you apply and are admitted into a graduate training program, you will join another elite group. Graduate school will not only prepare you to excel in your profession, but it will open other doors of opportunity for you to explore. This fact is highlighted by various growth projections made by the US Department of Labor.[18] For instance, from 2016 to 2018, employment of rehabilitation counselors is projected to grow 13 percent, which is faster than the average for all occupations.[17] You are needed! The training you received at the undergraduate level has equipped you with the skills needed to succeed in graduate school and serve consumers/clients.

WHY ATTEND GRADUATE SCHOOL?

Let us begin our exploration of rationales for attending graduate school with the consideration of a few brief cases which we can use for further discussion.

Bonnie aspires to owning her own business and wants to provide addictions counseling and outpatient therapy services to consumers in her community. However, Bonnie realizes she needs to become a licensed substance abuse counselor and have her agency licensed by a state where she intends to open the business.

Anthony wants to become a vocational expert with the Social Security Administration, but he must have a master's degree in rehabilitation counseling and experience in the field to become a vendor.

Leslie wants to work for the Department of Veteran Affairs as a Social Worker, but she must have a master's degree in social work from an accredited social work program and be a licensed social worker.

Karen wants to work as a tenured professor in human services. However, she needs to obtain a doctoral degree in human services or a related field.

Each of these individuals has one thing in common. In order to reach their professional goals, they need to obtain a master's or doctoral degree in their respective discipline (i.e. rehabilitation counseling, social work, or human services). Persons obtaining master's degrees receive advanced training in their selected field beyond the bachelor's level. Individuals pursuing doctoral degrees are considered experts in their field and contribute new knowledge to their field through research. Also, these individuals must invest in themselves. Listed below are five reasons you should attend graduate school.

INCREASE YOUR EARNING POTENTIAL
You may have heard persons with graduate degrees make more money than individuals with bachelor's degrees and high school diplomas. People with a graduate degree earn 38.3% more than people with a bachelor's degree in the same field. In 2017, the median salary of rehabilitation counselors was $34,860 while the median income for social workers was $47,980 annually. Median salaries for substance abuse and mental health counselors was $43,300 while median salaries for recreational therapists were $47,680 per year. Additionally, employment is expected to increase significantly in human services related

professions over the next seven years (See table 13.1). This is due to a rapidly aging population and veterans with disabilities.

TABLE 13.1

QUICK FACTS

	Rehabilitation Counselors	Social Workers	Substance Abuse and Mental Health Counselors	Recreational Therapists
2017 Median Pay	$34,860 per year $16.76 per hour	$47,980 per year $23.07 per hour	$43,300 per year $20.82 per hour	$47,680 per year $22.92 per hour
Typical Entry Level Education	Master's degree	Bachelor's degree	Bachelor's degree	Bachelor's degree
Work Experience in a Related Occupation	None	None	None	None
On-the-job training	Supervised field work and internships	Supervised field work and internships	Supervised field work and internships	None
Number of jobs 2016	119,300	682,100	260,200	19,200
Job outlook 2016-2026	13 percent (faster than average)	16 percent (much faster than average)	23 percent (much faster than average)	7 percent (faster than average)
Employment Change 2016-2026	15,100	109,700	60,300	1300

Note: The information in this table was obtained from the Bureau of Labor of statistics and Council for Accreditation of Counseling & Related Educational Programs.

Within the United States, Baby Boomers are more likely than any other generation to have a disability as they age. Baby Boomers are living longer than the generation before them, but they are not healthier.[12] Baby Boomers are highly likely to be obese, have diabetes and high blood pressure. Human services professionals are needed to assist baby boomers to continue to live as independently as possible.

Over the past few years, there has been a surge in applications from veterans for service-connected disabilities. This is attributed to injuries sustained on active duty and veterans being educated about their rights for compensation due to sustaining an injury while on active duty. The Department of Veteran Affairs hires rehabilitation counselors, social workers, substance abuse counselors, and recreational therapists to meet the needs of the veteran population. Due to the increase of veterans with service-connected disabilities, more rehabilitation counselors are needed to meet the demand.

As you can see, careers in the fields of human services and rehabilitation are lucrative and the job outlook is positive over the next seven years. Additionally, the earning potential is endless.

ENHANCE YOUR RÉSUMÉ

Actors and models develop portfolios and update their portfolios constantly to submit to casting directors in hopes of being hired for a job. Casting directors receive thousands of portfolios daily from hopeful actors and models. However, only a few will be chosen. How do they stand out? How do they get selected? They train and work.

If you want to succeed in your chosen profession, you must enhance your résumé so you can stand out from the rest of the crowd. Your résumé is your calling card and a hard-copy elevator speech. The first page of your résumé should pull the readers in and motivate them to contact you for an interview.

Should you include a glamour shot photograph on your first page to stand out from the crowd? No, but your first page should have enough information to make the reviewer feel like they have seen a glamour shot. Seeing a graduate degree on the first page of a resume under an education heading shines. More information about developing an effective résumé can be found in the chapter on Resume Development.

In 2016, 785,595 people in the United States had a master's degree. In 2016, 125 million people were employed in the United States.[17] Look at those odds! A master's degree will truly shine on your résumé.

While enrolled in a graduate program, students should take advantage of every opportunity afforded to them. Throughout the tenure of a graduate student's program, various opportunities present themselves. Internships, fellowships, and scholarships often present in the form of an email, lecturer, or professional conference. In doctoral programs, students are often conducting research, working as teaching or research assistants, and completing rigorous coursework.

It is easy to become overwhelmed by the demands of a graduate program. Participating in on campus and off campus activities is not only the best way to enhance your résumé, but it is a great way to develop your professional character. Counselors and social workers are charged with being ethical, giving back to the community, and to not cause harm to consumers.[2] Volunteering, interning, and participating in campus organizations provides students with opportunities to enhance their professional skills. Therefore, the most important reason for enhancing your resume is to enhance your professional skills.

INCREASE JOB MOBILITY & SECURITY

As we delve into our discussion about job mobility and job security, let us first consider a few case studies:

> *Kevin is a senior who majored in rehabilitation services. His parents are encouraging him to obtain a master's degree in business because they believe he will make more money in business and have more job opportunities. After sitting down with his academic advisor, Kevin learns that his earning potential is endless and that there is a high need for social workers. Kevin's counselor further explains that Kevin can go into business with a master's degree in social work and open a private practice, group homes, and a plethora of other businesses. After learning about the advantages of obtaining a master's degree in social work and job security, he decided to obtain a master's in social work.*

> *Whitney is athletic and loves team sports, hiking, and adventure. In undergrad, Whitney interned at a nursing home and was supervised by a recreational therapist. Whitney learned recreational therapists plan and coordinate recreation-based treatment plans for persons with disabilities. After watching the recreation therapist assist an elderly man in a wheelchair enter the pool using a wheelchair lift and participate in water aerobics with his friends, Whitney decided she wanted to obtain a bachelor's degree in recreational therapy.*

> *Kim grew up in foster care and experienced many challenges during her childhood. When she was 13 years old, she was assigned to a social worker who was kind and attentive to Kim's needs. Her social worker encouraged her to do well in school and was always available when Kim needed assistance. Due to her good experience, Kim decided she wanted to become a licensed social worker and open an adoption agency. Kim enrolled in a master's degree training program in her state. Human services professionals can work in private, state, government, and non-profit agencies. Or, they can choose to become entrepreneurs.*

You have already learned that job opportunities in the human services and rehabilitation field will increase rapidly over the next seven years. Obtaining a master's or doctoral degree will afford human service and rehabilitation professionals the opportunity to have options when it comes to their career. Rehabilitation counselors, social workers, substance abuse counselors, and clinical mental health counselors who have obtained a master's degree can become licensed. With a license, helping professionals can work in private, non-profit, and government agencies as a licensed counselor or social worker. They also could open a private practice and become a provider for insurance agencies such as Medicaid, Blue Cross Blue Shield, Aetna, and many other insurance companies.

HAVE A JOB YOU LOVE

The average American works 35 years.[16] Based on a 40-hour work week, that breaks down to 67,200 hours. The average person spends more hours awake at work than they do at home. Imagine being like Derrick:

> *Derrick is a 45-year-old attorney who specializes in contract law. For ten years, he worked for Crawley, Fischer, & Associates and recently made partner. Every week for the past ten years, Derrick has worked 80 hours a week. Due to his work hours, his marriage has suffered, and he is unable to make his children's sporting events. The only reason Derrick went into law was because his father is a retired attorney and he was expected to follow in his father's footsteps. When Derrick went to college, he learned about rehabilitation counseling. However, his parents told him they would not pay for his education if he chose rehabilitation counseling as a major. So, he went into law and made a lot of money. However, he hates his job.*

Millions of Americans work in jobs that they hate and retire out of those jobs. Many people are afraid to leave jobs due to fear of not being able to provide for their family, not being able to match their current salary, loss of benefits, and not having advanced training. With a graduate degree, you could not be fearful of changing jobs. Not only can you work in your chosen profession, but you qualify to work in other human service-related fields. Human services professionals work in the field of social work, business, social science, statistics, research, and other occupations.

OBTAIN RESEARCH SKILLS

Unless you are interested in working in a research career, many people do not enroll in research courses unless they are integrated into their curriculum. Often, graduate students are not exposed to research courses until they begin a graduate program. Once exposed, students gain skills that enables them to conduct research studies and present at local, state, and national conferences. Students even publish articles at the masters and doctoral level. Presenting at national conferences and writing publications enhances an individual's résumé and increases their competitiveness in the job market. Presenting research at conferences opens doors for human services and rehabilitation professionals and student counseling professionals.

Individuals may be invited to present and serve as a lecturer at conferences and workshops. They may also be invited to serve on committees or receive consulting opportunities. Gaining research skills also assists human services and rehabilitation professionals in becoming better at their jobs.

For instance, being an effective rehabilitation counselor, social worker, counselor, or recreational therapist requires professionals to be observant, use critical thinking skills, and analyze their clients. Implementing research skills in these professions creates effective service situations and has the potential to benefit human services and rehabilitation professionals regardless of their area of specialty. If you are considering graduate school, it is important that you research various graduate schools. Strategies for selecting a graduate program are provided in the next section of this chapter.

STRATEGIES FOR SELECTING GRADUATE SCHOOL

Thousands of college advertisements flood the internet, television, and billboards across America. Students have the option to attend traditional college programs or attend fully online programs. When selecting a graduate program, applicants must be cautious and purposeful. Applicants should take the following steps when selecting a graduate program.

➢ Research chosen profession,

➢ Research accredited programs,

➢ Contact accredited programs,

➢ Make a list,

➢ Select a program.

RESEARCH CHOSEN PROFESSION

Before applying to graduate programs or even researching graduate programs, prospective applicants should research their chosen profession. It is important to know and understand every aspect of a career before deciding to pursue.

Prospective applicants are encouraged to reach out to professionals in their chosen field. Schedule an appointment to interview them and ask them about their job. Request to shadow them and learn about their daily job tasks. Ask questions about work life, work happiness, and their self-efficacy. Find out how they achieved their goals.

Personal interviews and job shadowing experiences empower prospective applicants to make informed decisions and determine whether they want to pursue their career of interest. Additionally, the Occupational Outlook Handbook provides valuable insight into your chosen field. In the handbook, a summary providing an overview of your chosen profession outlines the tasks and job. The handbook also includes information about your field's work environment, salary, job outlook, state data, and similar occupations. By doing research on the front end, you can avoid ending up like Derrick who ended up in a job that he hated.

RESEARCH ACCREDITED PROGRAMS

If you have noticed, research is a keyword that keeps popping up in the chapter. There is an important reason the word research is used repeatedly. There are some individuals who completed a graduate degree from human service and rehabilitation programs and learned that they are not eligible to seek licensure because they did not graduate from an accredited program. Many states require applicants to graduate from a graduate training program that is accredited by their licensure body. Due to misinformation and not thoroughly investigating their selected program, some individuals must retake courses at another university that is accredited to obtain certain certifications and licensure.

By visiting national association websites for a selected profession, prospective applicants can find out what professional organization accredits their selected profession, program, program characteristics, accreditation status, and keywords. If you are not sure if a program is accredited, contact the program coordinator at the institution of interest. Accreditation is of paramount importance because it will impact an individual's job security and options in their selected profession.

CONTACT ACCREDITED PROGRAMS

After doing preliminary research online, reach out to programs of interest. One of the quickest ways to reach out to a program is to visit the program's website and identify the contact person for the program. Send them an email expressing your interest in the program. A sample email is below.

Dear *(insert program coordinator or search committee chair name),*

After learning about your program at (*insert place, person, or website*), I am interested in obtaining more information about your program. Presently, I am a (*insert job position or academic standing*) at (*list employer or university*). I believe I can be an asset to your institution and your program can assist me with meeting my professional goals. I have taken the liberty of attaching a copy of my resume to this email. If possible, I would like to schedule a meet and greet and tour your campus and department.

You may contact me via email or phone at (*insert phone number*). Thank you for your time and consideration and I am looking forward to hearing from you soon.

Respectfully,

(*insert name and credentials earned*)

It is important to be professional and follow proper etiquette when communicating electronically with search committee members. Your email may be the first interaction you have with the search committee and it becomes a part of your application. Search committees begin to evaluate your application during the initial contact. Therefore, it is important to make a great impression.

After you reach out to the search committee, schedule a visit with the campus and the department. When you go to the campus and meet members of the department, go professionally dressed. Remember, you are being evaluated. Programs must ensure that you are a good fit. You may be invited to meet with faculty, the department chair, and even the college dean.

Research the faculty and administration before visiting a university. Read some of the faculty's published articles and jot down questions about their research to ask when you visit the campus. Make sure you take a list of questions with you about the program and the faculty's research interest. More than likely, you will be conducting research and you will want to work with faculty who have similar research interests as yours. Remember, the initial contact is just as important as applying for admission.

MAKE A LIST

You have reached out to graduate program coordinators, toured the campus, met with departmental faculty, and finally decided you are ready to apply to graduate school. How do you narrow down your options? Making a list will enable you to identify your wants and needs to successfully obtain a graduate degree. There are five factors prospective applicants must take into consideration when narrowing down their options.

Location. Prospective applicants must take location into consideration if they want to attend graduate school online, locally, nationally, or internationally. Moreover, prospective applicants must evaluate if their current situation affords them the opportunity to move to attend graduate school. Many prospective applicants have families, jobs, and other obligations that may prevent them from being able to attend graduate school away from home. Others may desire to attend school out of state and must decide to move prior to obtaining a degree. Before applying to graduate school, determine your desired demographic location.

Cost. Graduate school can be expensive, and it is pertinent that prospective applicants take into consideration the financial impact of attending graduate school. Attending school out of state is going to be more expensive than attending school in-state. Nontraditional online private universities are often more expensive than attending a traditional training program.

When prospective applicants apply for federal financial aid, their financial package may consist of scholarships, grants, and loans. Scholarships do not have to be paid back while loans and some grants may have payback requirements. Determine how much money you will need to complete a graduate training program and budget accordingly. Be sure to do your research and seek out other scholarships available to graduate students in general, graduate students majoring in your program, graduate students with ethic or cultural backgrounds and characteristics, etc.

Traditional vs. Nontraditional. Due to an increase in online options, students do not have to attend a traditional brick and mortar college campus. Traditional graduate programs are semester based and students usually complete nine credit hours per semester to be considered full time. On traditional campuses, students have the option to take classes in a face-to-face, hybrid, or online format. Students are expected to attend classes, activities, and events on campus. Advising usually occurs in a faculty member's office.

In non-traditional programs, students may attend 100 percent of their classes online and may never step on a college campus during the duration of their program. There are many popular universities that enable students to receive academic advisement, training, and workshops 100 percent online. These programs are designed for persons with busy schedules who are unable to attend face-to-face classes on a traditional college campus. When deciding whether to attend a traditional or non-traditional program, prospective applicants must examine their personal needs and skills. It is essential to be mindful that online programs require significant intrinsic motivation, organization, and dedication.

Curriculum Length. Program curricula should be reviewed by prospective candidates before applying to a graduate program. Some rehabilitation counseling programs require more credit hours and courses compared to others. It is important that prospective applicants research various programs and compare the curriculum requirements. If you are planning to become licensed or certified in a specific area, make sure the curriculum at your selected school includes the courses you need to obtain licensure or certification.

In conclusion, selecting a graduate school should be a strategic and cautious undertaking. There are many universities recruiting prospective applicants like yourself and want you to enroll in their program. However, it is pertinent that you select a training program that can not only meet your current needs but assist you with reaching your career and professional goals.

HELPFUL RESOURCES

Below is a list of resources that can assist you with developing professionally in the field of rehabilitation counseling.

EMPLOYMENT OPPORTUNITIES

1. www.ncre.org
2. www.nationalrehab.org
3. www.counseling.org
4. www.usajobs.gov
5. www.governmentjobs.gov
6. www.indeed.gov
7. www.higheredjobs.gov
8. www.va.gov
9. www.namrc.org
10. www.goodwill.org
11. www.socialworkers.org
12. www.atra-online.com

PROFESSIONAL ASSOCIATIONS

1. The National Association of Multicultural Rehabilitation Concerns (NAMRC) – www.namrc.org

2. American Therapeutic Recreation Association – www.atra-online.com

3. National Association of Social Workers – www.socialworkers.org

4. National Association of Addictions Professionals – www.naadac.org

5. The National Council on Rehabilitation Education (NCRE) – www.ncre.org

6. The American Counseling Association (ACA) – www.counseling.org

7. The National Rehabilitation Association (NRA) – www.nationalrehab.org

DISCUSSION QUESTIONS

1. List four advantages of attending graduate school.

2. Compare and contrast the similarities between master's programs and doctoral programs?

3. Why is it important to attend an accredited program?

4. How can the cohort model assist graduate students with successfully completing their training program?

5. What are the advantages of obtaining a license?

REFERENCES

[1]Aliche, T (2018). Retrieved from http://thebudgetnista.com/

American Counseling Association (2018). ACA code of ethics. Alexandria, VA: Author

[2]Berkekey University (2019). What is graduate school. Retrieved from www.career.berkeley.edu.

[3]Bureau of Labor Statistics, U.S. Department of Labor, Occupational Outlook Handbook, Rehabilitation Counselors, on the Internet at https://www.bls.gov/ooh/community-and-social service/rehabilitationcounselors.htm

[4]Commission on Accreditation of Allied Health Education Programs (2019). About CAAHEP. Retrieved from: https://www.caahep.org/About-CAAHEP.aspx

[5]Commission on Rehabilitation Counselor Certification. (2019). Rehabilitation counseling scope of practice. Retrieved from https://www.crccertification.com/eligibility-requirements

[6]Council for Accreditation of Counseling & Relational Programs (CACREP). (2019). Retrieved from: https://www.cacrep.org/

[7]Council for Standards in Human Services Education (2018). Retried from https://cshse.org/wp-content/uploads/2018/06/CSHSE-National-Standards-Baccalaureate-Degree-2018-1.pdf

[8]Desilver, D. (2016). 10 facts about American workers. Pew Research Center. Retrieved from www.pewresearch.org.

[9]Doyle, A. (). What is the average hours per week worked in the U.S. Retrieved from: https://www.thebalancecareers.com/what-is-the-average-hours-per-week-worked-in-the-us-2060631

[10]First-Generation Students (2018). Postsecondary national policy Institute.www.pnpi.org.

[11]King, D. (2013). The Status of baby boomers' health in the United States: The Healthiest generation? JAMA Internal Medicine, Population Reference Bureau. Retrieved from: https://trends.psc.isr.umich.edu/pdf/pubs/baby-boomer-health-united-states-2013.pdf

[12]Michigan State University (2018). The Graduate school. www.grad.msu.edu.

[13]Ramsey, D (2018). Retrieved from https://www.daveramsey.com/blog/get-out-of-debt-with-the-debt-snowball-plan

[14]Redford, J., Mulvaney-Hoyer, K., & Ralph, J. (2013). First generation and continuing-generation college students: A comparison of high school and postsecondary experiences.

[15]Social Security Administration (2019). Employee benefits: Work schedule. Retrieved from: https://www.ssa.gov/kc/ee_benefits_wk_sched.htm

[16]US Census Bureau (2017). Retrieved from https://www.census.gov/quickfacts/fact/table/US/INC110217

[17]U.S. Department of Labor. (2019). Wage and hour division. Retrieved from: https://www.dol.gov/whd/regs/compliance/hrg.htm

PROFESSIONAL RESOURCES

CHRISTAN HORTON

ABSTRACT

The purpose of this chapter is to provide readers with professional resources related to the rehabilitation curriculum that aids in the preparations of novice professionals as they approach the internship/fieldwork stage of their academic career. This information is essential during the internship/fieldwork process because it will assist novice professionals to enhance acquired knowledge and a skill base using a practical rehabilitation education resource guide. The guide will outline historical and current resources that assist in professional skill development, maintenance, and competence building to effectively support individuals with various rehabilitation and other human service specific needs. The professional resource guide will assist novice professionals in navigating diverse disability and human service populations through empowerment, advocacy, and goal attainment skills. Included at the conclusion of this chapter is a listing of professional national rehabilitation and human services organizations along with websites that may contribute to professional identity, development, and relevance within rehabilitation and human services.

LEARNING OBJECTIVES

➢ To provide readers with resources associated with the rehabilitation curriculum that can be used for knowledge review and expansion.

➢ To assist readers in developing an effective library of resources to utilize in their professional development.

➢ To provide novice professionals with a foundation to work effectively with diverse populations.

➢ To provide readers literature that outlines skills, techniques, and interventions to best support individuals with disabilities and other human services populations to reach their maximal potential.

➢ To introduce professional rehabilitation and human service organizations that support professional identity development and engagement.

MEDICAL ASPECTS

A TO Z OF DISABILITIES AND ACCOMMODATIONS. (N.D.). RETRIEVED FROM
https://www.askjan.org/a-to-z.cfm.
The Job Accommodation Network offers A to Z listings according to disability, topic, and limitation. This resource enables employers and

individuals to identify the most effective accommodations to remain in compliance with Title I of the Americans with Disabilities Act (ADA).

Andrew, J. D., & Andrew, M. J. (2017). *The Disability Handbook* (2017 ed.). Linn Creek, MO: Aspen Professional Services.

This resource for rehabilitation counseling students and practicing rehabilitation counselors contains a description of 50 common disabling conditions. In addition to the description, functional limitations, vocational impediments, initial interview questions, observations during the initial interview, IPE considerations, and resources are included for each condition. The book also contains seven resource chapters covering eligibility determination, initial interview dictation guide, glossary of common medical terms, common drugs in general use, an overview of psychotropic medications, herbal medicines, and common abbreviations and prefixes.

Brain Injury Association of America. (2018). Retrieved from https://www.biausa.org/.

This resource provides vital information, tips, tools, and topics related to brain injury.

Brodwin, M. G., Siu, F. W., Howard, J., & Brodwin, E. R. (2009). *Medical, psychosocial, and vocational aspects of disability* (3rd ed). Athens, GA: Elliott & Fitzpatrick, Inc.

This text serves as a resource guide for students, counselors, and other allied healthcare professionals. The chapters represent common disabilities rehabilitation professionals typically experience while working in the field. Authors integrated case studies within each chapter to promote critical thinking and enrich discussion. Additional emphasis is placed on multiculturalism to enrich the presence of diversity within the text.

Falvo, D., & Holland, B. E. (2018). *Medical and psychosocial aspects of chronic illness and disability* (6th ed). Burlington, MA: Jones and Bartlett.

This source is a guide for professionals with limited medical knowledge, but practical experience providing services to individuals with chronic illness and disability. The intent is to acquaint readers with various concepts of medical terminology, International Classification of Functioning, and Disability and Health (ICF). Each chapter provides details that explain the physical and psychological aspects of disability and chronic illness in addition to its impact on activities of daily living (ADLs) and overall quality of life.

Flanagan, S. R., Zarestky, H., & Moroz, A. (2011). *Medical aspects of disability* (4th edition). New York, NY: Springer Publishing Company.

This updated edition aims to highlight the advancements in healthcare pertaining to specific chronic illnesses and disabilities. Several innovative topics were added that represent the changes of rehabilitation medicine and implications for rehabilitation research.

Chapters include: Geriatric Rehabilitation, Challenges and Opportunities for Quality in Rehabilitation, and Musculoskeletal Disorders.

Flanagan, Zaretsky, H., & Eisenberg, M.G. (2010). *Medical Aspects of Disability: A handbook for the rehabilitation professional* (4th ed). New York, NY: Springer Publishing Company

This popular resource covers medical conditions and rehabilitation from a clinical, functional, and psychosocial position. Authors describe methods to navigate medical issues, causative agents, psychological factors, and other rehabilitation concerns.

Health and medicine | Science. (2018). Retrieved from https://www.khanacademy.org/science/health-and-medicine

The Health and Medicine module of Khan Academy is a resource that introduces readers to an in-depth review of human body systems ranging from human anatomy and physiology, respiratory system diseases, and the endocrine system. The online tool incorporates various video series that cover vital bodily functions and the impact of chronic illness and disability.

Healthy People 2020. (2018, November 30). Retrieved from https://www.healthypeople.gov/

Healthy People 2020 is an online resource that provides readers with science-based, 10-year objectives focused on Improving healthcare outcomes among individuals in the US. The Health People 2020 effort aims to eliminate Health disparities, promote health equity, and improve healthcare outcomes for all populations.

International Classification of Functioning, Disability and Health (ICF). (2018, March 02). Retrieved from http://www.who.int/classifications/icf/en/

The online ICF addresses aspects of functionality across the human lifespan. Readers can review classification of health and health-related domains along with environmental factors to enhance practical experiences in the workforce.

Jongsma, A. E., Wodarski, J. S., Rapp-Paglicci, L. A., & Dulmus, C. N. (2015). *The social work and human services treatment planner, with dsm 5 updates* (2nd ed). John Wiley & Sons.

This treatment planner provides readers with the elements necessary to quickly and effectively develop formal treatment plans that fulfill the demands of HMOs, managed care companies, third-party payers, and state and federal review agencies.

Lahey, M. P., Kunstler, R., Grossman, A. H., Daly, F., Waldman, S., & Schwartz, F. (2013). *Recreation, leisure, and chronic illness: Therapeutic rehabilitation as intervention in healthcare* (1st ed). Taylor & Francis Group.

This text helps readers to understand how leisure can serve as a positive counterforce to the physical and mental declines that impact health and work. Contributors explore the philosophy of leisure and how freedom, enjoyment, self-determination, and interrupting the routines of daily life are central to true leisure, for persons from all backgrounds. The authors illustrate within the text the need for leisure in a variety of settings and in the quantity and the quality of life.

Learning Disabilities Association of America. (2018). Retrieved from https://www.ldaamerica.org

LDA's online resource aims to raise awareness and provide education to individuals, families, and support systems impacted by learning disabilities. Through empowerment, advocacy, and the development of best practices, LDA strives to reduce the prevalence of learning disabilities.

Mayo Clinic. (n.d.). Retrieved from https://www.mayoclinic.org/

Through the online Mayo Clinic, readers can review comprehensive guides of hundreds of conditions.

IMPACTING THE HUMAN BODY

Merck Manual. (2018). Retrieved from https://www.merckmanuals.com/professional

This online resource is one of the oldest and consistently published medical textbooks. The online manual allows students, professionals, and consumers to locate information on various medical topics and symptoms. Professionals can interactively participate in case study exercises, view podcasts, and other fundamental learning activities.

Moroz, A., Flanagan, S. R., & Zarestky, H. (2016). *Medical aspects of disability for the rehabilitation professional* (5th ed). New York, NY: Springer Publishing Company.

Given the advances in rehabilitation research and the wave of technology, this text was updated to address medical conditions and aspects of disability that rehabilitation professionals typically encounter. Updates include, but are not limited to integrative medicine, traumatic brain injury, prognosis, and vocational issues.

National Library of Medicine. (n.d.). Retrieved from https://www.nlm.nih.gov/

The U.S. National Library of Medicine (NLM) is the world's largest biomedical library. The NLM is a resource that hosts literature, data, and other electronic health information ranging across various medical topics. The 6,500-member national network of libraries provide access to research and medical information for millions across the world.

Porter, H. R. (2015). *Recreational therapy for specific diagnoses and conditions.* Enumclaw WA: Idyll Arbor, Inc.

The author provides readers with a detailed overview of 39 diagnoses and conditions treated by recreational therapists. Along with the diagnosis description, chapters include the incidence or prevalence, and the ages most impacted. Chapters also include the condition; social, emotional, and bodily systems affected; secondary problems; and prognosis. The following chapter focuses on the treatment team's assessment and the recreational therapist's role in assessment.

Shkreli, M. (2018). *The college student's guide to understanding the dsm-5: A summarized format to understanding dsm-5 disorders.* Twentynine Publishing, LLC.

This straight-forward guidebook aims to provide students with a clear understanding and knowledgebase of DSM-5 disorders. This reference guide is also useful for psychology majors, school counselors, family therapists, social workers, and mental health counselors.

Taber's Online. (n.d.). Retrieved from https://www.tabers.com/tabersonline/ub/

Taber's online Medical Dictionary offers more than 65,000 definitions, 32,000 audio pronunciations, 1,200 images, and 120 videos for review. The 23rd edition aims to support students and professionals navigate the ever-changing healthcare profession with effective communication skills and clarity.

United Spinal Association. (2018). Retrieved from https://www.unitedspinal.org/

The association is dedicated to the principles of advocacy for persons with disabilities. Efforts include expanding opportunities for accessible education and employment along with advancing ideals of the Americans with Disabilities Act (ADA). Through alignment with the ADA, the agency focuses on areas such as adequate transportation and modifying Medicare policies to promote community integration and reduced institutionalizations (e.g., nursing facilities).

Understanding Medical Words: A Tutorial from the National Library of Medicine. (2015, July 01). Retrieved from https://www.medlineplus.gov/medicalwords.html

This interactive online resource assists readers with understanding complex medical terminology. Readers can practice skills through participation in quizzes and additional educational components that test acquired knowledge.

University of Washington Model Systems Knowledge Translation Center. (n.d.). Retrieved November 30, 2018, from http://uwmsktc.washington.edu/

The University of Washington's Model Systems Knowledge Translation Center strives to bring awareness and understanding of the spinal cord injury (SCI), traumatic brain injury (TBI), and Burn Injury Model Systems through research and effective dissemination.

World Institute on Disability. (n.d.). Retrieved from https://wid.org/

The World Institute on Disability aims to advocate for inclusion and reduction of barriers among persons with disabilities. The site promotes health equity, accessibility, employment access, and community integration of persons with disabilities.

Your Trusted Guide to Health and the Human Body. (n.d.). Retrieved from http://www.innerbody.com/

Readers can interactively explore this resource to acquire an understanding of the anatomy, systems, major organs, diseases and conditions of the human body.

COUNSELING THEORIES AND TECHNIQUES

Austin, D. R. (2013). *Therapeutic recreation: Processes and techniques.* (7th. edition). Champaign, IL: Sagamore Publishing.

The author provides an in-depth review of the theories and therapies, facilitation techniques, therapeutic recreation process, leadership skills, clinical supervision, and health and safety considerations which are currently vital in the field. The text focuses on assessment, documentation, and conceptual models. The author incorporated useful appendices and practical clinical examples as an additional reference to further support the reader.

Chan, F., Berven, N., & Thomas, K. R. (2015). *Counseling theories and techniques for rehabilitation and mental health counseling professionals.* (2nd ed). New York, NY: Springer Publishing Company

This text introduces counseling theories and techniques for rehabilitation and mental health professionals. The authors provide definitions, breakdown terminology, significance of the counseling function, and importance of efficacy in the art of counseling and psychotherapy.

Corey, G. (2016). *Theory and practice of counseling and psychotherapy* (10th ed). Cengage Learning.

The author aims to guide students and professionals to compare and contrast various models within theories of counseling. Major theories are introduced such as: psychoanalytic, Adlerian, existential, person-centered, Gestalt, reality, behavior, cognitive-behavior, family systems, feminist, postmodern, and integrative approaches. Cases are incorporated to enhance student learning and understanding. The text highlights application of theories within practice and how to integrate theories into personal counseling style.

Corey, G. (2009). *Student manual for theory and practice of counseling and psychotherapy* (8th ed). Belmont, CA: Brooks/Cole.

This manual aims to support students in the application of theory to practice. The author strategically designed the manual to increase student's self-awareness through exercises that promote deeper self-awareness and understanding of various concepts that emerge from several approaches. The manual includes self-inventories, study questions, and self-test questions based on the case of Stan.

James, R. K., & Gilliland, B. E. (2016). *Crisis intervention strategies* (8th ed). Cengage Learning.

This crisis resource provides an overview of the latest skills and techniques for managing crisis situations. The text highlights the process of working with individuals in crisis, ranging from defining the problem to obtaining commitment. The authors provide strategies for processing different crisis situations in addition to the dialogue that a practitioner might use when working with an individual in crisis. The text places the reader on the front lines with the crisis worker throughout the chapters, and then outlines the techniques and strategies utilized by the worker. Partnered with the text is the option to review videos in MindTap for the reader to further understand the theoretical underpinnings of crisis intervention theories, as well as application of skills in crisis situations.

Jones-Smith, E. (2016) *Theories of counseling and psychotherapy: Concepts and cases an integrative approach* (2nd ed). Sage Publication, Inc.

The author integrates contemporary approaches to psychotherapy through introduction of chapters that focus on spirituality and psychotherapy, strengths-based approaches to therapy, neuroscience and neuropsychotherapy, motivational interviewing, and the expressive arts therapies. Case studies are represented in each chapter to demonstrate the application of theory. The text encourages reflection and enhances skills to develop a personal approach to psychotherapy.

Psychotherapy.net. (n.d.). Retrieved from https://www.psychotherapy.net/

Since 1995, this online resource has published over 300 quality training videos in psychotherapy. In addition to the publication of training materials, reviewers can locate articles, interviews, blogs and cartoons free of charge.

Yalom, I. (2009). *Gift of Therapy: An open letter to a new generation of therapists and their patients.* New York, NY: HarperCollins Publishers

This guidebook provides illustrations through real case studies describing how patients and therapists alike can benefit and maximize the use of therapy. The author provides insight and tips for beginner therapists.

GROUP COUNSELING

Corey, G. (2015). *Theory and practice of group counseling* (9th ed.). Boston, MA: Cengage Learning

This text provides readers with a detailed review of the eleven group counseling theories. While the author illustrates theory application, the text guides readers through creation of personal theory synthesis. Through author's clear and candid writing style, readers can effortlessly comprehend theoretical concepts and their relationship to group practice.

Corey, M. S., Corey, G., & Corey, C. (2010). *Groups: Process and practice* (8th ed). Belmont, CA: Thomson Brooks/Cole.

The authors tailored this text to reach both the undergraduate and graduate students seeking human services, counseling, social work, and counseling psychology degrees. This practical manual serves as an outline to facilitate groups.

Gladding, S. (2015). *Groups a counseling specialty* (7th ed). Boston, MA: Pearson.

This comprehensive text provides a detailed review on areas such as: groups, history of group work, group dynamics, group leadership, ethical and multicultural facets of group, group developmental stages, groups across the life span, and the theoretical foundation of group work. The clear and cogent text challenges reviewers to reflect on knowledge obtained, and personal experiences in groups.

Jacobs, E. J., Schimmel, C.J., Masson, R. L. L. (2015). *Group counseling: Strategies and skills* (8th ed). Cengage Learning.

The authors provide an in-depth review of group counseling while placing emphasis on practical knowledge and developing techniques for effective group leadership. The text provides an overview of the various aspects of group counseling and offer illustrations of skill application across a wide range of group settings. This reader-friendly text meets the needs of practicing or future counselors, social workers, psychologists, and others who are currently practicing or in preparation to lead groups in diverse settings.

COUNSELING SKILLS

Bradley T. Erford, (2017). *Orientation to the counseling profession: advocacy, ethics, and essential professional foundations* (3rd ed). New York, NY: Pearson.

The author aligned this text with the 2016 Council for Accreditation of Counseling & Related Educational Programs (CACREP) standards as CACREP defines the standard of quality in the area of counselor preparation. The text is specifically designed to orient counselors-in-training to the counseling profession, regardless of specialty area of interest. Most importantly, the text focuses on current and future counseling practices.

Degges-White, S., & Davis, N. (2017). *Integrating the expressive arts into counseling practice: Theory-based interventions*. New York, NY: Springer Publishing Company.

This text was expanded and revised to provide readers with a broader understanding of the complementary approach to therapeutic treatment. To date, this is the only text resource to combine expressive arts counseling techniques with major theories of counseling and psychology. New chapters reflect neuroscience in counseling, trauma-informed counseling, animal-assisted therapy, mindfulness, videography, family counseling, and an overall emphasis on cultural diversity. This text presents over 90 clear step-by-step interventions for use.

Egan, G. & Reese, R. (2018). *The skilled helper: A problem management and opportunity-development approach to helping* (11th ed). Cengage Learning, Inc.

This text provides an overview of a step-by-step counseling process that enhances confidence and competence. Focus is placed on the therapist-client relationship along with a three-stage framework that outlines client issue management and opportunity development.

Egan, G. & Reese, R. (2018). *Student workbook exercises for Egan's skilled helper* (11th ed). Cengage Learning, Inc.

This manual parallels with the main text, The Skilled Helper. Authors developed the manual to allow practice with self-development exercises as well as communication skills.

Halbur, K. V., & Halbur, D. (2018). *Developing your theoretical orientation for counseling and psychotherapy* (4th ed). Pearson.

This guide is designed to assist therapists in training, mental health counselors, psychologists, social workers, school counselors, substance abuse counselors, psychotherapists, and peer helpers to develop their theoretical orientation. Readers are provided a detailed review of theory and practice and an overview of major counseling theories. The authors integrated learning activities such as reflection questions and case examples. The text was updated to provide readers with a deeper discussion of the implications of empirically validated treatments and approaches.

Hutchinson, D. (2014). *The essential counselor: Process, skills, and techniques* (3rd ed). Thousand Oaks, CA: Sage Publications.

The text offers a comprehensive review of the process of becoming a counselor from beginning to end. The author emphasizes the significance of creating a therapeutic alliance through practical real-world examples, reflection activities, and skill-building exercises. The activities presented seek to challenge and instigate critical thinking skills that are required to thrive within the professional counseling setting. The updated third edition includes cases studies and video features that fully demonstrate essential skills that enhance the counselor-client relationship.

Hutchinson, D. (2011). *The counseling skills practice manual*. Thousand Oaks, CA: Sage Publications.

This manual serves as a practical guide for students who are striving to advance their counseling skills. As the companion to the text, *The Essential Counselor* and DVD, the manual works to offer discussion on skill sets in addition to examples and activities designed for practice.

Murdock, N. L. (2017). *Theories of counseling and psychotherapy: A case approach*, (4th ed). Boston: Pearson

This text utilizes case studies, examples of application, original sources, and the author's personal pedagogical style to further expound on fifteen of the highly leading and innovative theories of psychotherapy and counseling.

This clear guide to counseling theory provides students with the opportunity to develop skills to navigate complicated historical theory and understand how various theories have informed each other and contributed to modern practice.

Sharf, R. S. (2011). *Theories of psychotherapy and counseling: Concepts and cases student manual*. (5th ed). Belmont, CA: Brooks/Cole.

This text offers students and professionals sample case studies and multiple-choice questions that enhance the ability to learn important concepts within psychotherapy and counseling. The text offers an in-depth description of case summaries and discussion that demonstrate effective techniques and appropriate treatment in practice. Application of theory within individual therapy or group therapy is exemplified within the text.

Wedding, D., & Corsini, R. J. (2013). *Case studies in psychotherapy*. (7 ed). Stamford, CT: Cengage Learning.

The Seventh Edition of this casebook offers interesting new cases that further illustrate Psychoanalysis, Client-Centered Therapy, Existential Therapy, Interpersonal Therapy, Contemplative Therapies, and Therapy within a Multicultural framework. The text provides a new chapter on Positive Psychotherapy. The text preserves the parallel structure with the Tenth Edition of the author's work within current psychotherapies. As a result, readers are provided a more comprehensive view of psychotherapy.

CASE MANAGEMENT

Chan, F., Leahy, M. J., & Saunders, J. L. (2005). *Case Management for Rehabilitation Health Professionals* (2nd. Ed.). Linn Creek, MO: Aspen Professional Services.

This two volume set is one of the most comprehensive textbooks on the topic of case management.

Coombs, T. (2013). *Applied crisis communication and crisis management: Cases and exercises.* SAGE Publications.

This text provides students and public relations professionals the knowledge and skills necessary to become effective crisis managers. This practical resource includes a wide variety of cases that explore crisis communication and management through a practical approach.

Crimando, W., & Riggar, T. (2005). *Community resources: A guide for human service workers* (2nd ed). Long Grove, IL: Waveland Press.

This comprehensive resource provides human-service professionals with the answers necessary to effectively assist and guide clients. Developed by credentialed practitioners, this resource book offers detailed descriptions of the most prominent and beneficial human-service agencies. Additionally, the text provides information on agency personnel, as well as specific organizational certifications, licensing, or accreditation.

Eack, S. M., Anderson, C. M., & Greeno, C. G. (2012). *Mental health case management: A practical guide.* SAGE Publications.

> This resource is characterized as the first modern guide developed to provide students and practitioners with a practical tutorial on the essential functions of case management to effectively work with adults with severe mental illness. This resource intentionally omits extensive theoretical and historical discourse, and rather focuses on a direct and to-the-point approach that readers will find useful while learning the fundamentals of mental health case management.

Summers, N. (2015). *Fundamentals of case management practice: Skills for the human services* (5th edition). Boston, MA: Cengage Learning.

> This workbook serves as a step-by-step guide through the case management process. The text outlines the steps beginning with intake and assessment to the end with referrals and termination process. The edition provides examples of realistic exercises elicited from active professional's experiences. The intent is to introduce readers to a wide array of true-to-life situations and complications.

Tahan, H. M., & Treiger, T. M. (2016). *CMSA Core Curriculum for Case Management* (3rd ed). Philadelphia: Wolters Kluwer.

> This comprehensive guide provides individuals involved in case management with the best practices, key terms, critical skills, and the necessary tools that satisfy the current Case Management Society of America's (CMSA) standards and requirements. This text serves as a vital study guide and resource tool for case managers in various specialty areas. Provided information further supports the developmental transition from student to veteran case manager status.

Wilson, K. B., Acklin, C. L., Chao, S. (2018). *Case management for the health, human, and vocational rehabilitation services.* Linn Creek MO: Aspen Professional Services.

> This two-part text provides an overview of case management tools utilized across many areas of expertise in the human, allied health, and rehabilitation services. Additionally, the text highlights practices that occur in social work, psychology, counselor education, and rehabilitation services.

Woodside, M., & McClam, T. (2017). *Generalist case management: A method of human service delivery* (5th ed). Cengage Learning.

> This text provides realistic and current insight to the fundamental skills necessary to coordinate and provide services to a variety of populations. The text includes case studies, nationwide interviews with human service case managers, and opportunities to apply learned skills to real-life issues that enhance the ability to serve as a client advocate. This resource aligns with the NASW (National Association of Social Workers) case management standards to assist in the preparation for earning the C-SWCM (Certified Social Work Case Manager) certification. The text is also

designed to prepare individuals for the HS-BCP credential (Human Services Board-Certified Practitioner).

VOCATIONAL PROCESSES

Anderson, L. E., & Bolt, S. B. (2015). *Professionalism: Skills for workplace success* (4th ed). Prentice Hall.

This resource prepares students for professional jobs, career planning, and the acquisition of soft skills. Practice exercises are available for students to prepare for the transition from the classroom into the field. The text is designed for students to develop human relations skills and obtain career planning skills that enhance employment search strategies, resume development, and job interviewing techniques.

Andrew, J. D., & Faubion, C. W. (2014). *Rehabilitation services: An introduction for the human services professional.* Linn Creek, MO: Aspen Professional Services.

Bolles, R. N. (2018). *What color is your parachute? A practical manual for job hunters and career-changers.* Ten Speed Press

This text is a great resource for students, recent grads, or individuals experiencing a shifting economic landscape. Workers experiencing lay-offs, searching for a work-life change will gain insight on the effective and least effective job-hunt strategies. The author deciphers the total process of the job search, highlighting the development of resumes, completing interviews and networking to successfully progress toward the dream job.

Dictionary of Occupational Titles DOT. (2018, April 11.) Retrieved from https://www.occupationalinfo.org/

This online resource is a publication produced by the United States Department of Labor which provides support to employers, government officials, and employment development specialists in defining various types of work.

Edwards, D. W., & Edwards, Y. V. (2015). *A case study approach to vocational rehabilitation counseling.* Linn Creek, MO: Aspen Professional Services.

This resource offers examples through case study that accompany the major topics within the rehabilitation counseling course work.

Job Accommodation Network. (n.d.) Retrieved from https://www.askjan.org

The Job Accommodation Network (JAN) offers A to Z listings by disability, topic, and limitation. Listings serve as a benefit for individuals and employers as it supports identification of the most effective reasonable accommodations. Additionally, the online tool provides support to maintain compliance with Title I of the Americans with Disabilities Act (ADA). The online resource provides ADA information, ideas for reasonable accommodations, and additional beneficial resources.

Occupational Outlook Handbook. (2018, April 13) Retrieved from
https://www.bls.gov/ooh/

    This online resource is a publication of the United States Department of
Labor's Bureau of Labor Statistics. The Occupational Outlook Handbook
can assist individuals to identify career information, job duties, education
and training, salaries, and an overall outlook of various occupations.

O*NET. (n.d.). Retrieved from https://www.onetonline.org/

    This free online resource provides hundreds of detailed descriptions of
occupational definitions within the workforce for jobseekers. The online
source offers career exploration and the ability to create a job analysis to
better identify interests and preferences to enter the workforce.

Power, P. W. (2012). *A guide to vocational assessment* (5th ed). Austin, TX:
Pro-Ed.

    This fifth edition text highlights the social and economic systemic
changes facing adults with disabilities. The resource provides multiple
approaches to evaluation to possibly adjust what is typically difficult to a
possible or probable outcome. The updated text edition emphasizes
evaluation as a strengths-based approach that focuses on consumer's ability
to develop certain key skills. The author integrated a new chapter that
focuses on transition-age students, which is currently receiving great levels
of attention in the field of vocational rehabilitation.

Rehabilitation Measures Database. (2018). Retrieved from
https://www.sralab.org/rehabilitation-measures

    This online resource provides a detailed overview of instrumentation
utilized for rehabilitation research. The online source serves as a
community nurtured by academicians and the healthcare professionals.

Rubin, S. E., & Roessler, R. T. (2016). *Foundations of the vocational
rehabilitation process* (7th ed). Pro-ed.

    This restructured text provides an updated chapter on the 2008 changes
of The Americans with Disabilities Act (ADA). The text also includes
updated information and references on disability types such as emotional
disorders, intellectual disabilities, learning disabilities, and visual
impairments and blindness. Authors incorporated within the new text 300
new supplemental references. Readers are provided both theoretical and
practical support to translate mandates into positive action.

ASSESSMENT

American Psychological Association. PsychTESTS (n.d.). Retrieved from
https://www.apa.org/pubs/databases/psyctests/

    PsycTESTS provides access to published and unpublished
psychological tests, measures, scales, and surveys, as well as descriptive
information about the resources including their development, reliability and
validity, and administration. PsychTESTS supports professionals, students,

and educators within the behavioral and social sciences to identify tests and measurements with ease.

Blakenship, D. C. (2009). *Applied research and evaluation methods in recreation* (Har/Psc ed). Human Kinetics Publishers

This text is a core resource for undergraduate and graduate students. The contents include a foundational overview of research, evaluation, and step-by-step guidance of concepts and statistical methods. This text resource provides an in-depth linkage between classroom learning and field experiences. The author incorporated exercises and recreation scenarios for the reader to experience real world examples.

Burlingame, J. & Blaschko, T. M. (2009*). Assessment tools for recreational therapy and related fields.* (4th ed.) Idyll Arbor, Inc.

Students and professionals are offered essential information pertinent to the process of assessment, tools, and standards that govern assessment within this text. The new fourth edition highlights five new assessments and provides an updated version of national and international standards.

Hays, D. G., & Hood, A. B. (2013). *Assessment in counseling: A guide to the use of psychological assessment procedures* (5th ed). Alexandria, VA: American Counseling Association.

This text provides students and clinicians with updates on the fundamental principles of psychological assessment and current procedural changes, and the most commonly used tests applicable to counseling. The author guides the reader through each assessment stage and incorporates practical tools such as bolded key terminology within the chapters. Chapter pretests, summaries, review questions, self-development and reflection activities, and client case examples are all included within the text. An additional bonus provided by the authors are practitioner perspectives illustrating assessment along with tip sheets.

Marlow, C. R. (2010). *Research methods for generalist social work* (5th ed). Cengage Learning.

This resource provides a straight-forward, clear, and concise introduction to the concepts of research methodology. The author makes a clear connection throughout the text between social work research and generalist social work practice. As a result, the methods are clear and for readers to comprehend.

Power, P. W. (2012). *A guide to vocational assessment* (5th edition). Austin, TX: Pro-Ed.

This fifth edition text highlights the social and economic systemic changes facing specifically adults with disabilities. The resource provides multiple approaches to evaluation to possibly adjust what is typically difficult to a possible or probable outcome. The updated text edition emphasizes evaluation as a strengths-based approach that focuses on consumer's ability to develop certain key skills. The author integrated a new chapter that focuses on transition-age students, which is currently receiving great levels of attention in the field of vocational rehabilitation.

Research on Disability. (2017). Retrieved from https://researchondisability.org/

This online tool provides readers with a broad list of disability-focused research projects that are housed at the Institute on Disability at the University of New Hampshire. This resource provides a view of current and past grant-funded research projects. Contributors share work online through publications, events, expert staff, and research results. The staff has experience in disability research specific areas such as employment, statistics and demographics, health and individual-level features.

University of Nebraska-Lincoln. (n.d.). Buros Center for Testing. Retrieved from https://buros.org/

The Buros Center for Testing is an online resource that shares critical appraisals of tests and descriptive information, offer psychometric consultation services, and developing a deeper understanding of testing and assessment practices. Buros Center for Testing is a premier test review center that focuses on improve testing, assessment and measurement practices through efforts of consultation and education.

ASSISTIVE TECHNOLOGY

AbleData. (n.d.) Retrieved from https://abledata.acl.gov/

This online resource is the premier database for unbiased, comprehensive information on products, solutions and resources to improve productivity and ease life's tasks.

Bryant, D. P., & Bryant, B. R. (2011). *Assistive technology for people with disabilities.* (2nd ed). Pearson.

This text resource includes eight comprehensive chapters that focus on devices and software that enhance the lives and promote the independence of people with disabilities. Devices and software support readers to understand how areas such as mobility, communication, education, independent living, and access to information media affect learning and living for individuals with disabilities. Readers will also gain awareness of foundational and historical views of assistive technology, assessment, and universal design.

Cook, A. M., & Polgar, J. M. (2015). *Assistive technologies: Principles and practice* (4th ed). Mosby

This resource aims to give readers the confidence to master assistive strategies, acquire confidence in making clinical decisions, and overall, improve the quality of life for persons with disabilities. The text incorporates the Human Activity Assistive Technology (HAAT) model and provides readers with a detailed description of a variety of devices, services, and practices that comprise assistive technology. Additionally, the authors focus on the specific contexts of the relationship between the human user and the assisted activity. This updated edition features new ethical issues, clear applications of the HAAT model, and a variety of global issues surrounding applications and service delivery in emerging countries.

Robitaille, S. (2009). *The illustrated guide to assistive technology & devices: Tools and gadgets for living independently* (1st ed). Demos Medical Publishing, LLC.

This resource illustrates assistive technologies and devices utilized by persons with disabilities to perform challenging functions. The resource empowers individuals to utilize AT to remove barriers of physical or mental limitations. The text includes real examples of individuals utilizing AT and provides insight to the emotional concerns pertinent to AT/AD.

Scherer, M. (2011). *Assistive technology and other supports for people with brain impairment.* Springer Publishing Company, Inc.

The author provides an overview of the research and the experiences of individuals with cognitive disabilities using AT. The author incorporated reports of individual's perceptions of AT advantages and limitations. Additionally, the text offers practitioners a comprehensive method for application and utilization of technology along with the emphasis of individuals with brain injury and cognitive impairment.

DIVERSITY

Diller, J. V. (2014). *Cultural diversity: A primer for the human services* (5th ed). Cengage Learning

This text provides readers with an overview of variety of topics varying from the general principles of cultural diversity to steps on how to effectively provide cross-cultural services to clients from various diverse cultures and backgrounds. The resource encourages students to better understand their own prejudices in order to develop into effective counselors when working with culturally diverse clients.

Ivey, A. E., Ivey, M. B., & Zalaquett, C. P. (2018). *Intentional interviewing and counseling: Facilitating client development in a multicultural society* (9th ed). Cengage Learning.

This text offers tools to adapt skills and address individual and multicultural uniqueness, facilitate interviews utilizing five various theoretical orientations, and the development of a personal style and approach to interviewing and counseling that is the best fit for the reader's own abilities. The text challenges students to re-evaluate their behaviors and perceptions, thereby gaining insight on personal strengths, and areas for further development and growth.

Leung, P., Flowers, C.R., Talley, W.B. & Sanderson, P.R. (2007). *Multicultural issues in rehabilitation and allied health.* Linn Creek, MO: Aspen Professional Services

This text attempts to integrate the meaning of living in a multicultural society as it relates to rehabilitation practitioners and educators.

Schneider, I. E., & Kivel, B. D. (2016). *Diversity and inclusion in the recreation profession* (3rd ed). Venture Publishing, Inc.

The authors provide an overview of the significance of the construct of diversity as it pertains to managing recreation and leisure services. The text highlights the current state of awareness on diversity issues, incorporates case studies, and lived diversity experiences from professionals in recreation, leisure, tourism, and sports organizations. The authors also include issues and concerns of diverse groups along with a new chapter on religion and spirituality as they relate to diversity.

Sue, D. W., Sue, D. (2015*). Counseling the culturally diverse theory and practice* (7th ed.). Hoboken, New Jersey: John Wiley & Sons, Inc.

This text is the new update to the seminal work on multicultural counseling. Authors included current research, cultural and scientific theoretical formations, and extended exploration of internalized racism. With the inclusion of real-world examples, this text explains why discussions surrounding racial concerns remain difficult. An addition, the text provides techniques and advice for facilitating effective and productive discussions.

Sue, D. W., Rasheed, M. N., & Rasheed, J. M. (2015). *Multicultural social work practice: A competency-based approach to diversity and social justice* (2nd ed). Wiley.

This text is aligned with the Council on Social Work Education's (CSWE) 2015 Educational Policy and Standards. An additional caveat to the resource is the incorporation of the National Association of Social Workers Standards of Cultural Competence. Chapters within this edition place emphasis on critical race theory, microaggressions, societal attitudes, and evidence-based research-supported approaches to promote an overall understanding of cultural differences and the impact on the practice of social work.

PSYCHOSOCIAL ASPECTS OF DISABILITY

Chan, F., Cardoso, E. D. S., & Chronister, J. A. (2009). *Understanding psychosocial adjustment to chronic illness and disability: A handbook for evidence-based practitioners in rehabilitation*. New York, NY: Springer Publishing Company.

This text presents dominant theories, models, and evidence-based techniques professionals need in order to encourage the psychosocial adjustment of chronic illness or disability. Authors prepared each chapter from an evidence-based practice (EBP) perspective, and examines how important issues (i.e., social stigma, social support, sexuality, family, depression, and substance abuse) impact adjustment to chronic illness and disability.

Marini, I., Graf, N. M., & Millington, M. J. (2018). *Psychosocial aspects of disability: Insider perspectives and strategies for counselors* (2nd ed). New York, NY: Springer Publishing Company.

This revised text provides updated information about assisted suicide, genetic testing, new legislation, veterans, persons with disabilities living in poverty, and the significance of family and community-based engagement. The text provides students and practitioners of rehabilitation and mental health counseling insight into the lived experience of persons with disabilities.

ADDICTION DISORDERS

American Psychiatric Association. (2013). *Diagnostic and statistical manual of mental disorders* (5th ed.). Arlington, VA: American Psychiatric Association.

This text is published by the American Psychiatric Association. The purpose of the DSM 5 is to provide a detailed classification of mental disorders with the intention of improving diagnoses, treatment, and research.

Fetting, M. A. (2011). *Perspectives on addiction: An integrative treatment model with clinical case studies*. Los Angeles, CA: SAGE Publications, Inc.

This text provides a comprehensive, rigorous, and reflective overview of the complex field of chemical dependency. The author developed the text for students and clinicians who work with individuals and families experiencing substance use disorders. The content encourages active participation within the learning experience.

Maisto, S. A., Galizio, M., & Connors, G. J. (2017). *Drug use and abuse* (8th edition). Boston, MA: Cengage Learning, Inc.

The textbook integrates historical, social, psychological, cultural, biological, and medical perspectives to cover current topics regarding drug use, associated problems, and prevention and treatment options. Readers will understand the classes of drugs and the most recent data on drug use patterns and social trends.

McHenry, B. & Brooks, F. (2015). *A contemporary approach to substance use disorders and addiction counseling.* (2nd ed). American Counseling Association.

This text serves as an introduction to the profession of addictions counseling. Chapters cover basic foundational knowledge and skills required to provide counseling to individuals impacted by addiction.

ADDICTION TREATMENT

American Society of Addiction Medicine. (2018). Retrieved from
http://www.asam.org/
> The American Society of Addiction Medicine (ASAM) is dedicated to
> increasing accessibility to and the improvement of quality addiction
> treatment. In addition, the movement focuses on educating the public and
> physicians, supporting research and prevention strategies, and promoting
> appropriate role/function of physicians caring for individuals impacted by
> addiction.

Goldberg, R., & Mitchell, P. (2017). *Drugs across the spectrum.* (8th ed.)
Boston, MA: Cengage Learning.
> This text invites readers to explore the underlying motivation for drug
> use, the social implications, legal ramifications and factors affecting how
> drugs impact the human body. The new eighth edition reviews the history
> and culture surrounding drug use and abuse, includes key details regarding
> specific types of drugs and treatment, education and prevention approaches
> and programs.

Lusk, S. (2014). *Counseling the addicted family: Implications for practitioners.*
Linn Creek, MO: Aspen Professional Services.
> This text contains three sections: Family Development and Dynamics;
> Models of Individual and Family Therapy: and Special Topics.

Rx List. (n.d.). Retrieved from https://www.rxlist.com/script/main/hp.asp
> The Rx tool offers readers an online medical resource of detailed and
> current pharmaceutical information on brand and generic drugs.

SAMHSA - Substance Abuse and Mental Health Services Administration.
(n.d.). Retrieved from https://www.samhsa.gov/
> The Substance Abuse and Mental Health Services Administration
> (SAMHSA) is an agency within the U.S. Department of Health and Human
> Services that leads efforts to progress the behavioral health of the nation.
> SAMHSA's focus is to decrease the influence of substance abuse and
> mental illness on communities in America.

Stano, J. F. (2011). *Substance abuse: Treatment and rehabilitation.* Linn Creek,
MO: Aspen Professional Services.

DOCUMENTATION GUIDE

Gehart, D. R. (2015). *Case documentation in counseling and psychotherapy: A
theory-informed, competency-based, approach* (2nd ed). Boston, MA:
Cengage Learning.
> The text provides readers with a comprehensive introduction to case
> documentation utilizing four commonly used clinical forms: case
> conceptualization, clinical assessment, treatment plan, and progress note.

Case studies are available to illustrate how to effectively complete documentation using the seven counseling models: psychodynamic, Adlerian, humanistic, cognitive-behavioral, family systemic, solution-focused, and postmodern/feminist.

Kettenbach, G., Schlomer, S. L., & Fitzgerald, J. (2015). *Writing patient/client notes: Ensuring accuracy in documentation* (5ᵗʰ ed). F. A. Davis Company.

This resource provides a detailed description of the steps necessary to write clear and concise patient care notes. An array of straight-forward tools is provided within the text, including soap notes. This ideal resource provides supports to improve skills through clear and cogent justifications of why documentation is significant and clarification on how to complete the task of documentation.

Nagy, M., & Thomas, D. (2016). *Documentation for the advancement of the therapeutic recreation professional.*

This resource serves as a guide for students & practitioners by offering instruction on how to develop the skill of documentation in a professional, clear and concise manner. Reviewers will be introduced to assessments, treatment plans, progress note writing, professional vocabulary, and client specific goals.

Sidell, N. L. (2015). *Social work documentation: A guide to strengthening your case recording* (2ⁿᵈ ed). NASW Press

The author skillfully highlights the significance of documentation in the social work profession, clients, and the agencies rendering services. The text is comprised of ethical, technological, and supervisory scenarios. This perspective resource is beneficial for individuals at any level beginning from undergraduate to an experienced professional.

ETHICS

Anderson, E. E., & Corneli, A. (2018). *100 questions and answers about research ethics* (5ᵗʰ. ed). Thousand Oaks: CA, SAGE Publications, Inc.

This resource is an essential guide for students and researchers in the social and behavioral sciences. The text highlights ethical issues that individuals must consider when developing research agendas as well as offers guidance to effectively address ethical issues that may occur during research implementation. Readers are challenged to process questions pertaining to assessing risks, protecting privacy and vulnerable populations, obtaining informed consent, using technology including social media, negotiating the IRB process, and handling data ethically are covered within the text.

Corey, G., Corey, M. S., & Corey, C. (2018). *Issues and ethics in the helping professions* (10ᵗʰ ed). Cengage Learning.

This modern and practical text assists reader to explore and determine individual strategies for helping within the extensive limits of professional codes of ethics and varied theoretical positions. The authors address central issues, diverse views regarding specific issues, and opportunities to refine thinking and actively develop an informed position.

Dolgoff, R., Harrington, D., & Loewenberg, F. M. (2011). Ethical decisions for social work practice (9th ed). Cengage Learning.

This text enhances reader's ability to recognize ethical issues and dilemmas, execute careful application of reason regarding ethical issues, clarify ethical aspirations at the level commanded by the profession, and accomplish an advanced ethical stance during practice. Additionally, the text offers two ethical screens to assist readers in identifying significant priorities among competing ethical duties.

Jewell, P. (2010). Disability ethics: A framework for practitioners, professionals, and policy makers. Common Ground Publishing.

Within this text the author explores ethical theories, tests their application, and offers readers key strategies tailored for practitioners, managers, policymakers and professionals who provide services to individuals with disabilities.

Johnson, W. B., & Koocher, G. P. (2011). Ethical conundrums, quandaries, and predicaments in mental health practice: A casebook from the files of experts. Oxford University Press.

In this casebook, readers encounter real-life scenarios which include a comprehensive ethics casebook for mental health professionals. An eminent group of mental health clinicians provide readers with personal experiences of ethical dilemmas. Each chapter includes ethically complex cases and details that outline the process of ethical reasoning used to determine the final decision. Each case concludes with recommendations for promoting ethical practice within challenging work environments.

Parsons, R. D., & Dickinson, K. L. (2017). Ethical practice in the human services: From knowing to being (1st ed). Los Angeles, CA: SAGE Publications, Inc.

This textbook provides readers with insight to ethical behavior through awareness of personal morals, values, and choices. The text covers ethical issues and principles within social work, counseling, psychology, and marriage and family therapy. Readers are provided case illustrations and guided exercises to offer a deeper understanding of morals and values that serve as a basis for the various ethical codes.

Stumbo, N. J., Wolfe, B. D., Pegg, S. (2017). *Professional issues in therapeutic recreation: On competence and outcomes.* (3rd ed). Champaign, IL: Sagamore Pub.

This updated text includes insight from a diverse range of authors who intelligently articulate the latest issues and directions of the field. The text consists of 30 chapters that represent current challenges faced by the field. The text consists of four major sections which consist of: introduction, education, practice, and research. To continue with discovery and reflection, each chapter includes discussion questions at the conclusion of each chapter.

Stano, J. F. (2016). *Ethics: A case study approach.* Linn Creek, MO: Aspen Professional Services.

Svedin, L. (2011). *Ethics and crisis management.* Information Age Publishing, Inc.

This resource text presents a public policy framework for analyzing ethical dilemmas in crises. The text introduces ten empirical chapters developed by prominent public administration and crisis management scholars. Cases reviewed within the text include Abu Ghraib, the 9/11 Commission, the 2008 Financial Crisis and the Memorial Hospital Tragedy during Hurricane Katrina. The concluding chapter outlines imperative teachings about criteria for crisis decision-making and strategies, bureaucratic discretion, and post-crisis evaluations. This resource is tailored toward students, scholars, and practitioners involved with public management, public sector ethics, public policy, and crisis management.

SUPPLEMENTAL REHABILITATION AND HUMAN SERVICES PROFESSIONAL SITES
(List not exhaustive)

ADA National Network. (2018, November 28). Retrieved from https://adata.org/

The online ADA National Network provides individuals with information, guidance, and training on the Americans with Disabilities Act. In addition to ADA National Network serving as a professional resource, novice professionals should particularly note: The ADA National Network provides guidelines to use when writing or discussing persons with disabilities.

American Psychological Association. (2011). *Publication Manual of the American Psychological Association* (6th ed.). Washington, DC: American Psychological Association.

The Publication Manual of the American Psychological Association is a resource for writers, editors, students, and educators in the social and behavioral sciences. The manual offers instrumental guidance on the writing process. Examples of guidance include navigating ethics of authorship to the word selection that reduces language bias.

Directory of Open Access Journals (n.d.). Retrieved from https://doaj.org/

The Directory of Open Access Journals is an online community directory that provides access to high quality, open access, peer-reviewed journals. DOAJ is independent. DOAJ services are free of charge including the process of being indexed in DOAJ. In addition to the free services,

DOAJ facilitates an education and outreach program across the world that focuses on quality application development.

Disability is Natural (n.d.). Retrieved from https://www.disabilityisnatural.com/home.html

Disability is Natural aims to influence a new way of viewing intellectual disabilities. The online resource offers access to articles, media, books, presentations, and testimonies from individuals creating positive change.

Eric Institute of Educational Services (n.d.) Retrieved from https://eric.ed.gov/

The Education Resources Information Center is an online digital library of education research and information. The Institute of Education Sciences of the United States serves as the sponsor for ERIC.

Institute on Disability/UCED. (2018). Retrieved from https://iod.unh.edu/

The Institute on Disability (IOD) strives to improve knowledge, policies, and practices associated to the quality of life among persons with disabilities and their families. The IOD further aims to strengthen local, state, and national capabilities in order to effectively respond and address the needs of persons with disabilities.

National Rehabilitation Information Center (n.d.). Retrieved from https://naric.com/?q=en/REHABDATA

The mission of the Center is to collect and disseminate research results funded by the National Institute on Disability, Independent Living, and Rehabilitation Research (NIDILRR). The online tool consistently provides information services and document delivery to the various disability and rehabilitation communities across the United States.

NCHPAD - Building Inclusive Communities. (n.d.). Retrieved from https://www.nchpad.org/

NCHPAD is an online public health practice and resource center on health promotion for individuals with disabilities. NCHPAD aims to support people with disabilities and other chronic health conditions achieve health benefits through increased participation and inclusion in all types of physical and social activities.

The Social Work Helper. (n.d.) Retrieved from https://www.socialworkhelper.com/.

This award-winning online progressive news resource takes an interdisciplinary approach to provide news and information to provide support for individuals. Readers gain access to information, resources, and entertainment related to social work, social justice, and social good. The audience is comprised of academics, policymakers, social workers, students, practitioners, helping professionals, and caregivers. Contributors are not required to obtain a social work degree or title of social worker to provide input.

Therapeutic Recreation Directory. (n.d.). Retrieved from www.recreationtherapy.com

This directory provides therapeutic recreation, recreation therapy, and activity director resources which includes job bulletins, internship listings, activity and treatment resources, and articles.

NATIONAL ORGANIZATIONS RELATED TO THE REHABILITATION AND HUMAN SERVICES PROFESSION
(List not exhaustive)

American Counseling Association (ACA)

 The American Counseling Association (ACA) promotes counselor professional development, advocacy for the profession, and the assurance of ethical, culturally inclusive practices that safeguard individuals seeking counseling services. Website: https://www.counseling.org/

American Deafness and Rehabilitation Association (ADARA)

 The American Deafness and Rehabilitation Association (ADARA) is a national organization that unites professionals within vocational rehabilitation, mental health, chemical health, education, interpreting, and related fields to share best practices in working with individuals who are Deaf and Hard of Hearing, address policy and programmatic concerns, and to create networking opportunities. Website: https://www.adara.org/

American Rehabilitation Counseling Association (ARCA)

 The American Rehabilitation Counseling Association (ARCA) is an organization of rehabilitation counseling practitioners, educators, and students concerned with enhancing the quality of life among persons with disabilities. Website: http://www.arcaweb.org/

American Therapeutic Recreation Association (ATRA)

 The ATRA is the premiere national membership organization that represents the interests and needs of therapeutic recreation specialists (also known as recreational therapists). Website: https://www.atra-online.com/

Council on Accreditation of Parks, Recreation, Tourism and Related Professions (COAPRT)

 COAPRT recognizes academic programs in colleges and universities that prepare new professionals to enter the parks, recreation, tourism and related professions. Website: https://www.nrpa.org/certification/accreditation/coaprt/

Council on Social Work Education (CSWE)

 (CSWE) is known as the national association representing social work education in the United States. Members include over 800 accredited baccalaureate and master's degree social work programs, in addition to social work educators, practitioners, and agencies dedicated to the advancement of excellence in social work education. Website: https://cswe.org/

International Association of Addictions and Offender Counselors (IAAOC)

The International Association of Addictions and Offender Counselors (IAAOC) is an organization of professional counselors along with other individuals with interest to work in the area of addictions or forensic/criminal justice fields. Other members consist of correction counselors, students and counselor educators concerned with additive or criminal behaviors. Members focus on advocating for appropriate treatment for clients within the specific client population. The organizational mission is to lead in the area of advancement of the addictions and offender counseling profession. Website: http://www.iaaoc.org/

International Association of Rehabilitation Professionals (IARP)

The primary goal of IARP is to become the leading international rehabilitation professional association through life-long learning and career development for rehabilitation professionals. The organization aims to increase membership, provide high quality research, advance legislation and policy, and strengthen the community of rehabilitation professionals over the period of a lifetime. Website: https://rehabpro.org/

National Association for Alcoholism and Drug Abuse Counselors (NAADAC)

The "NAADAC is the premier global organization of addiction focused professionals who enhance the health and recovery of individuals, families and communities." - NAADAC Vision Statement adopted 1998 Website: https://www.naadac.org/

National Association of Social Workers (NASW)

With more than 120,000 members, NASW is the largest membership organization of professional social workers. The organization aims to improve the professional growth and development of NASW members, create and maintain professional standards, and advance social policies. NASW activities include advocacy, ethics, continuing education, and publication. Website: https://www.socialworkers.org/newhomepage

National Board for Certified Counselors (NBCC)

The National Board for Certified Counselors, Inc. and Affiliates (NBCC) is the credentialing body for counselors. NBCC ensures that successful board-certified counselors have attained the highest standard of practice through modes of education, examination, supervision, experience, and adherence to ethics. Website: https://www.nbcc.org/

National Council for Therapeutic Recreation Certification

The NCTRC is the credentialing body for the profession of Therapeutic Recreation. The organization is dedicated to professional excellence for the protection of consumers through the certification of recreational therapists. Website: https://nctrc.org/

National Council on Rehabilitation Education (NCRE)

The National Council on Rehabilitation Education (NCRE) is a professional organization consisting of educators dedicated to ensuring quality services for persons with disabilities through education and research. NCRE promotes current education and training, and the maintenance of professional standards in the field of rehabilitation. Website: https://ncre.org/

National Institute on Drug Abuse (NIDA)

The mission of the National Institute on Drug Abuse (NIDA) is to advance science regarding the causes and consequences of drug use and addiction and improve individual and public health through the application of the knowledge.

Website: https://www.drugabuse.gov/

National Rehabilitation Association (NRA)

The National Rehabilitation Association (NRA) aim is to promote the vocational rehabilitation of persons with disabilities through advocacy, professional development, and public education. In addition to advocacy, members promote high quality, ethical, and collaborative practice across the rehabilitation profession. Members consist of counselors, educators, researchers, and diverse individuals with a specific interest in enhancing the quality of life of individuals with disabilities, families, and communities. Website: https://www.nationalrehab.org/

National Child Traumatic Stress Network

The mission of The National Child Traumatic Stress Network's aim is to raise the standard of care and advance access of services for traumatized children, families, and communities within the United States.

Website: https://www.nctsn.org/

National Organization for Human Services (NOHS)

This online resource is a professional association consisting of human services practitioners and educators who are devoted to advancing the quality and accessibility of human services to individuals of need. The mission is dedicated to increasing professional development opportunities, promoting identity through certification, advancing both internal and external communication, social policy advocacy, and financial stability and organizational growth. Website: https://www.nationalhumanservices.org/

APPENDICES

HELPFUL RESOURCES

SAMPLE LETTER OF INTEREST

The purpose of the cover letter is to introduce yourself to an organization, demonstrate your interest in the company or a specific vacancy, draw attention to your resume, and motivate the reader to interview you. Often this letter is the first contact you have with a prospective employer.

SAMPLE RESUME

The purpose of a resume is to provide a summary of your skills, abilities, and accomplishments. It is a quick advertisement of who you are. It is a "snapshot" of you with the intent of capturing the employer's interest and securing you an interview. It is not an autobiography.

SAMPLE INTRODUCTION LETTER

The primary purpose of an introduction letter, or letter of introduction, is to introduce yourself and/or your business (or another person or business) to another party. In fact, a poorly written introduction letter will seriously damage your credibility.

STUDENT SELF-INTRODUCTION: PROGRESSION ASSESSMENT

Informational form for a student scheduled to participate in an upcoming clinical education experience. This information may assist the supervisor in preparing for and conducting the experience for the student.

STUDENT RECORD OF CLINICAL EDUCATION-IMMUNIZATION RECORD REFERENCE

Vaccination records (sometimes called immunization records) provide a history of all the vaccines you have received. This record may be required for certain jobs, travel abroad, or school registration.

STUDENT CLINICAL FILE CHECKLIST

A checklist is a type of job aid used to reduce failure by compensating for potential limits of human memory and attention. It helps to ensure consistency and completeness in carrying out a task. A basic example is the "to do list".

OFF CAMPUS LIVING BUDGET

The purpose of budgeting includes the following three aspects: A forecast of income (what you take in) and expenditure (what you have to spend). It is a tool for decision making that is a means to monitor financial resources.

FIELDWORK WEEKLY TIME LOG:
A time log is a chronological list of records that are kept in a journal for each day that document the sequence of student activities with a time and date entry.

INFORMED CONSENT: OBSERVATION AND AUDIO/VIDEO TAPE RECORDING
The purpose of informed consent is to gain permission of the client before taking a video or recording. The client should understand the purpose, benefits, risks, and other options. It is recommended that a written signature be obtain for this type of activity.

CONFIDENTIALITY STATEMENT
The purpose of a confidentiality statement is to hold healthcare providers accountable for private and sensitive healthcare information. This information cannot be used for purposes not related to health care without explicit authorization from the patient. All individually identifiable health information shall be maintained in medical records at the field site facility This prevents unauthorized use and disclosure to third parties.

RECORD OF WEEKLY CONFERENCE FORM
The purpose of a Weekly Conference Form is for the clinical instructor and student to discuss the student progress that has been made during the week. It is a form that can be used to identify any areas of improvements and to highlight areas of strength. Goals and objectives can also be set for the next week.

IN-SERVICE EVALUATION
The purpose of the In-service Evaluation is for the student to conduct a presentation to peers and receive feedback on communication and the appropriateness of the topic of discussion.

WRITING SUCCESSFUL INTENTIONAL BEHAVIOR OBJECTIVES
The purpose of writing successful behavioral objectives is to identify what level of learning the student needs in order to accomplish specific task he/or she will be performing.

LEARNING STYLE INVENTORIES
Learning style inventories are designed to help students determine which learning style they have. These inventories typically take the form of a questionnaire that focuses on how people prefer to learn.

CODE OF ETHICS
A code of ethics is usually established by a professional organization to protect the public and the reputation of the professionals. People who breach their code of ethics incur disciplinary actions that can range from a warning or reprimand to dismissal or expulsion from their profession.

ETHICAL AND LEGAL ISSUES

The purpose of recognizing legal issues is to commit to professional Codes of Ethics or Standards of Professional Practice. A healthcare, rehabilitation, or human service professional who acts outside his/or her scope of practice will be subject to disciplinary action, up to license revocation.

APPENDIX A

SAMPLE
LETTER OF INTEREST

Name Recipient
Address Recipient

Dear _____,

I am writing to apply for a professional internship with the _____ (name of school or system) after completing my _____ (number at the University of _____ (or name of school). I have always wanted to be _____. I have researched your facility and feel that I would benefit from a professional learning experience at (name of site), this summer. I have a special interest in _____ (specialty, or area of interest).

My academic and observation experiences have helped me develop a keen understanding of how _____ works in (your discipline). My background includes being selected as an officer of my school organization, conducting research in (area of study), and maintaining my GPA, etc. My GPA is currently a 3.0, which has been a difficult accomplishment in a rigorous program.

My future goals include:

I would enjoy working with you as my professional mentor and preceptor for the following dates: _____. I will bring my best effort to represent every client and your organization. I have received practice approval from _____ and I await your phone call or response to my request

Sincerely,

_____
Student Name
Contact information

APPENDIX B

RESUME TEMPLATE

NAME:

ADDRESS:

OBJECTIVE:

EDUCATION:

PROFESSIONAL/ACADEMIC MEMBERSHIP:

PEER REVIEWED/NON PEER REVIEWED PUBLICATIONS, OR WRITINGS:

VOLUNTEER AND COMMUNITY SERVICE:

EXPERIENCE:

HONORS AND ACHIEVEMENTS:

CERTIFICATIONS:

REFERENCES:

APPENDIX C

SAMPLE
INTRODUCTION LETTER

Date:

Dear _____,

    Thank you for accepting me as a Student _____ and serving as my preceptor. I am excited about learning and more importantly working with you to further my professional internship/field site education experiences. I am a student at _____. I graduated from _____ university with a degree in _____.
I have experience working in _____ or I have observed _____.
    Some of my professional goals are:

1) Practice writing SOAP notes/documentation accurately with minimal assistance from preceptor, by end of professional experience.

2) Practice strategies to improve my communication skills with co-workers and clients.

3) Practice giving patient instructions for _____ by end of the rotation.

4) Practice the use of _____ by the end of the internship.

    If there are any special instructions or requirements for your facility such as time of arrival or any special attire, please send them to me at your earliest convenience. I look forward to reporting to your site on _____ date.
    If you have any questions or concerns, please feel free to contact me at (email/contact number). Thank you again for this opportunity.

Sincerely,

_____
Student Name,
Name of University
Student Email
Student Telephone Number

APPENDIX D

STUDENT SELF-INTRODUCTION
PROGRESSION ASSESSMENT

The following information has been provided by the student who is scheduled to participate in an upcoming clinical education experience at your facility. This information may assist you in preparing for and conducting the experience.

Name of Student: _____

Dates: Start _____ / _____ / _____   Finish _____ / _____ / _____

Professional Experience Internship/Field Site Course: _____

_____

—

Type of Internship/Field Site Scheduled: _____

_____

—

   A. Please list your previous clinical education experiences, including facility(ies), length of experiences, types of patients treated and any special activities or skills you accomplished:

   B. Briefly describe your preferred learning style (how do you want your CI to teach you)?

   C. List your specific goals for this clinical education experience. Goals can be in any area: i.e. examination, intervention, administration, etc.

   D. Outline any expectations or "special requests" you have for this experience, i.e., viewing surgery, exposure to specific patient types, exposure to specific evaluation or treatment procedures, service-learning projects, community services, etc.

   E. List the specific recommended areas for improvement from your last clinical experience and your strategies to facilitate improvement?

STUDENT RECORD OF CLINICAL EDUCATION REQUIREMENTS FORM.
STUDENTS IMMUNIZATION RECORD READY REPORT REFERENCE.

Name: _____ Date of Birth _____
Address: _____
Phone: _____

TB Skin Test Date/ Results	Chest X-ray if warranted	MMR Date	DTP Date	Hepatitis-B Dates #1, #2, #3	Chicken Pox Yes/No

Tetanus Booster	CPR Certification (Renewal Date)	Health Insurance Coverage	Background Check (Type)	Drug Screening (Type)

APPENDIX F

STUDENT CLINICAL FILE CHECKLIST

Use this checklist to ensure that your professional and personal file is complete before attending a field work assignment.

Student Name: _____

_____ Contact Field Site
_____ Review Fieldwork Handbook
_____ Review HIPPA/Confidentiality Statement
_____ Verification of Hepatitis Vaccination or Waiver for Hepatitis B Vaccination
_____ CPR card verification
_____ Health insurance information (with current dates)
_____ TB skin test (X-ray if warranted)
_____ Immunization Records
_____ Emergency Contact Information
_____ Health Insurance updated and validated
_____ Liability Insurance
_____ Background/Drug Screening, if required by facility

Visit the site below and complete the following quizzes as a refresher:
These refresher quizzes are very short and should not take long to complete.
Print your Certificates for both and insert into your personal file folder.
Quizzes are located toward the bottom of the page on this website.

https://www.mysafetysign.com/first-aid-quiz

_____ Workplace Safety: Hazardous Materia
_____ Workplace Safety: First aide
_____ Complete the HIPPA refresher below (see sample below at website) HIPPA

http://studylib.net/doc/8559457/test-questions-lesson-%231---tenet-s-privacy-policies

OFF CAMPUS LIVING BUDGET

The following form has been developed to help students work out a semester/monthly budget that they can realistically follow. It will help you plan and track expenses each semester. Complete the worksheet as thoroughly as possible.

INCOME (List all income available to you from all sources)
One-time income:

Scholarships $_____
Grants $_____
Monetary gifts received $_____
Personal savings $_____
Loans $_____
Other $_____

Subtotal One-time income: $_____

Monthly Income:

Salary/work wages $_____
Allotment (from parents) $_____
Stipend $_____
Other $_____

Subtotal Monthly income: $_____

TOTAL INCOME: $_____

EXPENDITURES (List all expenses you expect to have each semester or month)

One-time expenses per semester:
School related

Tuition $_____
Fees $_____
Books and supplies $_____
Meal plan $_____
Parking permit $_____
Other $_____

Subtotal school related: $_____

Non-school related

Telephone set-up	$_____
Cable/internet installation	$_____
Renters insurance	$_____
Health/medical insurance	$_____
Vehicle insurance	$_____
Furniture	$_____
Other	$_____

Subtotal non-school related: **$**_____

Travel related (break periods)

Transportation	$_____
Hotel	$_____
Food	$_____
Other	$_____

Subtotal travel   **$**_____

Monthly expenses:
Housing

Rent	$_____
Electric	$_____
Gas	$_____
Telephone (landline)	$_____
Telephone (cellular)	$_____
Cable/Internet	$_____
Furniture rental	$_____
Other	$_____

Subtotal housing: **$**_____

Transportation

Car payment	$_____
Fuel	$_____
Vehicle maintenance	$_____
Other	$_____

Subtotal transportation: **$**_____

Household

Food	$_____
Toiletries	$_____
Laundry/dry cleaning	$_____

Cleaning supplies $_____

Other $_____

Subtotal household: $_____

Monthly expenses (continued):
Recreation

Eating out $_____

Entertainment $_____

Movies $_____

Other $_____

Subtotal recreation: $_____

Clothing

School clothes $_____

Work clothes $_____

Other $_____

Subtotal clothing: $_____

Monetary Commitments

Credit card payments $_____

Loan payment $_____

Membership dues $_____

Subscriptions $_____

Gifts (holidays) $_____

Gifts (birthdays) $_____

Other $_____

Subtotal commitments: $_____

Total One-time Expenses: $_____

Total Monthly Expenses: $_____

TOTAL EXPENSES: $_____

TOTAL INCOME: $_____

Compare your total expenses with your total income. Your income should be greater than your expenses. If that is not the case, try to reduce your expenses and/or increase your income.

APPENDIX H

INTERNSHIP WEEKLY REHABILITATION COUNSELING LOG

Name:
_____

Course Info:
_____

Week #: _____ Date: _____ / _____ / _____ to _____ / _____ /
_____

Site Name: _____
Supervisor Name:
_____

Supervisor Signature:
_____

	MON	TUES	WED	THURS	FRI	SAT	SUN	*THIS WEEK*	*PREV WEEK*	*CUM TOTAL*
Intake Evaluation										
Individual /Couples therapy counseling										
Group/ Family therapy counseling										
Vocational Planning										
Referrals										
Records										
Consultation										
Job Readiness Activities (resume writing, interviewing skills										
Job Development/Job Placement										

Individual Supervision										
Group Supervision										
Observation										
Listening to Tapes										
Other (Specify)										
Total:										
Types of Disabilities: 1 2. 3. 4. 5.										
Time Key: .25=15 minutes .50=30 minutes .75=45 minutes 1.0=1 hour										

APPENDIX I

SAMPLE
INFORMED CONSENT

Observation and Audio/Video Tape Recording

    In order to provide quality counseling services, counselors in training for their degree program in Rehabilitation Counseling at _____ University are required to receive clinical supervision. To aid in this, counseling sessions are monitored using audio/video tape recordings and/or actual observations of clinical sessions. Information from the client's clinical case file also may be reviewed. Such information will be treated in accordance with professional ethical standards (e.g., *Code of Professional Ethics for Rehabilitation Counselors*) and confidentiality will be maintained. This authorization for the use of this information expires when the client is no longer receiving services by a counselor trainee of the Rehabilitation Counselor Training Program. Information will not be released to any other agency without the client's further written consent.

    "I understand that I am not required to participate in this counseling program but am giving my consent to the matters noted above as a free and voluntary act."

_____   _____

Date   Signature of the Client

_____   _____

Date   Signature of the Counselor in training

_____   _____

Date   Signature of a Witness

SAMPLE
RIGHTS REGARDING CONFIDENTIALITY

The counseling services offered to counselors in training for their degree program in Rehabilitation Counseling at _____ University are confidential. This means that we do not release any information about you to any persons who are not directly involved in clinical supervision without your written consent. Danger to self and/or others (i.e. suicide or homicide) may necessitate the breaking of confidentiality without your consent. In addition, by law, we must report suspected child abuse and/or neglect communicated to us by you.

"I have read and understand my rights regarding confidentiality."

_____   _____
Date   Signature of the Client

_____   _____
Date   Signature of the Counselor in training

_____   _____
Date   Signature of a Witness

APPENDIX K

<small>SAMPLE</small>
CONFIDENTIALITY STATEMENT

I, _____, understand that during
the course of my educational training I may have exposure and access to highly
confidential information which includes but is not limited to medical and
personnel records. It is my responsibility to protect the rights and
confidentiality of patients, employees, physicians, and the clinical setting.
Confidential information should only be used in conjunction with the learning
experiences while in the clinical setting. I also understand that any information
brought to the university setting in order to fulfill course requirements for the
physical therapy program must exclude patients' names, physicians' names,
medical record numbers and other personal information that will aid in the
identification of patients.

I understand that a violation of patient, personnel, and physician's
confidentiality may result in disciplinary action which may include a
recommendation for dismissal from this internship experience.

I have read and understand the above statement concerning confidential
information and agree to maintain the confidentiality of all such information.

_____   _____
Signature   Date

_____   _____
Witness   Date

WEEKLY CONFERENCE WITH INSTRUCTOR
(Copy as needed)

DATE: _____

STUDENT NAME:

THERAPIST NAME:

WEEK #_____ OF CLINICAL EXPERIENCE: _____

STUDENT'S REVIEW OF THE WEEK:

THERAPIST'S REVIEW OF THE WEEK:

FEEDBACK TO THE CLINICAL INSTRUCTOR:
(Supervision, Communications, Feedback)
1)
2)
3)

GOALS FOR THE UPCOMING WEEK:
1)
2)
3)

APPENDIX M

IN-SERVICE EVALUATION
Template Form

Student Name

Topic   Date

Instructions: Please rate the in-service presentation as:
(1) strongly disagree, (2) disagree, (3) agree, or (4) strongly agree

1. The topic was appropriate for presentation.

    1   2   3   4

2. The student was knowledgeable of the topic.

    1   2   3   4

PRESENTATION

3. Objectives were identified prior to start of presentation.

    1   2   3   4

4. Objectives were clear and at the appropriate level for the audience.

    1   2   3   4

5. The presentation was well paced within the time available.

    1   2   3   4

6. The student utilized audiovisuals, which contributed to audience understanding.

    1   2   3   4

7. The student utilized handouts, which contributed to audience understanding.

    1   2   3   4

8. The student presented accurate information based on current research findings.

    1   2   3   4

9. The student responds appropriately and interacts with the audience.

    1   2   3   4

10. Objectives were met.

    1   2   3   4

COMMENTS:_____

_____
_____
_____
_____
_____
_____
_____
_____
_____
_____
_____
_____

APPENDIX N

WRITING SUCCESSFUL INTENTIONAL BEHAVIORAL OBJECTIVES

In order to be successful during a professional education experience, the student should write intentional behavioral objectives related to the specific learning experience.

Students should write behavioral objectives for each professional education experience. The following information is provided to assist the student in the preparation of useful behavioral objectives. An objective is an intent communicated by a statement describing a proposed change in a learner (a statement of what the learner is to be like when he/she has successfully completed a learning experience). A given objective should include only one intended outcome. Well-written objectives contain an audience, a behavior, a condition, and a degree. Objectives should be specific, measurable, attainable, relevant, and should encompass a defined time period.

TERMS RELATING TO PREPARING OBJECTIVES

a. Audience: The person from whom the behavior is requested/required. This should always be the student.

b. Behavior: One specific, observable activity to be displayed by the learner.

c. Condition: Relevant factors affecting the actual performance, i.e., given a case study, diagram, clinical problem; upon completion of the examination; following a demonstration by the instructor.

d. Degree: The level of achievement that indicates acceptable performance, such as:

  ➤ To a degree of accuracy, i.e., 90%

  ➤ To a stated proportion, i.e., 3 out of 5

  ➤ Within a given time period

PRACTICE WRITING A BEHAVIORAL OBJECTIVE FOR YOUR PROFESSIONAL LEARNING EXPERIENCE BELOW. (Use an extra sheet of paper, if needed)
1.
2.
3.

SUGGESTIONS FOR WRITING MEASURABLE OBJECTIVES

The following are suggestions for verbs that may be used to describe desired behaviors pertaining to various levels of demonstration and integration of knowledge:

Knowledge Level	Application	
Level	Problem-Solving	
Define	Apply	Analyze
Describe	Classify	
Appraise		
Discuss	Compute	
Assess		
Explain	Demonstrate	
Breakdown		
Identify	Employ	
Calculate		
Indicate	Find	Compare
Label	Operate	
Compose		
List	Perform	
Construct		
Locate	Predict	
Create		
Name	Schedule	
Criticize		
Note	Sketch	
Design		
Recall	Solve	
Diagram		
Recite	Use	
Differentiate		
Recognize	Write	Distinguish
Record	Establish	
Inspect		
Repeat	Evaluate	
Inventory		
Report	Examine	
Research		
Restate	Formulate	
Prepare		
Review	Invent	
Propose		

State	Judge	Rate
Show	Organize	Select
Summarize	Plan	
Synthesize		

Most students focus their objectives on the behaviors related to the application of examination or intervention skills.

Objectives may be written, however, for all the elements of the Patient/Client Management Model, as well as for other administrative aspects that pertain to the effective delivery of professional services (i.e., verbal or written communication skills, marketing, conflict management, etc.).

LEARNING STYLE INVENTORY

To better understand how you prefer to learn and process information, place a check in the appropriate space after each statement below, then use the scoring directions at the bottom of the page to evaluate your responses. Use what you learn from your scores to better develop learning strategies that are best suited to your learning style. This 24- item survey is not timed. Respond to each statement as honestly as you can.

	Often	Sometimes	Seldom
1. I can remember best about a subject by listening to a lecture that includes information, explanations and discussions.			
2. I prefer to see information written on a chalkboard and supplemented by visual aids and assigned readings.			
3. I like to write things down or to take notes for visual review.			
4. I prefer to use posters, models, or actual practice and other activities in class.			
5. I require explanations of diagrams, graphs, or visual directions.			
6. I enjoy working with my hands or making things.			
7. I am skillful with and enjoy developing and making graphs and charts.			
8. I can tell if sounds match when presented with pairs of sounds.			
9. I can remember best by writing things down.			
10. I can easily understand and follow directions on a map.			

11. I do best in academic subjects by listening to lectures and tapes.			
12. I play with coins or keys in my pocket.			
13. I learn to spell better by repeating words out loud than by writing the words on paper.			
14. I can understand a news article better by reading about it in a newspaper than by listening to a report about it on the radio.			
15. I chew gum, smoke or snack while studying.			
16. I think the best way to remember something is to picture it in your head.			
17. I learn the spelling of words by "finger spelling" them.			
18. I would rather listen to a good lecture or speech than read about the same material in a textbook.			
19. I am good at working and solving jigsaw puzzles and mazes.			
20. I grip objects in my hands during learning periods.			
21. I prefer listening to the news on the radio rather than reading the paper.			
22. I prefer obtaining information about an interesting subject by reading about it.			
23. I feel very comfortable touching others, hugging, handshaking, etc.			
24. I follow oral directions better than written ones.			

LEARNING STYLES ASSESSMENT

Read each statement and select the appropriate number response as it applies to you. Often (3) Sometimes (2) Seldom/Never (1)

DIRECTIONS: Place the point value on the line next to the corresponding item below. Add the points in each column to obtain the preference score under each heading.

VISUAL MODALITY

_____ I remember information better if I write it down.

_____ Looking at the person helps keep me focused.

_____ I need a quiet place to get my work done.

_____ When I take a test, I can see the textbook page in my head.

_____ I need to write down directions, not just take them verbally.

_____ Music or background noise distracts my attention from the task at hand.

_____ I don't always get the meaning of a joke.

_____ I doodle and draw pictures on the margins of my notebook pages.

_____ I have trouble following lectures.

_____ I react very strongly to colors _____ Total

AUDITORY MODALITY

_____ My papers and notebooks always seem messy.

_____ When I read, I need to use my index finger to track my place on the line.

_____ I do not follow written directions well.

_____ If I hear something, I will remember it.

_____ Writing has always been difficult for me.

_____ I often misread words from the text, i.e., "them" for "then."

_____ I would rather listen and learn than read and learn.

_____ I'm not very good at interpreting an individual's body language.

_____ Pages with small print or poor-quality copies are difficult for me to read.

_____ My eyes tire quickly, even though my vision check-up is always fine.

_____ Total

KINESTHETIC/TACTILE MODALITY

_____ I start a project before reading the directions.

_____ I hate to sit at a desk for long periods of time.

_____ I prefer first to see something done and then to do it myself.

_____ I use the trial and error approach to problem-solving.

_____ I like to read my textbook while riding an exercise bike.

_____ I take frequent study breaks.

_____ I have a difficult time giving step-by-step instructions.
_____ I enjoy sports and do well at several different types of sports.
_____ I use my hands when describing things.
_____ I must rewrite or type my class notes to reinforce the material.
_____ Total

Total the score for each section. A score of 21 points or more in a modality indicates a strength in that area. The highest of the 3 scores indicates the most efficient method of information intake. The second highest score indicates the modality which boosts the primary strength. For example, a score of 23 in visual modality indicates a strong visual learner. Such a learner benefits from the text, from filmstrips, charts, graphs, etc. If the second highest score is auditory, then the individual would benefit from audio tapes, lectures, etc. If you are strong kinesthetically, then taking notes and rewriting class notes will reinforce information.

CHARACTERISTICS OF LEARNING STYLES
Three of your senses are primarily used in learning, storing, remembering and recalling information. Your eyes, ears, and sense of touch play essential roles in the way you communicate, perceive reality and relate to others. Because you learn form and communicate best with someone who shares your dominant modality, it is a great advantage for you to know the characteristics of visual, auditory and kinesthetic styles and to be able to identify them in others.

VISUAL: Mind sometimes strays during verbal activities

- Observe rather than acts or talks
- Likes to read
- Usually a good speller
- Memorizes by seeing graphics or pictures
- Not too distractible
- Finds verbal instruction difficult
- Has good handwriting
- Remembers faces
- Uses advanced planning
- Doodles
- Quiet by nature
- Meticulous, neat in appearance
- Notices details

AUDITORY
- Talks to self-aloud
- Enjoys talking
- Easily distracted
- Has difficulty with written directions

> Likes to be read to
> Memorizes sequentially
> Enjoys music
> Whispers to self while reading
> Distracted by noise
> Hums or sings
> Outgoing by nature
> Enjoys listening activities

KINESTHETIC

> Likes physical rewards
> In motion most of the time
> Likes to touch people when talking
> Taps pencil or foot when studying
> Enjoys doing activities
> Reading not a priority
> Poor speller
> Likes to solve problems by physically working through them
> Will try new things
> Outgoing by nature; expresses emotions by physical means
> Uses hands while talking
> Dresses for comfort

SOUND: Hints for the Auditory Learner

GENERAL

1. Say aloud the information to be learned/have someone read the information to you/read it into a tape recorder and replay it.
2. Read your work out loud. Summarize what you have read on tape.
3. Say words inside your head silently.
4. Brainstorm ideas with others. Form study groups.
5. When possible, learn information through tapes, television, oral reports, rhymes, and songs, radio, lectures, book reviews, panel and group discussions, guest lectures, and oral questions and answers.
6. Use a straight-edge marker or guide to assist you in keeping your place while you are reading or working with printed materials.
7. Tape class lectures (Ask instructor for permission).
8. Meet with classmates before and/or after class to discuss material.

WRITING

1. Plan each sentence you want to write by saying it out loud or silently in your head.
2. Say each sentence several times.

3. Write each sentence as you say it, or talk into a tape recorder, dictating each sentence of your paragraph; then play the tape back, one sentence at a time, and record your paragraph in writing.

1. Listen to the spelling of the word.
2. Say the word – then say each letter out loud
3. Close your eyes and spell the word out loud; check your spelling.
4. Close your eyes and spell the word out loud again; check your spelling.
5. Now write the word, trying to hear it in your mind.
6. Verbally review spelling words and lectures with a friend.

MATHEMATICS
1. Learn math while saying the concept, fact, theorem, etc., aloud.
2. Explain math problems, concepts, facts, etc., to yourself, relating the information out loud.
3. Use a tape recorder and replay the information.

SIGHT: Hints for the Visual Learner

GENERAL

1. Take notes, make pictures, graphs, and charts. Use flashcards and highlight key details.
2. Sit close to the teacher so that you can watch his /her face and gestures.
3. Take notes or make lists as you listen to directions.
4. Carefully check instructions written on the chalkboard and on handouts.
5. As the teacher lectures, pay attention to visual aids such as the following:
   - Drawing, maps, graphs, charts
   - Transparencies, posters, films, books
6. Imagine pictures of the information you are supposed to remember.
7. Use color coding as cues to important information.
8. When possible, read assignments silently.
9. Maintain class notes and outlines of important information to study.
10. Try to read and study in well lit, quiet place.
11. Record homework assignments in a date book, on a note pad, or a specially designed assignment sheet.
12. Always keep a notepad with you. Write out everything for frequent and quick visual review.

READING
1. Use sight words, flashcards, note cards and experience stories; don't try to sound words out, but try to determine if the new word or words has

words you already know. For example, the "systematic" has the word "system", "stem" and "mat" within it.

2. You are a "look-and-say" learner. Look at a word carefully; then say it.

WRITING

1. Jot down ideas as they form in your mind.
2. Outline your ideas.
3. Make a rough draft, skipping lines. Correct/revise your work.
4. Recopy your paper.
5. *Essay test.* Make quick outlines on scratch paper or in the margin of test the before writing your answer.

SPELLING

1. See the word – close your eyes.
2. Take a picture – then read from your picture.
3. Write the word – match the picture.
4. Check your work immediately.

MATHEMATICS

1. Visualize the problem.
2. Make pictures or tallies of the problem on scratch paper.
3. Write the problem.

TOUCH (Hints for the Tactile/Kinesthetic Learner)

1. Keep your desk clear of distracting objects.
2. Cover the page you're not reading.
3. If you are distracted by noise, turn off the radio; wear earplugs or wear an earphone in the learning center to block out the noise. If you want sound, listen to soft music.
4. Divide your work into short study sessions. Get a timer. After 20 minutes or when a task is completed, give yourself a reward, a cookie, a walk around the block, listen to one song, etc.
5. Sit as close to the teacher as possible or sit in the center of the room by quiet students.
6. When studying, use a multi-sensory approach (hearing, seeing, touching and doing) as much as possible.
7. Get plenty of sleep.
8. Eat a nutritious breakfast and lunch. Snack on fruit or nutritional food if you need extra energy.
9. Study in a carrel or in an office where there is a desk for your textbooks and notebook.
10. Use models, real objects, and materials that can be touched and moved. For example, learn geography through handling and studying a globe.
11. When possible draw what you are learning.
12. Trace spelling words as you practice them.

13. Record in writing information learned. Keep a supply of paper on hand.
14. When possible, role play, type, take notes, or construct models to learn the information.

CODE OF ETHICS

Interns should take responsibility to review the appropriate Code of Ethics for their background of study in order to ensure demonstration of skills, attitudes, and behaviors within their profession during their fieldwork site learning experience. Practicing students have an obligation to demonstrate ethical conduct that reflects professional values when working with clients, families, caregivers, administrators, colleagues, policymakers, payers, and other health care professionals.

Rehabilitation Counseling	www.crccertification.com/code-of-ethics-3
Guidance Counselors	www.counseling.org/resources/aca-code-of-ethics.pdf
Physical Therapy	www.apta.org/uploadedFiles/APTAorg/About_Us/Policies/Ethics/CodeofEthics.pdf
Occupational Therapy	www.aota.org/About-Occupational-Therapy/Ethics.aspx
Nursing	http://nursingworld.org/books/
Health Information Management	study.com/academy/lesson/american-health-information-management-associations-code-of-ethics.html library.ahima.org/doc?oid=105098#.W_DcjPZFzIU
Radiology Technologist	www.arrt.org/docs/default-source/Governing-Documents/arrt-standards-of-ethics.pdf?sfvrsn=12
Social Work	www.socialworkers.org/About/Ethics/Code-of-Ethics/Code-of-Ethics-English
Nutrition	www.eatrightpro.org/~/media/eatrightpro%20files/career/code%20of%20ethics/codeofethicsdieteticsresources.ashx
Recreation Therapy	https://www.atra-online.com/page/Ethics
Physician Assistants	www.aapa.org/wp-content/uploads/2017/02/16-EthicalConduct.pdf
Medical Technologist	ascls.org/about-us/code-of-ethics

ETHICAL & LEGAL ISSUES

Ethical codes are to protect the public from unethical or incompetent professionals, and to protect the profession from unethical practices by any of its members. Rehabilitation Counselors follow the Code of Professional Ethics for Rehabilitation Counselors students in practicum/internship will also follow this code of professional ethic

Counselors have a "duty to warn" individuals which have been threatened by clients in a counseling session.

This duty to warn comes from the Tarasoff case of 1969. An individual revealed he intended to kill his fiancée, the counselor reported this to police who then questioned the individual and later released him.

No one contacted the fiancée who was subsequently killed later by the individual who had threatened to do so earlier. From this incident many states make it necessary for counselors to warn individuals in harm's way.

Rehabilitation Counselors have the requirement to report any child abuse to child protective services.

Child abuse includes physical injury, mental injury, and sexual abuse. Failure to report child abuse is a misdemeanor and neglect. The person reporting is given immunity from any civil or criminal liability for breaking confidentiality. Counselors are faced with dilemma when consumers, in confidence, reveal that child abuse is occurring either to themselves or to someone else. The counselor, however, must report the abuse to child protective services.

I have been made fully aware of the content mentioned in the previous paragraph. With this understanding, I agree to comply with the content in the previous paragraph.

Student's signature: _____ Date: _____

Faculty Supervisor: _____ Date: _____